The Campaign in Gallipoli

By
Hans Kannengiesser
Prussian and Turkish Major General Retired

Translated from the German by
Major C. J. P Ball, D.S.O., M.C.

Edited by John Wilson

Gosling Press

ISBN 978-1-874351-30-6 (Hardback)
ISBN 978-1-874351-31-3 (Paperback)

Gosling Press
www.goslingpress.co.uk

Introduction to this new edition

With their defeat in the Balkans the Ottoman General Staff embarked on a new wave of reforms in the army. The idea was to engage expertise from around Europe to help modernise the Ottoman military. At this time there was a British naval Mission and a French *Gendarme* Mission. The proposal was to buy in German expertise to help reform the army and in 1913 a five year contract was signed with Germany and General Otto Liman von Sanders, who was commander of the 22nd Prussian Division, was dispatched to lead the Mission.

General von Sanders and his staff of 10 officers arrived in Istanbul on the 14th December, bringing the total number of German officers with the Ottoman Army to 41. All of the Germans were given ranks in the Ottoman Army, which were one step higher than that they held in the German Army.

Major General Hans Kannengeisser was initially employed to conduct an inspection of the Ottoman forces in Northern Anatolia, to assess their ability to mobilise for war, but on the outbreak of war he found that his role would significantly change. Initially expecting to be recalled to Germany he was given the Ottoman rank of Pasha and led the 9th Division of Von Sanders' fifth army during the Gallipoli campaign.

This book is an interesting, and rare, opportunity to study the campaign on Gallipoli from 'the other side of the hill' and Kannengeisser takes care to pay tribute to the courage of all the combatant nations

LIMAN VON SANDERS

The Campaign in Gallipoli

By
Hans Kannengiesser
Prussian and Turkish Major General, retired

Translated from the German by
Major C.J.P Ball, D.S.O., M.C.

INTRODUCTION

Only a few Germans know much of the eight months of heavy fighting on the Gallipoli Peninsula, which, in 1915, decided the possession of the entrance to the Dardanelles and the occupation of Constantinople.

There were only five hundred Germans who, distributed among a large Turkish Army, far from home, under burning heat, short of ammunition and under continuous ships' fire, held high the honour of the German name against a powerful Anglo-French invading Army.

Now that twelve years have passed, one of the bravest among the five hundred German comrades has taken his pen to write, and has depicted in the most vivid manner the story of this bloody campaign, which stands incomparable in the world's history. Only personal experience and knowledge of incidents hidden from history enable the writer to tell his story in such a clear and simple manner as to find its way immediately to the heart of the German people.

The brilliant work of the English Minister, Winston Churchill, *The World Crisis, 1915*, is here supplemented from the German side in a manner which deals equally justly with the German activity as with that of our late Turkish Allies and with the brave enemy. It is my hope that this clear, truthful and extremely interesting book of General Kannengiesser will meet with the reception which it deserves.

LIMAN VON SANDERS
Late Imperial Prussian General of Cavalry,
Dr Phil H.C., formerly Field Marshal and
Commander-in-Chief of 5th Turkish Army
MUNICH, 27 January, 1927.

PREFACE

On 20 December 1925, we Gallipoli veterans celebrated for the first time the day on which, ten years previously, the English had evacuated the Gallipoli Peninsula and thus retired from the fighting for the Dardanelles. It was a joy to all of us to meet again the greater part of the men who formerly, under most curious and difficult circumstances, fought a heavy fight under conditions which certainly up-to-date could only have been known in their extreme peculiarity to those who had fought with us.

Shall the deeds of those men be forgotten who there, under the Crescent, fought for Germany's name and honour?

Every regiment prizes its war record, with justice. I have to date vainly awaited a history of the Gallipoli campaign, something more than a casual story in the newspapers, which so depicted the terrible difficulties of the heavy fighting in Oriental surroundings as to make them for the first time completely understandable, and which first did real justice to the political importance of those battles. This is the reason why I have now seized a pen and believe myself to be fulfilling a comradely duty, not only to my German comrades but also towards the brave Turkish Army. What I have to say about the Turkish Army really only affects Turkey as she was in 1914 and 1915, measured by the impressions which I received before and on Gallipoli, and which I shall endeavour to relate and substantiate. I limit myself, therefore, to depicting the conditions and circumstances of that period. These I have embodied in a story of my personal experiences.

THE AUTHOR
BAD GRUND HARZ WALDHAUS,
Autumn 1926

Contents

Maps

List of Illustrations

CHAPTER I
At The Outbreak of War on The Black Sea

Deeply laden, with a heavy list to port, the Haleb, a ship of the Turkish Steamship Company, Shirket Hairie, left Trapezunt on 30 July 1914, for Constantinople. I was returning from a visit of inspection in the northern section of Anatolia, where, as Director of a War Office Department, I had been inspecting the local Turkish mobilisation organisation and taking part in the Cura (muster of conscripts). I had seen and learnt much and was considering how to embody in a long report the best possible suggestions for improvement.

The air felt heavy with political tension. It is curious how one is here cut off completely for weeks from the outer world, although the Black Sea borders are heavily populated. An old paper from Constantinople, the German-owned Turkish Lloyd, which I had found on the deck of the steamer arriving from Stamboul, reported the Austrian ultimatum to Serbia. It seemed to me particularly severe. The news agency of the steamer had further heard that war had broken out between these two countries – Russia had already put out all the lights along her coast and the Austrian steamers had been recalled from the Black Sea.

This last information appeared to be correct, because yesterday an Austrian ship should have overtaken us on the way between Batoumn and Rize. So we sat tapping in darkness, not knowing what was going on in the world and dependent on coastal gossip and rumour. Even the Vali (mayor) of Trapezunt had told me that he did not know of anything of particular importance occurring in world politics.

That same afternoon we passed the Austrian steamer going to Batoum. No war! I had that calming feeling that I had lost no incident of importance in the world.

Travelling slowly much too slowly for my impatience – we steamed along the beautiful, fertile coast of Asia Minor, which reminded me of the Riviera. What could one not make of this beautiful neighbourhood with its wonderful beaches! In my thoughts I saw sea baths, sanatoria, hotels and a cosmopolitan society. Now I know why the ancient Greeks particularly selected this region for colonisation.

The next afternoon we arrived in Kerison, the home of the cherry. Then our course lay past the land of the fabled Amazons; past Samsun with its big lighters, broad of beam with high-built prows mostly ornamented with dragons' heads; past the delta at the mouth of the Kyzyl Irmak, the Halys of the ancients, whose yellow flood coloured the water far out to sea; past the old ruined walls of Sinope, the birthplace of Demosthenes. The journey seemed unending. Everywhere I sent my interpreter ashore to obtain intelligence, but as he brought back no news of war or rumours of war my fears were calmed.

At last we reached Ineboli, the last stop before Constantinople, and on the morning of 3 August at 11 o'clock we were to begin the passage of the Bosphorus. The character of the country had altered. The hills of Pontus rose abruptly from the coast and we only saw scanty settlements here and there in the mouths of the valleys.

The next morning early, a Turkish torpedo boat met us. We were hailed through a megaphone to know if we had met a Turkish ship with a German Pasha on board. The ship in question carried a special Pasha pennant. It should return at once. We replied "No," and further questions were prevented by the torpedo boat immediately continuing its course. It was apparently in great haste.

A curious feeling of tension again filled my mind. There must be something happening. If only we had reached the Bosphorus! Our expected entry had been somewhat delayed and we were not passing through until the afternoon. In spite of attempts to adjust the cargo, the Haleb had not lost her list, and she still sailed very slowly past the steep cliffs. The hours seemed to drag more and more slowly by.

Suddenly an unknown man took hold of my arm and pointed excitedly to the north-west, exclaiming: *"Voilà, de nouveau un vaisseau de guerre, mais ce n'est pas un Turc."* I could only see a smoke-wreath on the extreme horizon and went up on the bridge. The captain was already examining the ship through his telescope. A warship certainly, nationality not discernible, but judging by the direction probably a Russian. After a short time the captain asked me to leave the bridge. "It would probably be better to know nothing." It became quite clear that a cruiser was following hard after us. She was a Russian. The whole deck was full of Russian infantry, their flat caps and bayonet points being clearly seen. Our ship travelled very slowly, whether by order or free will I do not know. My anxious interpreter, Major Zia Bey, requested me to withdraw to my cabin, but I declined. Surely if the others stop, I can. About 100 yards away the cruiser turned and drew up with her broadside to us and proceeded to lower a boat into the water for the purpose of visiting us.

Suddenly the four funnels of the Russian commenced to belch forth clouds of light smoke – an elegant curve and the cruiser had left us at full speed in pursuit of a cloud of smoke on the eastern horizon. She appeared to be looking for the Austrian we had met a few days before. War between Austria and Russia on Serbia's account seemed certain. Only later, as I learnt of the merciless imprisonment of the many German residents, was it clear to me what a critical moment this had been for me, as the only German on board.

What else was happening in the world? What was Germany doing? My excitement grew from hour to hour. At last, about 3 o'clock, we actually entered the Bosphorus. Almost immediately a small ship approached us from Anadoli Kawak flying the quarantine flag. I sent Zia Bey, my interpreter, to ask for news. He came back almost immediately. On his good-natured face I read anxiety and excitement. Quite a number of Turkish officers who were travelling with us had attached themselves to him. They saluted me and Zia Bey said: "We congratulate you. Germany has declared war on France and Russia. We wish you a glorious campaign." The quarantine doctor did not know any more than this. I thanked them and said: "One thing is surely incorrect, gentlemen. Russia and

France have certainly declared war on us."

Here it was, then, the war of which we had often spoken, but in which we had never really believed. A pleasant feeling of freedom ran through me. Now we Germans could show the world what we had created in many tens of years of steady, tireless work. I then said to myself:

"Naturally the whole of the Military Mission will have already returned to Germany--probably my wife and boy with them. However, I shall still be able to catch up those officers employed in Smyrna and Angora." My immediate route lay either in disguise through Bulgaria and Romania or through Greece and our true ally, Italy. Back to Germany at all costs.

The anchor of the Haleb rattled into the waters of the Golden Horn. I left my baggage with Zia Bey and my excellent orderly, Arif Effendi. I went ashore with the first *caique* and immediately on landing seized the Stamboul from the first newsboy I saw and read the headlines in large letters 'The World War,' and then my glance fell on the words Switzerland has mobilised her entire army. Hullo! This meant a world war. I must follow the others back to Germany as quickly as possible.

However, the surprises of that day were not yet ended. As I looked up from the paper I saw coming towards me as if called, but nevertheless to my great astonishment, my neighbour in Moda (suburb on the Asiatic shore), Col Nicolai, Commander of the 3rd Division. "Hullo! You still here!" I called to him. "We are all here," he replied. "Nobody from the Military Mission has been allowed to return to Germany. I have just left a General Council of Officers with His Excellency von Liman. We have each of us received our orders for the mobilisation of the Turkish Army. You are to remain at the War Office."

And now began a hard, a difficult period.

CHAPTER II
Turkey's Neutrality

Our first official duty was the mobilisation of the Turkish Army. This had been ordered for the purposes of general safety, otherwise Turkey declared her neutrality. We thus continued to work along our usual lines, even though the method and occasionally the places were different. Appendix I gives a list of the members of the Military Mission, showing their occupations.

The work had now altered in character, inasmuch as far-seeing changes in the existing organisation, planned to bear fruit in the future, had to be dropped. Now the main object was to use every available means to make the Turkish Army a good fighting instrument as rapidly as possible.
Threateningly, ever before our minds, was the remembrance of the complete breakdown during the but recently concluded Balkan Wars. This time, however, German influence was to be allowed a wider scope. The earlier reformers were merely allowed to put forward suggestions which, as a rule, were simply shelved by the Turks. The sole evidence of the personal influence of the German instructors was in the "model formations."

The Military Mission, which had been in existence since December 1913 – eight months before the outbreak of war – was built up on broad foundations. The members took over commands in the Turkish Army – a certain definite field of work thus coming under their personal influence, and placing them in a position to carry out any contemplated improvements without delay.

The head of the German Military Mission was the Cavalry General Liman von Sanders, who was at that time Marshal in the Turkish Army, where every German officer ranked one step higher than he did in the German Army. The Marshal, as I shall call him in future, for the sake of brevity, was a tall, stern, military-looking man, very self contained, quick in decision, clear in his orders, scanty of praise, sharp in reprimand and in following up a decision once taken. He did not leave us in the dark as to the tasks which lay ahead of us. During the negotiations in 1913, a certain time limit was laid down for the activity of the Military Mission. We had Turkish *muavine* allotted to us, who worked with us as our assistants and who were ultimately to take over the posts themselves. The usual translation of *muavin* by interpreter is not correct. That many of them, like my good Zia Bey, were incapable of filling the post of an interpreter is another matter.

We were not concerned with politics. The sole object of the Military Mission was to assist the Turks to get their army into good fighting trim. We Germans wanted a strong, vigorous Turkey. The outcry made in Entente diplomatic circles over the German Military Mission, and particularly in Russia, was therefore quite out of place. Why was there no agitation regarding the simultaneous activities of the British Naval Mission under Admiral Limpus, or of the French General Bauman, who had the whole of the Turkish police force under his command an excellent, militarily organised body of men?

It was a great pity, both in the interests of the work we had undertaken as well as in that of the Turkish Army, that the Military Mission's task of reorganisation, which had commenced so propitiously, could not at least be carried through to a definite conclusion, but was suddenly interrupted by the outbreak of the world war.

On the whole the Turks were keen and receptive, even though there were naturally many difficulties to be overcome. These were partly personal, but mostly due to the unfortunate financial conditions. I will not say more on this point here. In the War Minister, Enver Pasha, however, we had a man who, backed by the authority of his important position, successfully set himself to carry through the reorganisation. Even the then Naval Minister, Djemal Pasha, while admitting to political leanings towards the Entente at that period, says that we set about the theoretical and practical training of the army with quite unusual care. Already at the end of the first month or two it was apparent that a new spirit had been infused into it.

A parade of the 1st Division, which took place in the middle of July 1914, at Liberty Knoll, the grave of Mahomet Shefket Pasha, and was a brilliant success, may be described as the last of our peace time activities. I was away on duty at the time, but I was told that the excellent carriage and drill of the troops made an overwhelming impression on the numerous spectators, and particularly on the foreign military attachés, who had not considered such progress possible, a proof of what can be achieved with the excellent material to be found in Turkey, particularly with the splendid Anatolians.

The effects of the reorganisation grew naturally less discernible the greater the distance from Constantinople. The mobilisation of the army made slow but steady progress. The mobilised army corps often carried out manoeuvres on a large scale round about Constantinople and Adrianople – with blank cartridges, of course! How could it be otherwise during peace time manoeuvres! This recalls vividly to mind that period, which was the most difficult for us German officers in Turkey.

The waves of patriotic enthusiasm had risen high in the Fatherland. From all parts of the world Germans streamed home to their colours. We saw them leaving Constantinople. Who has not read with a fast-beating heart how every German who thought he could be of any use to his country vanished under the eyes of the Entente, having to resort to numerous subterfuges and running very great risks in order to get back to Germany.

And we, who were soldiers by profession, whose own element was supposed to be war, had to sit passively watching. We felt ashamed of ourselves. I can still see the gigantic liner, flying an enormous blue, white and red flag, which was conveying French reservists to Marseilles, rounding Seraglio Point. Jubilation, shouting, singing and military music had drawn me on to the terrace of my house, which projected far out into the water and lay opposite Seraglio Point. The strains of the Marseillaise fell on my car. I retired again quickly. Then the word went round: "The English are leaving tomorrow." It was not such a noisy business. Occasionally the rumour arose that a special train was standing ready with steam up in the station to take us back, and that luggage was limited to one portmanteau each. Vain hope!

German newspapers still arrived fairly regularly. We saw how in one short moment the spirit of August 1914 was born. Suddenly it was there, just as in 1813 and 1870. It is an experience one only has once in a lifetime, if one is lucky. And we were not allowed to take part. We, who had chosen soldiering for a career, were denied one of the few opportunities afforded to Germans of illustrating by deeds the gospel we had been preaching to our subordinates all our lives: "When the moment for action comes, teeth clenched and at it!"

Liège fallen! and my battalion there, which I had left only a few months previously. Constantinople newspapers of French origin stated for some time after this: "Liège still holding out." Later on, when we had to combat false reports of this nature, they developed into household words.

My brother, in command of his battery on the Western Front, had already been awarded the Iron Cross II – the dream of every true soldier. I made up my mind to remain in Turkey for the rest of my life, so that the finger of scorn should not be pointed at me in Germany as a shirker and a poltroon. None of us dreamed of anything but a short war.

Once again the Marshal wrote very explicitly to His Majesty, the Emperor, in a final endeavour to obtain our recall. The following is the Emperor's reply:

> While fully recognising the services rendered by you in the past I appeal to your sense of duty and to that of my officers who are serving under you, to persevere undisturbed by politics in the work I have allotted to you until you receive further orders from me. I consider your duties there at the present critical period to be equivalent to any services you could render me here, you successfully carry out your difficult task in Turkey which may perhaps often demand self-sacrifice, but which is of such importance to us here.
> (Signed) WILLIAM IR

Nothing remained, therefore, but to obey. We each took the precaution to provide ourselves with a copy of the above-mentioned A.K.O., which we fastened over our beds so as to be able to read it each morning and thus obtain renewed strength to carry on our work. In my bitter disappointment I wrote to my brother-in-law about that time: "Over there you are making history which we here are allowed to read about."

There were, however, also gratifying moments. On 10 August 1914, I was with the War Minister, Enver Pasha, for the purposes of my usual report when, contrary to custom, the attendant interrupted the interview to announce Lt Col von Kress (who became later the well known and greatly esteemed leader of the expeditions against the Suez Canal). It was clear therefore that the matter must be very urgent. The following conversation then took place: Kress: "Fort Tchanak Kale states that the German warships *Goeben* and *Breslau* are lying at the entrance to the Dardanelles and request permission to enter. The fortress asks for immediate instructions to be sent as to procedure of the commanders of the Kum Kali and Siddil Babr forts,"
Enver: "I can't decide that now. I must first consult the Grand Vizier."

Kress: "But we must wire immediately."

It was a very difficult problem for Enver Pasha—usually so quick in arriving at a decision. He battled silently with himself though outwardly showing no signs of the struggle within. Finally he said abruptly: "They are to allow them to enter."

A weight fell from the hearts of us two Germans, though Kress was not yet content. "If the English warships follow the Germans, are they to be fired on if they also attempt an entrance?"

Renewed cogitation on the part of Enver. "The matter must be left to the decision of the Council of Ministers. The question can remain open for the time being."

Kress: "Excellency, we cannot leave our subordinates in such a position without issuing immediately clearly defined instructions. Are the English to be fired on or not?"

Enver, after further thought: "Yes."

We heard the clanking of the portcullis descending before the Dardanelles. It was an incident in the world's history of which I chanced to be a witness. None of us had moved a muscle. Kress took his leave and I proceeded with my report as though nothing had happened.

Goeben and *Breslau* under Rear Admiral Souchon had adventurous and heroic voyages behind them, several accounts of which have already been published. I will therefore merely mention here, for general information, that Souchon, by the surprise bombardment of Bone and Philippeville on 4 August, considerably disturbed the transport of Algerian troops to France, and after coaling at Messina deluded the English ships lying in wait for him, gained the open sea and again snapped his fingers at the English by making for Constantinople instead of entering the Adriatic, as they anticipated.

He coaled at nights under cover of the darkness, obtaining his supplies from the duly prepared German ships, and on 10 August the *Goeben* and *Breslau* safely entered the Dardanelles. In vain had superior English forces lain in wait for or scoured the Mediterranean searching for them.

In taking such a step on his own initiative Enver Pasha had naturally assumed a grave personal responsibility, and for him everything now depended on whether and how his ministerial colleagues would share this responsibility with him.

At this critical period the senior ministers and Halil Bey, the President of the Chamber, were accustomed to meet every evening in the Yali of the Grand Vizier at Jenikoi. On 10 August Enver Pasha was the last to enter the circle, and as he did so he said in his characteristically quiet and smiling manner: "A son has been born to us." No one understood him at first, but when he explained to the more impatient present that the *Goeben* was the son referred to the consternation was great. No immediate way could be seen out of this delicate situation. According to international law the ships would either have to leave the Dardanelles again within 24 hours or they would have to be disarmed and interned. A suggestion to appear to do the latter was rejected the same night by the German Ambassador, von Wangenheim. A second suggestion which was put forward by Djemal Pasha, and accepted, was that Turkey should nominally buy these two ships from Germany. In this way Turkey's desire to maintain her neutrality was possible. The *Goeben* flew the Turkish flag as Javus Sultan Selim and the *Breslau* as Midilli.

A few mornings later I was crossing as usual from Kadikoi (on the Asiatic side) to Stamboul, in order to carry out my duties, when just at that moment the *Goeben* and *Breslau*, both flying the Turkish flag, were seen approaching from the Golden Horn. Our captain altered the course of our boat and steered us up close to these approaching cruisers. Everybody streamed to port and great was the jubilation and hand-clapping of the many Turks on board at this surprise reinforcement to their fleet.

In order to understand better this remarkable enthusiasm of the usually stolid Turk it should be stated that the Turks, at the cost of a great deal of money, obtained for the most part by collections made from the inhabitants up and down the country, had placed an order in England for two Dreadnoughts, the *Sultan Osman* and the *Reschadieh*. *Sultan Osman* was practically finished and the Turkish crew of 500 in England. *Reschadieh* was to follow shortly. These two completely modern battleships were impatiently awaited in Turkey. Over and over again, however, England, that is to say, Messrs. Armstrong Vickers, the shipbuilders in question, found excuses to delay delivery. Then came the threat of world war, and as early as 21 July 1914, in spite of the neutrality of Turkey, these eagerly awaited ships, purchased at great expense, were commandeered by England. This evoked tremendous indignation and fury against England in Turkey, and each one who had contributed his mite felt that he personally had been betrayed. It was the best propaganda England could possibly have made for us, for it increased a thousand fold the joy and gratitude of the Turks for the two warships sent as substitutes from Germany.

In spite of this the Entente did not abandon the hope of still keeping Turkey at least neutral – a neutrality à la Greece presumably.

One commonly heard that opinion in the Turkish Council of Ministers regarding the ultimate attitude of Turkey was divided. A bitter subterraneous battle commenced. Naturally the German Military Mission was a sharp thorn in the side of the Entente and their supporters in Turkey. The dead weight which our mere presence with the many commands of the army put into the scale in favour of the Central Powers was only too apparent.

On 30 October 1914, England demanded for the last time the dissolution of the German Military and Naval Missions within twelve hours, and there was also a rumour afloat that we were to be removed by force. This may have been merely one of those many fantastic rumours without which the Orient cannot exist, and the creation of which forms the sole mental occupation of so many Orientals. In any case, we never left our quarters without a revolver in our pocket.

CHAPTER III
The Political Position of Turkey

The development of the political position in the world war and the increasing mobilisation of the Turkish Army which, as a result of three months' work had now reached a certain stage, forced Turkey more and more to decisive political action. The further continuation of a state of neutrality became increasingly nonsensical. How this neutrality was regarded on the side of the Entente was seen from a telegram from Iswolski, Russian Ambassador in Paris, to his Government, dated 11 August 1914, in which he says that in the opinion of the French Government the offer of guarantee (to Turkey) would not prevent the Narrows question being settled in the way we (the Russians) wish it following the termination of war. Consequently neutrality was impossible for the Turks. It would have meant a disgraceful break up of the Turkish Empire without a fight. Even Djemal Pasha was in agreement on this point.

It was certainly a weighty decision for Turkey to decide to openly come in on the side of the Central Powers, because in the world mêlée which had already started Turkey would be fighting for her very existence.

The history of Turkey since 29 May, 1453, the date of the capture of Constantinople, had continuously pointed forward to this moment. On the other hand this decision could not be so very difficult, not merely because on 2 August 1914, they had concluded a secret agreement with Germany which was not even known to all the Turkish ministers, but because no Turkish statesman in the autumn of 1914 was able to conceive any other termination if he quietly and clearly considered what historical development the policy of the European Powers had, in the course of time, gradually followed regarding Turkey.

Russia is the old traditional enemy. This belief sits deep and firm even in the simple Anatolian peasant. It had been hammered into generations through the centuries by repeated acts in history. This is not the result of ill-will or unfriendliness, but the unalterable results of geographical conditions. Man and his plural, the people, is simply a product of the earth out of which he grows, and whether he will or no he is bound to its conditions.

Russia, this enormous colossus, this terrible Continental power, needed a safe approach to an ice-free sea. With dynamic energy she was forced to continually seek connection with that nation connecting always to a warm sea. Otherwise she would smother, given normal conditions, of a superfluity of her agricultural produce and a lack of industrial produce. That is why the history of Russia consists of continuously recurring attempts to get air for the country and relieve it from its geographical necessity.

Russia first conquered the east coast in the battles of the north. This is, however, not continually free from ice. A dramatic example of this lies in front of me on the day that I write – the middle of January 1926 – the freezing in of more than 30 ships among them many German in the Finnish waters. They are in the greatest danger, and our battleship *Hessen*, ice-breakers and aviators are working tirelessly to save them.

To the north there is a connection over the Murman railway-- Archangel to the White Sea. What this is worth in winter is excellently illustrated by Paléologue, the French Ambassador to the Russian court, when the French Government in December 1915, insisted on 400,000 Russians being sent by 10 January 1916, by this route to the French battlefields. As the mouth of the Dvina was frozen as far as 100 kilometres above Archangel, these troops would have had to march four or five days with the temperature 40° C. below zero, in total darkness, across the ice to reach transports. One must just conceive this picture! What enormous difficulties solely for food supplies, coal, light, billets, quite apart from the carrying out of the march itself! The departure of a ship is then only possible so long as ice-breakers can hold open the narrow passage. Such a connection is absolutely of no value.

The analysing glance passes still further across the Russian map and finds the unnaturally long Siberian railway, which stretches continually farther east till it reaches the coast of the Pacific Ocean. But as Russia was about to reap the fruits of this 10,500km. length of railway line and establish herself firmly on the shores of the Pacific in 1904, the Russian bear received from Japan a painful blow on her far-extended claws. Here again she was unable to achieve any definite result.

Encircled Russia has now only one remaining avenue of escape under the sky to the south. There a direct connection with the continuously warm Mediterranean is possible. "That we must have," was the logical conclusion of every thinking Russian. But the river-like outlets, the Bosphorus and the Dardanelles, were firmly held by the Turks. The Turks fully understood their value, carefully watched the rights of usage and had locked the entrances to both Narrows with strong fortifications.

Russia's development continuously forced her in this direction. Peter the Great is said to have laid this down in his will. This was Catherine II's real objective in the first Russo-Turkish war of 1768–1774, which brought the conquest of the Crimea. Her eldest nephew, Alexander, was to be Emperor of Russia and his brother, Constantine, Emperor of Byzantium.This urge continued through the centuries. Fresh attempts of Russia to conquer Constantinople by force followed the first Russo-Turkish war. Each time she grasped with hungry outstretched arms towards the Capital on the Golden Horn. With the one arm across the Balkans, creating new states such as Rumania and Bulgaria, with the other arm across the Caucasus, to the destruction of the Armenians. As ebb and flow occur in rhythmical change, based on nature's laws, so the Russian flood rose continuously against the Turkish possession.

We had to suffer a similar continuously recurring flood on our western frontier. We had to, whether we wished to or no. The French will have the Rhine. We cannot recognise, however, in this case a similar geographically natural urge. Both countries, however, Turkey as well as Germany, needed to resist this flood a Dyke Captain "who under stood his business, such as we had had in Dyke Captain von Schönhausen." (Bismarck)

At the moment, however, we see Moscow and Ankora arm in arm on the world's stage. An unnatural picture born of need, which must again vanish with the recovery in strength of Russia. One thing is certain, that Russia, as a result of her urge towards the sea, developed in the course of centuries as the natural enemy of

TCHANAK KALE BEFORE THE OUTBREAK OF WAR, 1914

THE MARSHAL AND ESSAD PASHA (IN PROFILE) DURING AN INSPECTION
OF TROOPS ON GALLIPOLI

Turkey. I have already said that even the Anatolian peasant instinctively felt this. It is, however, astonishing how this urge had seized on all classes in Continental Russia, even to the head and heart of the simple man of the people. On 20 February 1915, Paléologue wrote as follows: "The Byzantine delusion increasingly chains the public opinion of Russia and permits the loss of East Prussia to be regarded as almost nothing in comparison, as if the fulfilment of the Byzantine dream did not necessitate the defeat of Germany as a preliminary condition." And already, on 1 October 1914, a Russian spoke as follows: "This war can be of no use to us if it does not bring us Constantinople and the Narrows. Constantinople must belong to us and to us alone. It is our historical mission, our sacred duty to again plant the cross of the orthodox faith on the cupola of the sacred St Sophia. Russia would not be the chosen people if she did not finally revenge this century-old shame of Christendom."

What was the feeling as against the two other partners of the Entente, England and France?

The wrath which raged against the first-named as the result of the seizure of the warships, I have already described. In addition, the policy of these two States had, for a long time past, unmistakably disclosed the intention to seize for themselves, during the coming re-partition of Turkey, portions cut from the body of the sick man. "These portions were already generally well known. They were known as spheres of interest." They were the areas which the League of Nations has today allotted to them as mandated territories. The motives lie clearly disclosed: For England, securing her communications with India by land; for France, the control of the eastern portions of the Mediterranean. For these reasons both powers were largely interested in a weakened Turkey unable to defend herself, whose dissolution would then be for them only a question of time.

With this in view England had already approached Germany in July 1895, with the proposal to divide up a Turkey no longer capable of existence. Of what importance this thought was to England is clear from the fact that Salisbury a month later again approached Kaiser

Wilhelm II, who was at that times at Cowes, I.O.W., and sought to win him over to this plan. Both attempts failed. Germany could not be won over to any attempt against Turkey.

"We can reach our aim in another way," thought England, and proceeded to remove those difficulties which existed outside Europe with France and Russia so as to give herself a free hand in Europe. The birth of the Entente drew nigh. A neutral, the Swede Rudolph Kjellén, has admirably, clearly and convincingly, even dramatically, pictured this in his book on the diplomatic history of the period prior to the world war. On 8 April 1904, all points of friction existing between the powers, England and France, were cleared up by a series of diplomatic agreements. This agreement is generally distinguished by the decision: Morocco for France, but in exchange a free hand for England in Egypt.

Now came Russia's turn. On 31 August 1907, England reached an agreement with Russia on Persia, Afghanistan and Thibet. "With this agreement the shadows broadened over Europe," said Kjellén. That is what I could almost call the finesse, of all these apparently harmless colonial agreements, because they were actually directed against Germany and her associates, as they cleared the way in Europe for the Entente which was born as their result.

Turkey's last doubts must have disappeared after a conversation which took place in Paris in July 1914, between Djemal Pasha and de Margerie, of the French Foreign Ministry. The latter frankly conceded that the Entente was forging an iron ring round the Central Powers. And to the Entente belonged the inexorable Russia who, as is known from the comparative history tables of the Kaiser, had already, on 21 February 1914 with the consent of the Czar, formally laid down in protocol a decision to commence military and technical preparations for an attempt on Stamboul.

Turkey was in danger of being simply smothered by this group of Powers if she did not seek shelter from the other side.

Germany, in contradiction to the Entente, had a very definite interest in a strong Turkey capable of development, without any intentions whatsoever regarding increase of territory there. History has shown that this was truly our policy – not merely to obtain Turkey's good graces, but for very real political and economic considerations. From political, because with the increasingly apparent effort on the part of the Entente to confine the growing urge of Germany towards extension, this connection which offered a way out of our confinement across the Balkans to the far off rich Asia – even if it were only Asia Minor appeared to Germany as most welcome. Economic, because Germany hoped to find in the rich development possibilities of Turkey a favourable field for her Capital, the products of her constantly developing industry and her trade.

A very drastic piece of evidence in this connection is afforded by a study of the railway policy of the different powers in Turkey.

The English and French built short railways in their spheres of interest, which lay under the muzzle of their ships' guns. Germany, on the contrary, by deciding on the Anatolian railway to Angora and then on to Konia, opened up the interior of the country in the truest strategical and economic interests of Turkey. The continuation of the railway to Baghdad was only possible as the result of truly heated negotiations with Russia, France and England. In spite of all, however, the course of the railway in the Bay of Alexandretta came within the radius of fire of England's naval guns.

The eternal postponements had, however, still more severe results. The Baghdad railway was not finished at the beginning of the world war. As a result Turkey, and with her Germany, suffered immeasurable damage, because the unfinished portions which were intended to convey supplies to the 2nd, 4th, 6th, 7th and 8th Army remained broken in the Taurus. The long tunnel from the Taurus was only finished in the end of September 1918 too late.

The interests of Turkey and Germany thus went hand in hand. The policy of the Entente forged them together, otherwise what was the sense of the slogan then current in St Petersburg that the road to Constantinople passes through Berlin? Turkey was forced from a pure desire to save her own skin, to help to close this road.

If the Turkish statesman in the autumn of 1914 calmly and clearly reviewed the historical development of European politics against Turkey, he could not for a moment remain in doubt that the interests of his own country demanded Turkey's entry into the world war on the side of the Central Powers.

I lay particular emphasis on this point, because I still hear, here and there, that Germany forced Turkey to take part in the World War on her side.

CHAPTER IV
Decision In Favour Of The Central Powers

With Turkey in this state of high tension politically, it only required some incident to bring matters to a head, and this actually happened – the usual spark fell into the powder barrel.

On 29 October 1914, Russian ships were fired on by the *Goeben* and *Breslau*, as well as several Turkish warships, as they were laying mines at the entrance to the Bosphorus. An unheard of breach of peace! It resolved itself into a battle during which the Russian minelayer, which had "only 700" mines on board, was sunk. In following up the enemy fleet, Sebastopol, Odessa, Feodosia and Novorossik were bombarded, 50 petroleum depots and many granaries burnt, 14 military transports sunk, et cetera.

We learnt this as on 30 October we were assembled at the Sultan's court in Dolma Bagdsche for the ceremony of the Schärpenküsses, during the feast of Bairam.

That meant war! At last we had our justification for being present. That is what actually happened. The army received the declaration of war with great acclamation. At least so Djemal Pasha relates, to whom I must continually refer because he is the sole Turkish soldier and statesman whose reminiscences we know and to which we Germans can justifiably attach importance, because he was no pronounced friend of Germany. This decision was also received with joy even by the most distant Turkish circles.

That this feeling was nevertheless scarcely unanimous is clear from the utterances of certain Turkish papers. The Tanin wrote, for instance, at that time: "We can regard the incident in the Black Sea as a frontier incident. We do this out of consideration for the peace and quiet of the people. If Russia so wishes, she need not herself take any other view. If, on the other hand, she does not wish to, it will be all the same to us. That is the position."

Ikdam wrote: "It is very regrettable that the Russian Government, instead of replying to the protest of the Porte in the proper manner, recalled her Ambassador in Constantinople, and that the powers associated with Russia – England and France have also recalled their Ambassadors. This step of the Powers has doubtless arisen owing to a misunderstanding. They nevertheless have let the matter rest with the breaking off of diplomatic relations without one of them declaring war on Turkey. Between the breaking off of diplomatic relations and a declaration of war lies a great difference."

Naturally there were also circles friendly to the Entente. A Turkish nation of one common opinion was out of the question. As there are many parties in Germany, so the Turkish Empire possessed different nationalities and races with tendencies considerably differing one from the other.

Armenians and Greeks, Jews and Levantines constitute the main mass of non-Mahommedans. They control trade and commerce – without them no business.

It is said: "A Greek gets the better of two Jews, an Armenian of two Greeks, and only the Devil can get the better of an Armenian."

The Levantine race, which has gradually grown up on the shores of the Levant, is principally composed of a mixture of these races, with occasional dilutions of French and Italian blood. They ally all the worse characteristics of their progenitors in themselves

It is clear, therefore, that no trace of national spirit or sacrifice of personal affairs in the interest of the Ottoman Turkish Empire could be expected from such elements. For them the Turk and the Turkish State simply remained as an object of plunder for their numerous business talents. They inclined in the main to the Entente and fell an easy prey to the attempts to win them over.

There was thus a ceaseless conflict below the surface throughout the war, which ended in a weakening and finally a total destruction of the Turkish powers of resistance.

These magnificent Ottoman subjects shamelessly and openly displayed their true colours when in November 1918, English and French troops marched into Pera. The blue, white, red, and the

Grecian flags, which had been hidden somewhere since the hoped-for entry of the Entente at the time of the Dardanelles campaign, were again brought out to be glorified with a disgusting frenzy of joy. The fez was hurled into the corner.

As opposed to these spongers, and in numbers far more numerous, were the Mahommedans, who also were one only in faith and not in race. There was the ever-present difference between Turk and Arab, of whom the latter could not be depended upon from the national-Turkish point of view. In addition to these there were Albanians (Arnautes), Bosnians, Kurds, Circassians, Lacedemonians, Georgians, according to the land from which they had sprung. Finally, there was still a difference between the European Turks, the Thracians, and the Asiatic Turks, the Anatolians, who were the pearls of the whole lot.

These varied characteristics of this many-sided structure of the Ottoman Empire were to be found in the Capital itself. On the one side that "enormity" Pera, supposedly European in a tawdry and flashy style with a night life *à la franca*, and on the far side of the Golden Horn the peaceful Stamboul with its many magnificent mosques, its famous memories of past centuries and its contemplative life *à la turka*.

That the final entry of Turkey into the world war would not produce from such a mixed nation the united spirit we saw in Germany in 1914, was clear to the beholders. That was not to be expected from a people so constantly at war.

As a result, the pompous declaration of the Holy War, the *Djihad*, on 14 November 1914, by the reading of the five *Fetvas* in the Faith mosque at Constantinople, the unfurling of the green flag of the Prophet, the prayer of the Sultan, on the Holy Mantel of the Prophet in Top Kapu did not deceive the knowing observer.

Fetva is a solemn answer of the Sheik-el-Islam, the head religious official of ministerial rank, to questions of the Sultan and Caliph who, to speak in European parlance or *à la franca*, combined the offices of Emperor and Pope in his own person. In the above-mentioned case the Caliph asked five questions, all of them bearing on the duty of all Mahommedans to take part in the Holy War against Russia, England and France, and threatening with the heaviest terrors of hell those Mahommedans who, as subjects of these three powers, were to fight against the Sultan and Caliph or his allies. The Sheik-el-Islam answered quite shortly, "Yes, certainly they will," and as a result the following of these orders became a religious duty to all true believers, and the Mahommedan takes his religious duties very seriously. The lower his social position the more earnestly he takes his religion.

The hoped-for effect was however not attained, at least so far as those Mahommedans were concerned who were not at the same time political subjects of the Sultan. Moroccans and Indians and every possible kind of other racial branches professing the Mahommedan faith fought quite unmoved against the Caliph. It is to be hoped that hell will be good to them.

Turkey drew one immediate advantage from the declaration of war. This was the removal of the "Capitulations." These, originating from former times, granted to the nationals of foreign states special rights outside the regime of the government of the country, of which the most important were separate postal facilities, freedom from taxes and jurisdiction in their own consulates.

What was the composition of the Government which knowingly, after ripe consideration, had led this country into war?

At the head stood the Sultan, who was at the same time Caliph and Commander-in-Chief. A good, old man, of benevolent appearance, who actually however was the sole head in name only.

The Grand Vizier – or Prime Minister in our sense – was the Prince Said Halim, a small, gentlemanly, clever and sympathetic personality of ancient Egyptian stock, and with the assurance of a man of the world. If one met him in the street, always in a carriage surrounded by a squadron of Life Guards, taking the steepest streets, up or down, at a fast trot; as a friend of horses one felt sorry for the horses, but one realised the Oriental character as the procession sped past and one saw a small, wise, Asiatic yellow face under a red fez returning one's bow. A picture from *A Thousand*

and One Nights. I did not get to know him closer personally, but I have always heard that during these stormy times he was the man who wisely weighed every problem and maintained the balance.

Before I speak of other Ministers I must mention something which was, for us Germans, an incomprehensible, bodyless. Something, which was everywhere active and was actually a driving force which the Government possessed and which yet did not belong to the Government. This was the *Comité d'Union et Progres*, or translated, the Committee for Union and Progress, shortly 'the Young Turks.' Nobody knew who was the president. The individual members were also unknown, although naturally there must have been many among the officers. Actually the thing was so organised that a number of members of the Committee were Ministers at the same time, and were thus able to make their influence felt along the lines desired by the Young Turks.

At this time it was the famous triumvirate –Talaat, Enver, Djemal – who in this manner imprinted on the Turkish Government its decisive character and this in a sense friendly to Germany.

Talaat Bey, later Pasha, was at first Minister of the Interior, then Grand Vizier. He was big and imposing in person, vigorous, amiable and natural, with clear and alert eyes. Judged by his external appearance he could have been a Western European.

Djemal Pasha, a type of the clever, retiring, calculating, energetic Oriental, with fixed aims and not willing to let others see his cards, was head of the Admiralty. He is author of the oft-mentioned reminiscences. His sympathies lay at first on the side of the Entente. Was he not in July 1914 an esteemed guest at the French fleet manoeuvres, and had he not given free play to his feeling at the departure of the French reservists from Constantinople on 9 August 1914? It is therefore the more to his credit that this man of cool decision, in full recognition of the Turkish position, now voted with honest will for the alliance with Germany.

The third man of this triumvirate was the most important for us German soldiers, the Deputy Commander-in-Chief and War Minister Enver Pasha. He was definitely an open friend of

Germany, sometimes too much so, as when he vainly tried to arrange certain matters according to the German manner although such arrangement did not fit in at all with local conditions.

I had to deal with him practically every day. In the early thirties, of youthful, vigorous appearance, clever and energetic, with quick powers of appreciation and a first class memory, fate had brought him in his early years into a position of unique power and heavy responsibility, and yet as compared with our higher leaders, his whole personality did not appear to be such as to give or receive confidence. In his manner, particularly with strangers, there was a certain timidity and diffidence, so that I can understand that officers meeting him for the first time sometimes mistook him for his own adjutant. Enver Pasha was a true Oriental. His immovable features always hid a riddle and the unsolved question whether he had actually given complete expression to his thoughts.

He gave decisions shortly, clearly and with assurance. Whether they were always correct is another matter. As a result of his rapid promotion to high military rank he lacked that knowledge of the lower ranks which can only be acquired by slow promotion from grade to grade. He further lacked the knowledge of what could in actual practice be done in and with troops. In the German consistent organical further development he saw merely German pedantry which made unnecessarily difficult the carrying out of his ideas. He generally looked on a matter as finished as soon as the orders were issued, whereas in fact, particularly with the Turkish Army, the main difficulties only commenced with the attempt to put orders into practice.

He had become very distant to all the friends of his earlier years, particularly since he had as *Damad* – son-in law of the Sultan – enlarged his household to the size of a small court. Many who knew his rise to power from a lowly status regarded this action on his part with great suspicion.

As far as Parliament was concerned his duties as Minister were comparatively light. Parliament had one annual sitting which lasted from 13 March until the autumn. During the intervening period the Council of Ministers issued provisional laws which were later to be confirmed in Parliament.

Parliament was worked successfully to prevent any impression of difficulties reaching foreign observers. Consequently the War Office in this respect was able to work without disturbance. This was just as well, as Enver Pasha was not liked by Parliament. This was due to the impression left by his retiring manner, which awoke the feeling that as a soldier he did not esteem Parliament very highly. Finally, he was not a clever speaker. He spoke shortly, sharply, hesitatingly, in a tone of military superiority – probably more as a result of a certain embarrassment than intentionally.

I have described Enver Pasha so completely because he was both before and during the war militarily the leading personality, and because in a certain sense he had imprinted the seal of his personality on the army

Seen in his car, dashing at speed through the streets of Stamboul, closely followed by a second car containing A.D.C.s armed to the teeth, it was easy to believe him the youthful master or dictator of the Empire. Of the A.D.C.s only the first who generally sat beside him, Major Kiasim Bey, was adjutant in the German sense of the word – a prudent, clever, educated and amiable man. For the rest, bodily strength and ability to handle their weapons constituted their chief accomplishments.

Of the remaining Ministers of the Ressort [Council] only Djawid Bey, the Minister of Finance, played an important part in addition to the President of the Chamber, Halil Bey. The first was a *Domne*, a Jew of Spanish origin who had become a Mahommedan.

Such were the men in whom found expression the determined desire of the Turkish nation to maintain its place among the nations of the world. They understood how best to translate this national desire into fact. Nevertheless, I am forced to state that, probably under the influence of the Gallipoli success, they very considerably overestimated the capacity of their country.

Turkey did not content itself by regarding its task as strictly one of defence of its widely extended and far distant frontiers *à la*

Gallipoli, for which its resources would have sufficed, but she hoped – apparently under the impulse of Enver's fantasies – for an extension of the Turkish frontiers in the direction of their country of origin, the highlands of Iran and the valleys of Turan. Dreams of a greater Turkey, complete over-estimation of her own strength.

Thus took place in 1918, as a preliminary stage to the attainment of this aim, the campaign of Wehib Pasha in Transcaucasia and Asserbeidjan. This drew from the exhausted country the last of its strength which was then so urgently required in Mesopotamia and more particularly in Palestine.

Following the collapse, Enver Pasha, stubborn as he was, continued undisturbed his ideas of enlarging Turkey in Turania. He died a hero's death for his ideas, in this respect happier than his Minister colleagues who – in accordance with conditions not uncommon in Turkey – were all murdered; Prince Said Halim in Rome, Talaat Pasha in Berlin and Djemal Pasha in Tiflis, as far as I know all by Armenians.

Djawid Bey, however, the best financial brain in Turkey, was hanged on the gallows at Angora on 20 August 1926, for rebelling against the Government of Mustapha Kemal Pasha.

THE MARSHAL IN CONVERSATION WITH THE WAR MINISTER, ENVER PASHA, BEFORE THE
SULTAN'S PALACE AT DOLMA BAGDSCHE
30 October, 1914

CHAPTER V
The First Months Of War

What was the general military-political position of the Central Powers at the commencement of November 1914, when Turkey finally joined. The front of the Central Powers extended from a right flank standing on the North Sea, across Germany and Austria to Hungary.

The original idea of a crossbar through the centre of Europe with the left flank resting on the Mediterranean had not been realised, as that "perfidious" Italy suddenly discovered that it had a long coastline quite defenceless against British guns. The van of the Central Powers was confronted by England, France and Serbia, while their rear was threatened by mighty Russia. A devilish position!

Generally in the course of a battle an attempt is made to encircle the enemy and then crush him. An old law. so simple and yet so difficult. Every struggle teaches this lesson, from the famous world-renowned examples of Cannæ (216 B.C.) to Tannenberg (A.D. 1914). Edward VII of England, the spiritual father of the world war, also acted in accordance with these principles when, soon after his accession to power, he prepared the peoples surrounding Germany for an appeal to arms.

To encircle correctly, the centre must stand fast and possess wings as long and powerful as possible.

Germany was in a position to still further extend. By her fleet, her right arm, the northern wing. This did not happen.

The left wing of the Central Powers pointed to the Balkans. There Rumania had so far always been an ally of hers. But Rumania refused to join her by a decision of the Privy Council of 3 August 1914, against the desire of its old, grey-headed King. The King, a Hohenzollern, died under the shock.

Thus Turkey filled the empty place although the road to the new ally was closed. That fact increased the moral value of this courageous act.

All the same, Turkey could not take action in the sense of being a wing of an encircling movement. Prior preparations were entirely lacking. Her quite extraordinary value to the Central Powers lay much more in the geographical position of Turkey, because once the above-described front reached a definite settlement in the south-west, Russia would be finally shut off from the rest of the Entente.

The importance of this is clear from the preceding general historical considerations. But already in these first months of war with Turkey the practical results were making themselves felt in the worst possible manner for Russia.

The Russian Empire had already suffered prodigious losses, particularly under Hindenburg's blows. Men could be replaced, but the Russian industry could not even begin to meet the colossal demands for rifles and artillery munitions. The latter demand reached a daily total in December 1914 of 45,000 shells. The whole Russian supply reached at most a total figure of 13,000, and following 15 February 1915, perhaps 20,000 shells. It is not to be wondered at that about this time the Grand Duke Nicholas advised the French Ambassador that this was the reason for the stoppage of the operations.

Paléologue disclosed countless further proofs. I will only add one remark of the Russian Foreign Minister, Sazanow, 20 February 1915, he, in company with the French Ambassador, crossed the grand parade ground in Petersburg, the 'Champ de Mars,' where several companies of infantry were drilling. Sazanow said with a sob: "Just look at that, it drives me almost mad. There are perhaps 1,000 men and not even recruits; those are soldiers who will probably leave in a few days for the front. Just look at them! Not a single rifle! Is that not lamentable! For God's sake, my dear Ambassador, do your very utmost to urge your Government to come to our help. Where are we driving to, otherwise?"

Such moderate expressions of sentiment, almost anecdotes, are often more convincing than the carefully considered statistical reports of officials.

In the face of this fact an immediate and simultaneous attack by the Entente on the Bosporus and Dardanelles could, strictly speaking, be regarded as a certainty. The more so as other considerations must also lead the Entente to this decision. These considerations touched the Balkan peoples, whose assistance would be sought for by both warring parties.

From Churchill's interesting book *The World Crisis*, we know the astonishing fact that the Greek Premier, Venizelos, had already on 19 August proposed to England that Greece should come into the war on the side of the Entente, so that her army and navy, with the assistance of the British Mediterranean Squadron, should occupy the Dardanelles and Gallipoli.

There is an old prophecy existing that a King Constantine with his wife Sophia should someday make his entry through the Golden Gate in Jedikule (part of Stamboul), The Turks consequently had this gate walled up. The road goes round. So it stands today. The ruling pair in Greece were actually named Constantine and Sophia, the latter well known as a sister of the German Kaiser. The belief was common in Greece that the moment of the fulfilment of this prophecy had arrived.

It was known that Gallipoli was only weakly held. The Greek General Staff were already in possession of carefully prepared plans for the conquest of the peninsula. The Greek plan, however, shattered on the fact that Constantinople could hardly be given simultaneously to Russia and Greece.

In addition it was generally believed that in such event Bulgaria would certainly join the Central Powers. It was hoped to avoid such action on Bulgaria's part by the formation of an alliance between the Christian Balkan Powers, Serbia, Greece, Bulgaria and Rumania. This plan was again unsuccessful owing to the suspicion of each State of the other – a quite understandable result of the second Balkan War.

So the plans against Turkey, and especially against the Narrows, at first ended in nothing – to the great advantage of Turkey.

Her military tasks developed first one after the other. With the same calmness as during the mobilisation period, the armies marched to their assembly points.

Turkey found herself strategically on the defensive. Her forces were distributed as follows:

1st Army. 5 Army Corps under Marshal Liman von Sanders Pasha, west and south of Constantinople.

2nd Army. 2 Army Corps under the Minister of Marine, Djemal Pasha, east of Constantinople.

3rd Army. 3 Army Corps and 2 Cavalry Divisions under General Hassan Izzet Pasha, round Erzerum.

Bosphorus and Dardanelles were under the command of the German Admiral, Marshal von Usedom Pasha, as Commander-in-Chief of the Narrows.

The fleet, of which *Goeben* and *Breslau* formed the backbone, was under the command of the German Admiral Souchon.

The first fighting began in the east, as the Russians began to march on Erzerum from Kars. They were brought to a halt not far from the frontier by Köpriköi. It was established with great satisfaction that the Turks, who were fighting for the first time since the unlucky Balkan War, had fought courageously and well. It is not my intention here to follow this campaign any further. Only from the point of view of historical context I mention that in December 1914 a general offensive was commenced by the 3rd Army (9, 10 and 11 Army Corps), commanded by the Deputy Commander-in-Chief, Enver Pasha, in person, across narrow mountain roads and passes lying deep in snow, with the conquest of Kars as the objective. The Russians were assisted by the Russian winter. The offensive completely failed. Only remnants – about 12,400 men out of a total of 90,000 – returned at the beginning of January 1915. That was a good beginning.

This Turkish offensive, however, curiously enough raised another question, that of a possible attack on the Dardanelles. The Russian Commander-in-Chief, Grand Duke Nicholas, greatly disturbed by the threatened Turkish offensive in the Caucasus, had approached England in the turn of the year with an urgent request to prevent the despatch of further reinforcements to the Caucasus by some demonstration against Turkey.

In London the Dardanelles were considered to be the right objective. It was hoped by attacking these to additionally prevent the Turks from commencing an offensive against the Suez Canal. In view of coming events it is interesting to note the proposal of the First Sea Lord, surly old Lord Fisher, who unfolded the following plan on 3 January 1915, the carrying out of which at that time did not appear to be impossible either politically or militarily.

The Indian troops at that time in Egypt and 75,000 English troops were to be landed under command of Sir W. Robertson in the Besika Gulf, while simultaneously the English fleet was to attack the Dardanelles, the Greeks Gallipoli, the Bulgarians Constantinople and the combined Russians, Serbians and Rumanians Austria. Speed was the main essential.

But there were too many heads, too many opinions, too many self-seeking wishes. The plan, which was excellent from the English point of view, remained a plan. The practical result was that the Dardanelles project began to take shape.

A further Turkish battleground developed in the south. From the idea of closing the Suez Canal and where possible destroying the British control in Egypt, developed the proposal of an offensive against Egypt, a proposal strongly supported from Germany.

A 4th Army was formed in Syria under Djemal Pasha, and troops of the 8th Army Corps were placed under the command of Lt Col Freiherr von Kress, as an Expeditionary Force. This magnificent officer, thanks to splendid preliminary organisation, actually succeeded in leading 10,000 men by seven night marches across the desert of El Tih, and reaching the Suez Canal at the beginning of February 1915, where they began to cross. However, the numerical superiority of the English became rapidly so great that Lt Col von Kress received orders to retire across the desert.

The English had at last appeared in Irak, taken Basra, and advanced to Gurna, the junction of the Tigris and Euphrates. Thus already at the commencement, theatres of war began to take shape on the far-reaching frontiers of the Empire, in which fighting was to continue to the bitter end.

Only on the Bosphorus and Dardanelles, the most endangered points, reigned for the moment an idyllic peace, disregarding the single bombardment of the outer forts of the Dardanelles on 3 November 1914. A bombardment whose purpose was not very clear, but which with brazen tongue heralded the declaration of war against Turkey in the eastern portion of the Mediterranean.

The calm was however only external. On the Bosphorus, as on the Dardanelles, much work was in progress. The chief aim was to secure the defence of the waterways by improving the available obsolete works, particularly the batteries, and bringing them as far as possible up-to-date; throwing up new batteries, and placing mines and submarine nets, as far as the limited available means permitted. The garrisons, among them 5 German officers and 160 men had to be drilled. An extraordinary amount was achieved. Naval Captain Weniger and Commander Schneider have described this in a most complete and interesting manner. I have simply taken a few points characterising the whole. The batteries were grouped at random, from guns of varying calibre, by different makers, some Krupp, some Schneider and Creuzot, Vickers, et cetera, all old models. They stood in quite obsolete earthworks, without any of the recently introduced technical aids for fighting a modern war. The fort of Tchanak Kale, for example, had as munitions supply only 12 long-range shells for each heavy gun. During the time it took the German gunners of the strongest Turkish Fort Hamidié to fire one round, their chief opponent, the *Queen Elizabeth*, could fire six broadsides. Each broadside hurled a total weight of shell of nearly 16,000lbs on the exposed batteries. Any further explanation would be superfluous.

The collection of mines was most amusing. Among them were Russians recovered from in front of Trapezunt, French fished up from in front of Smyrna, and even Bulgarian mines left over from the last war. All the same, no less than 145 mines had been collected by December 1914 thanks to the tireless activity of the Torpedo Captain Gehl, and prepared ready for relaying.

Old hoisting wires from mines were used to prepare the barrier nets. In other words, any form of materials that would act as a substitute and could be assembled in a hurry was used.

In addition to these duties carried out by the navy, the land army took over the defence of and fortified the coasts of the Black and Aegean Seas. The technical material available for this purpose was still more wretched than that on the Bosporus and Dardanelles. There was practically nothing at all actually available.

Turkey had completely used the whole of her war material in the recently ended Balkan War. The replenishment during the comparatively short period of peace was not possible, for there was no Turkish industry and gold was lacking for the purchase abroad. That was always the final conclusion of the weekly meetings in council of the Cabinet at the War Ministry.

With the outbreak of the world war an import of material was practically impossible. It is true that the way across Rumania was still open. The Rumanians, however, showed no inclination to assist; on the contrary, they raised difficulties wherever possible. If the Rumanian Government had adopted the attitude of a strictly neutral state against all the powers at war and entirely closed its frontiers, that would have been a correct attitude. But, on the contrary, she forwarded the connection between Russia and Serbia in an entirely one-sided manner. It was therefore necessary to use methods of bribery and corruption. Officers, soldiers, shipbuilding and munition workers travelled as civilians under other categories from Berlin to Constantinople. This actually led to many incidents with the Rumanian frontier authorities, as, for instance, the case of the French teacher who, actually one of the lowest shipbuilding workers from Kiel, was naturally unable to speak a word of French when asked to function as an interpreter. Material, in particular munitions and technical instruments, was hidden and with the assistance of heavy sums in bribery, was smuggled across the frontier. This money was accepted by all classes from pointsmen to officials in high positions, generally, however, without success, because agents of the Entente paid still higher prices. Often a wagon full of ammunition, which was supposed to contain cement, still stood the following morning on the same spot. We Germans are supposed to have shown ourselves as not at all suitable for utilising such underhand methods of getting round difficulties. The truth of all these events I am naturally unable to vouch for. They nevertheless show our efforts to help Turkey in every possible way and give a picture of the little war on neutral ground.

U-boats later brought supplies of the finer technical instruments required for war.

Apart from this import from abroad attempts were also made to erect shell factories in Turkey. The greatest credit belongs to the German Naval Captain, General Pieper Pasha, who accomplished an exceptional amount of work in this direction. If the artillery ammunition thus supplied did not offer a completely efficient substitute for the German it was nevertheless extremely welcome to us on Gallipoli. There they had already been forced to use blank cartridges to give a deceptive impression of fire support to their own infantry.

CHAPTER VI
Geo-Military Description of The Gallipoli Peninsula and The Dardanelles.
(See map p.39)

Before I begin to relate my experiences in the Dardanelles and on Gallipoli I propose to include a geographical description of this area, viewed from a military standpoint. I recommend the study of this chapter, with the use of the maps, to those readers who wish to reconstruct a clear picture of the events and form their own opinion.

Thracia, the land west of Constantinople, runs in a southerly direction into the Gallipoli Peninsula, which stretches for 80 kilometres between the Gulf of Saros, on the Aegean Sea, and the Dardanelles.

Soon after leaving the main Continent the peninsula becomes very narrow in the neighbourhood of Bulair, with a waist of roughly 4 kilometres, and then proceeds to widen out to a maximum breadth on a line from Large Kemikli to north of Akbash, reaching a width of over 20km. From this point the peninsula runs fairly sharply to its most southern point at Cape Helles, not unlike a foot with the toes pressed out. In this southern portion there is also a narrow waist of only 7km. between Kabatepe and Maidos. Both waists are of great military importance, being the shortest way from the sea to the shore of the Dardanelles. Only the most northern is protected by the forts of Aj-Tabia, Merkes-Tabia and Jildis-Tabia. These are the only land fortresses on Gallipoli, but they are obsolete, with walled chambers. Mouse-traps is what an experienced artillery officer called them, who refused to occupy them with his battery.

The fighting in 1915 took place in the southern portion of the peninsula, because there, there were many more favourable landing places, and because from this portion

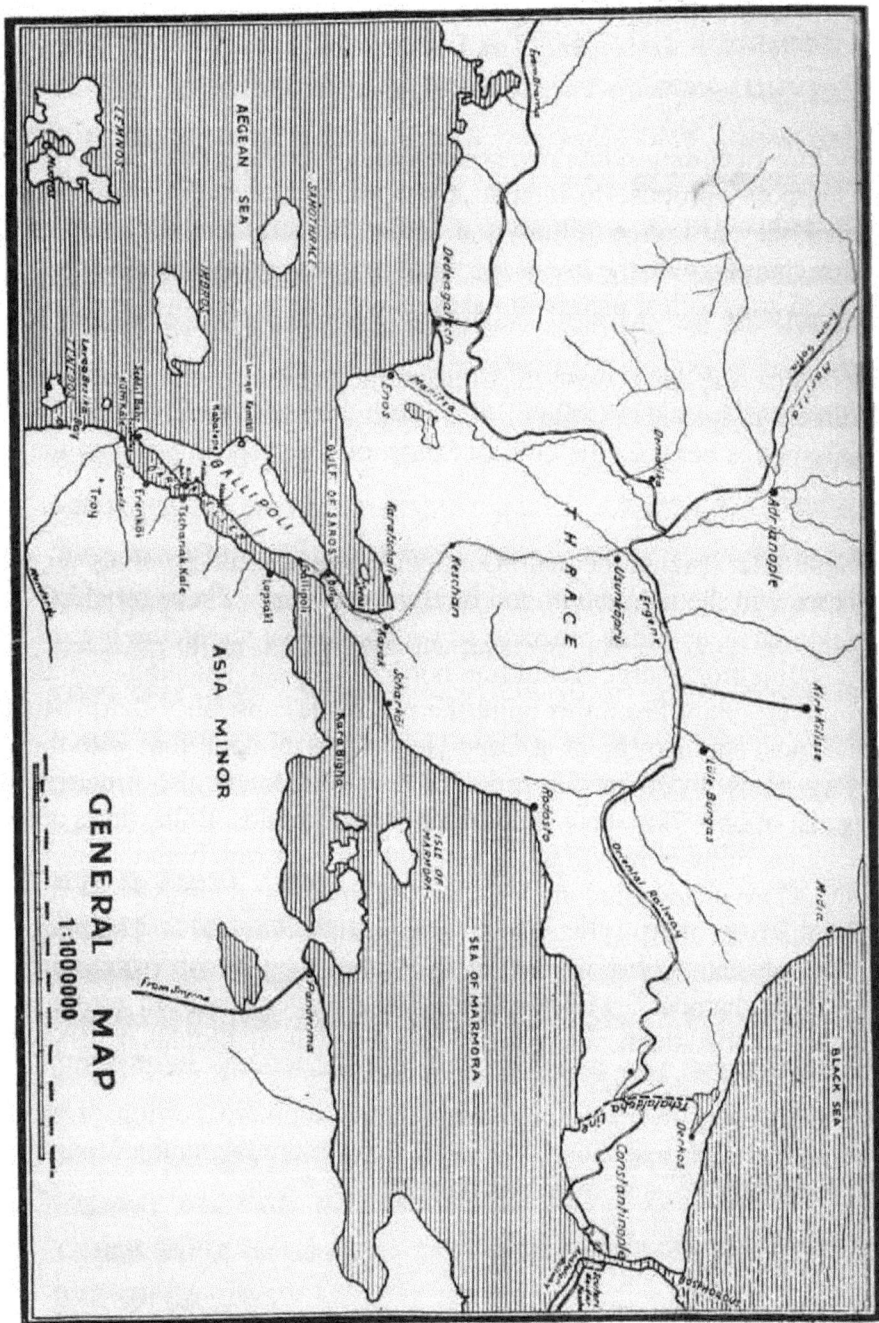

GENERAL MAP
1:1000000

AEGEAN SEA

LEMNOS

SAMOTHRACE

IMBROS

GALLIPOLI

ASIA MINOR

Troy

GULF OF SAROS

THRACE

Adrianople

Enos

SEA OF MARMORA

ISLE OF MARMORA

Constantinople

BLACK SEA

39

the main fortresses blocking the Dardanelles at Tchanak Kale could be most quickly reached.

The peninsula consists mainly of a hilly country, unfertile, deeply cleft and torn with sharp valleys, steep hills and stony cliffs which rise to a height of 1,000 feet and fall abruptly and steeply towards the coast. As a result the waters are carried off by a large number of small brooks and rivers called *dere* which have cut deep channels in the lime stone and have brought a clay sub-soil into the valleys. Because of this, small level spots are to be found, and where the streams reach the sea, small coastal flats. These were the entrances sought for the landing Englishmen. The country by Bulair and further north at the end of the Gulf of Saros offered such opportunities. In a southerly direction as far as Large Kemikli the cliffs rose sharply from the edge of the sea and were only broken once by the small but beautiful valley, Edje Liman (Port Liman).

The picture changes when the coastline bending round Large Kemikli continues in a southerly direction. Here one finds what is for Gallipoli the fairly large Anafarta Plateau with the port-shaped Suva Bay and the flat coastal area reaching as far as the mouth of the Azmakdere. On the other side the steep Ariburnu, with a very narrow coastal strip and the already mentioned invaluable Kabatepe, runs parallel with the coast and slopes away inland until it almost reaches the east coast. From the mouth of the Azmakdere, south of the Kabatepe, as far as Kumdere, the coast is steep but not very high, with a narrow sandy strip running along the shore. The coast again falls sharply away up to the mouth of the Singindere, and from this point right round the southern portion of the peninsula and into the Dardanelles, including Morto Bay, offers many opportunities for landing.

The character of the hinterland of the peninsula is defined by the steep, high ridges and the deeply walled ravines. These determine the geographical construction or lay-out of the peninsula and thus its military importance. It can generally be said that the heights fall away towards the south, although here and there occur massive ridges and isolated conical heights, which drew with magnetic power the fighting forces towards them when tactical developments brought these into their neighbourhood. We regarded Suvla Bay in the broad plateau of Anafarta as a fortress surrounded by high hills, in particular the Karakoldagh and the Kiretshtepe in the north; to the right flank curving in a southerly direction is the strong ridge of Kavaktepe Jussuftepe with a projecting nose like a bastion overlooking Mestantepe and Punartepe. On the farther side of the northern Asmakdere a mountain range forms a mighty group reaching its highest point in the fiercely contested Kodjadshemendagh, covering the country as far as Ariburnu and Kanlisirt and terminating in the south height of Gabatepe. South of Asmakdere rise the heights of Egerlitepe and Kajaltepe which gradually fall away to the Soanlidere and beyond to the southern extremity of the peninsula.

This southern portion bears a considerably different character. The land grows flatter and flatter until it lies like
a plateau. There is only one high point, namely, Eltshitepe (Achi Baba), which reaches a height of 700 feet. This gives the whole area a distinctive character, together with the stubbornly disputed village of Krithia which lies 2km. further to the east. Following the lines of the country the little rivers and streams all flow in a southerly direction, like the ribs of a fan, from the approximate neighbourhood of Hill 145 – Eltshitepe – the Sigindere, Kirthedere, Kanlidere, Kerevisdere and Domusdere, towards the sea. The soldier must follow the geographer, and so up all these valleys now famous in history the English and French fought their way towards Krithia and the Eltshitepe.

The flora of the country is very poor and limited short coarse grass, low oak and thorn bushes, crippled fir trees which here and there form small woods; single trees clinging to the stony heights and, in the valleys, scattered cypresses and groups of olive trees.

The population, for the most part politically untrustworthy Greeks, had been thrown out by the Turkish Government and accommodated in Asia Minor. The task of looking after the empty houses was removed by the English who left no stone upon another in the whole of Gallipoli. In July 1915 I was unable to find a single complete house anywhere on the peninsula.

The soil produced a very small and meagre harvest olives, as the trees and the characteristic oil mills showed, and the bark of the low bush-like stone oaks (Valonia), which forms an export article highly valued for tanning purposes.

Apparently the fauna had also been thrown out because there was practically nothing to be seen. Only at nights I often heard the miserable cry of a jackal, a cross between a crying child and a dog's howl, or I noticed horrible scorpions in my tent.

Thus was the arena cleared for the fighters.

Only the sun was there. It burnt with extraordinary regularity day after day and month after month in increasing strength on us poor Europeans. The Turks, as Asiatics, did not notice it as we did. We could not save ourselves. Gallipoli lies more to the south than Naples. The path of the sun was such that during the day its rays reached every fold of the country. It was almost as hard-hearted as the English, who, most indiscreetly, watched us with their aeroplanes and captive balloons until they could almost look into our trouser pockets.

A very important point for the formation of a military opinion of a country is the means of communication. These were of vital importance for the numerically inferior forces of the defenders. But in this respect it looked worse than evil as far as roads were concerned, because the only passable road through the peninsula could be seen from many points from the sea and was therefore useless for military purposes. There was no direct road from the town of Gallipoli to Maidos, and the existing road between Maidos and Kilid Bahr was not extended towards the southern portion of the peninsula. Most of the communications between the various villages were merely paths across the sand, sufficient for foot passengers and donkeys.

It is to the undying credit of the Marshal that he wisely set to work immediately and concentrated his energies on increasing and improving the roads. By so doing he increased the number of his troops many times – a point of particular importance in view of the easy transport communication of the English by sea.

Until now I have been discussing the communications in the fighting area. These communications must, however, be dependent on good safe approaches for supplies of munitions, food and other kinds of material, otherwise fighting troops cannot remain effective. The connecting routes – main lines of communication – run towards the mother country. In this case they led to Constantinople by two main routes, the sea route via the Sea of Marmora, and the land route to the north via the Gulf of Saros and Keschan to Usunköprü, the station of the Orient railway line running to Constantinople.

By the first route Constantinople could be reached in 12 hours. Following 25 April 1915, the date of the English landing on Gallipoli, English submarines appeared in the Sea of Marmora, which greatly hindered this method of communication although they never actually broke it completely. The land route was more certain, but 160km. had to be covered before the single line railway was reached. I first learnt to know this route in October 1918, as I had to cover a line from Adrianople to the mouth of the Ergene with 25th Turkish Army Corps against anticipated attacks by the Entente from Bulgaria. The road was quite good at that time, but I was astonished at the steep hills. In the year 1915 it was still partially being built. Columns of camels and buffalo wagons drove supplies forward with difficulty. As a main artery for the supply of an army which at one time reached 22 divisions, this was only a drop of water on a hot stone. The sea must remain the main artery of communication, and danger and losses must be reckoned with.

The Gallipoli Peninsula is, therefore, in itself practically valueless. Its great political and strategical importance is due to its neighbour, the Dardanelles, that strip of water separating continents but acting as a main water channel of communication between races.

The Dardanelles flow in a broad steam roughly 60km. long and varying in width from 1,250 to 7,500 metres, towards the Aegean Sea. We already know the right, European, bank. The left, the Asiatic, is flatter, friendlier and more fertile.

At the entrance lies to the right the town of Gallipoli, from which the peninsula takes its name. To the left are olive groves and vineyards with the pleasant village of Lapsaki. After about 30km.

A GIANT CYPRESS AT KUMKOI, WITH A SUARI (ORDERLY)
AND HORSES
30 October, 1915

A TROOP OF CAVALRY NEAR THE OIL MILLS AT TURSCHUNKOI
12 October, 1915

44

the Dardanelles narrow to 2,500 metres. The Fort Nagara is built on that corner of the Asiatic side which juts well out at the point. At Maidos, which is the narrowest portion, the Dardanelles are only 1,250 metres wide, and as a result the most important fortifications are to be found at this point. On the right Kilid Bahr (Key of the Sea) and on the left Tchanak Kale. This last serves at the same time as the headquarters of the commander of the forts and water defences. Then the waterway broadens out twice, in the Bay of Sari-Siglar and that of Erenkoi, both of which are divided by Cape Kefes. Following this the two continents approach one another again like a doorway with Seddil Bahr (Sea dam) on the right and Kumkale (Sand castle) on the left bank. Here lies the outer ring of fortifications, at Ertrogul on the right, Orhanié on the left, which look far out into the Aegean Sea. Unfortunately with their obsolete guns they could not shoot as far.

Shortly before this we pass, on the Asiatic side, a flat plain lying broad, along the shores of the Dardanelles, which awakens memories of our school days. It is the delta of the Menderes, the 'Skamander' of the Ancients, with the grave cairns of Achilles and Patroclus. Here the Achæans drew their broad-built ships to land and erected beautiful, shelters for themselves. From this place one looks far into the Trojan Plain, recognising on the right, in front of the village of Hissarlik, the high-lying, ruin-covered hill of Troy, and behind this again the heights of Mount Ida. The Dardanelles, known to the Ancients as the Hellespont, hide many ancient memories which I will endeavour to shortly cover in this story.

The Gallipoli Peninsula is the Thracian Chersonese of the Ancients which Miltiades, five and a half centuries before the birth of Christ, defended against the plundering forays of the Thracians by a wall built across the narrow strip at Bulair.

The high hill south of Akbash was the site of the old Sestos to which Leander is supposed to have swum to Hero from Abydos (Nagara).

> *Seht ihr dort die altersgrauen*
> *Schlösser sich entgegenschauen,*
> *Leuchtend in der Sonne Gold,*

Wo der Hellespont die Wellen
Brausend durch der Dardanellen
Hohe Felsenpforte rollt?

It was in this spot, by Nagara, that Lord Byron later swam the Hellespont. It is not the narrowest part. This lies, as we already know, by Tchanak Kale, but because of the narrowness the current is too strong. For this reason this portion by Nagara has been used by every army commander who has tried to lead his army or his people from one continent to another during the course of the centuries: Xerxes 480 years B.C., Alexander the Great 334 years B.C., Kaiser Friedrich Barbarossa A.D. 190, who led his army of Crusaders, and A.D. 1354, Sultan Orchan, who led his Ottoman horde. At this spot in 1915 was put down the net which should close the Dardanelles against the British submarines.

Truly an historical spot!

The Ottoman conquerors at first took up residence in Adrianople and went on from there in 1453, under Mohamed II, to the conquest of Constantinople. Nine years later this exceptionally active and powerful Sultan shut the Dardanelles by his two castles of Kilid Bahr and Kale Sultanié (Tchanak Kale), and built so well that even the 15-inch shells of the *Queen Elizabeth* burst harmlessly against these thick walls on 18 March 1915.

Between these two dates, 1462 and 1915, the Turks have had many cares and much work, both military and to diplomatic, to maintain for themselves possession and the rights of usage of the Dardanelles. This Dardanelles question has formed a continuous bone of contention throughout the centuries. Already at the time of the Trojan War, 1194–1184 B.C., there was a battle for the entrance to the Dardanelles, and the reason which history gives for the war, namely the beautiful Helen of Troy, is either a poetical dream of Homer or a clever story of the Greeks to provide them with an adequate reason for war.

Later, the colonisation by the Greeks of the Sea of Marmora and the Black Sea began. Even today the Greeks, although quite a different race, wish to expand to the north towards Constantinople, whilst the Russians wish to attain the same aim in a southerly direction. So the importance of this world-connecting line north-south continues through the centuries, just as we have noticed the importance of the line east–west in the crossing of the Dardanelles at Nagars which remains of equal importance to us today owing to the world connection Europe-India by the Orient, Anatolian and Baghdad Railway.

These lines of undying importance cross, however, in Constantinople, known as the navel of the world. As Napoleon I once discussed in Tilsit with the Czar a partition of the world and the Czar insisted on having Constantinople, Napoleon replied: "Never Constantinople! It is the Empire of the World."

In this reply he was not referring to Constantinople as a town, but the far-reaching fortress of Constantinople, whose approaches are protected on the north by the heavily fortified Bosphorus, on the west by the Tshataldsha, on the south by the heavily fortified Dardanelles and with its eastern approaches covered by the loyal body of Anatolia.

For these reasons we understand the political importance to the world of the small, bare peninsula of Gallipoli.

CHAPTER VII
Unsuccessful Attempt by The Fleet To Break Through

What was the first action of the Entente following Turkey's joining the ranks of their opponents? I have already explained how a simultaneous attack on the Bosphorus and the Dardanelles was a natural assumption. The quicker an attempt was made to obtain success there immediately following the Turkish entry into the war, the greater was the chance of success.

However, following the arrival of the *Goeben* and *Breslau* the Russian fleet no longer controlled the Black Sea, and 47,000 men who were already waiting on transports in their harbours were despatched immediately to the west frontier of the Empire.

To explain how England came to include the Dardanelles in her plan of general operations I must diverge somewhat further. Already in August 1914, Churchill had got in touch with the Grand Duke Nicholas and agreed that the English fleet should fight for and obtain the control in the Baltic. Then the Russians were to land on the German Baltic coast and either attack the rear communications to the east front in the valley of the Weichsel or advance on Berlin from Stettin. The preparations were energetically pushed forward under Churchill's powerful pressure. The 5th Battle Squadrons under Admiral Bayly were to form the backbone of the coming operations. Borkum and the Brunsbütteler locks were the immediate aim. Extremely exact models of the mouths of the German rivers and the islands lying in front of them had already been prepared during peace by the British Admiralty.

Then a new problem appeared – the Dardanelles problem as a result of Turkey's entry into the world war. Here a strong fleet was also required. Both enterprises at the same time were impossible, because the 'Grand Fleet' was untouchable. It lay and menaced the German High Seas Fleet. The enemy flanks could only be turned either in the north, in the Baltic, or in the south, the Dardanelles. By both ways it would be possible to lend the Russians a helping hand.

The danger of an attack against the Dardanelles seemed the lesser of the two. There, "the terrible resistance of Germany on land and sea" need not be reckoned with. The first victory of the Dardanelles was already ours without our knowing it and without a shot having been fired. Even if the danger of a Russian landing had perhaps later, for other reasons, become very improbable, England looked at the further possibility of an attack in Schleswig Holstein which might bring with it an alliance with Denmark in the event of a decisive action being fought.

On 26 November 1914, a meeting of the War Council took place. It consisted of Asquith (Prime Minister) Lloyd George (Treasury), Sir E. Grey (Foreign Minister), Lord Crewe (India Office), Lord Kitchener (Secretary of State for War) and Winston Churchill (Admiralty). The Council had the control of all operations by land and by water and immediately decided on a large-scale expedition against the Dardanelles.

The Entente now commenced, under England's leadership and in the usual English methodical way, well thought out and lasting, taking advantage of every possible means, to firmly establish themselves on the islands of Tenedos, Imbros and Lemnos, just at the entrance to the Dardanelles.
That the Grecian flag flew over these islands did not matter. "Right or wrong my country."

A base for a large-scale operation was in due course established. Landing stages, barracks, aerodromes were erected. Lighters, barges, tugs and every kind of shipping, material and foodstuffs were bought up in the harbours of the Mediterranean. Levantines and Greeks unexpectedly discovered a new and rich source of income.

On 3 November 1914, the Entente with iron fist had knocked for the first time demanding entry on the doors of the Dardanelles – certainly without any serious intention, because after a short bombardment the English and French ironclads retired. Nevertheless this was a warning. In Seddil Bahr a powder magazine with 5 officers and 61 men was blown up by a direct hit.

Many weeks now passed peacefully, greatly to the advantage of the

Turks to whom this period was welcome for the completion of their defences. Lt Col Wehrle with his regiment, eight 15cm howitzer batteries, was placed by the 1st Army at the disposal of the fort of Tchanak Kale, and dug in his main forces on the heights west of Erenkoi, with the remainder on Gallipoli so placed in field positions as to obtain a flanking effect on the waters of the Dardanelles. (See map) This efficient officer and his first class men were to earn here their first laurels.

At the commencement of January 1915 the Dardanelles question was again brought to the front by the Russian call for help already previously described. Of the splendid plan to crush Turkey there now only remained the fleet attack on the Dardanelles, which had already been decided on as an attempt to break through to Constantinople and destroy the
Goeben.

Vice Admiral Carden, the Commander of the Fleet at the Dardanelles, replied to questions from London that a breakthrough by the fleet through the Dardanelles was possible, but not in one attack. On 11 January 1915, he submitted a very complete proposal for a methodically developing battle to be carried out on the arrival of reinforcements, which would take about a month to carry through. The outer forts were first to be reduced, then the batteries as far as Cape Kefes and, following the removal of the mines by sweeping, the destruction of the inner forts.

On 13 January 1915, the War Council at their meeting in London agreed in principle to this proposal. The latest battleship, the *Queen Elizabeth*, which had just been completed and which was to calibrate its guns at Gibraltar, was sent to the Dardanelles for that purpose. In addition a further number of battleships were sent as reinforcements.

In the meantime Constantinople had not remained inactive. The Marshal, at that time Commander of the 1st Army, had fully protected the whole coast on the European side, and on the Asiatic side as far as Prince's Islands by many large, concealed batteries, and Army Corps were standing to in expectation. These troops had received splendid training by constant marches, sham fighting and alarm exercises which extended along the coast of the Black Sea to meet possible Russian attacks. In addition the Turkish fleet, which could not be entirely disregarded under command of Admiral Souchon had prepared a warm reception for the Entente fleet should it emerge from the Dardanelles into the Sea of Marmora. The matter was therefore not quite so simple as it looked. The successful breakthrough did not at all mean the occupation of Constantinople. In any case the conditions were far from those of 1807, when at that time the English fleet successfully forced the passage.

In Constantinople the civil population was in a constant state of excitement, particularly when reports were received from the Dardanelles of bombardment, or the troops were alarmed. This was a splendid forcing house for the wildest rumours which mostly came from Salonica and Athens. Both towns were probably often represented in the Greek quarter at Pera.

Nevertheless the Government took the correct precaution of transferring the whole of the Government staff to Asia Minor. A portion of the Treasury was removed from the Old Serail, I believe to Eskichehir, to which place it was intended that the Sultan should retire, if and when necessary. It was also noticeable that that portion of the civil population which could afford it had suddenly a wish to travel. There was the greatest anxiety regarding possible billeting by Russian forces. Baggage was packed, or at any rate stood with the lids open. Perhaps the beautiful spring weather was also partially responsible for this?

It was no particularly elevating feeling for us Germans to feel that a portion of the population heartily hoped for an Entente victory. These were the already mentioned Greeks, Armenians and Levantines, who only wore the fez outwardly.

I could see not far from my house a splendid report station as soon as twilight closed in, because so long as the lights of St Stephano and on the Serail across on the European side still burnt, this told me that the Dardanelles still held out. The lights were first put out much later as the English submarines were successful in reaching the Sea of Marmora.

In the second half of February the Entente began to take serious action at the Dardanelles and put into operation the methods recommended by Carden, for the systematic reduction of the forts.

The first attack on 19 February 1915, engaged the outer forts at the entrance by Seddil Bahr and Kumkale, which disappeared in smoke, dust and splinters under the hail of shells from the long-range bombardment. What could the thirty-year old guns with obsolete methods of traversing and firing do against such a bombardment? As Cardon withdrew his ships at the approach of dusk the loss in men and material was very unimportant. Naval Lieut. Woermann was killed in the battery Orhanié. Covered with a Turkish flag, with his face towards Mecca, he was that evening buried by the Hodscha. A dead and yet speaking witness of the German-Turkish brotherhood in arms.

On 25 February the picture was repeated. That time, following the first bombardment the ships approached nearer. The garrison of the forts, supposedly dead, sprang however out of the heap of ruins to their guns and opened fire against the approaching ironclads. Useless. In the evening the forts of Seddil Bahr and Kumkale had ceased to exist. Next morning with bells tolling the *Majeste* sailed, as the first enemy ship, through the burst open door.

With this success the Entente had completed the first portion of the Carden programme and was filled with the best of hopes. Carden reported that, given good weather, he hoped to reach the Sea of Marmora by the middle of March. The Entente agents reported from Sofia, Bucharest and Rome, that as the result of this extraordinarily lucky success the scales were beginning to sink in favour of the Entente. Greece offered, on 1 March, to land three divisions on Gallipoli. Wonderful possibilities! But Russia two days later declared that Constantinople had already been promised to her as a prize of victory by her allies, and stated categorically that she could not agree to Greece taking part in the Dardanelles operations. Greece should go to the assistance of Serbia. Thus this splendid plan was shattered. Oh! this war of coalitions! It suited us very well.

In the meantime mine sweepers proceeded to sweep the mines from the Dardanelles. This task was very much more difficult than had been anticipated because Wehrle's batteries were there and the 15cm quick-firing battery, Dardanos. Admiral Limpus did not know of these, although he had been for many years head of the English Naval Mission in Constantinople. Further weeks passed in continual small battles as the work of clearing up proceeded.

The Russians urged an early opening of the Dardanelles. They yearned for the many heavily laden freighters full of war material of all sorts and conditions which were lying ready in the various ports of the Mediterranean. The methods of the careful Carden appeared too slow for the War Council in London. Heartening telegrams were received – Carden reported sick, a change in the admiral and system. The fiery Admiral de Robeck took over the command on 16 March. On 17th orders were issues at Tenedos. On 18 March the whole armada, consisting of two squadrons each of six armoured ships, with a further six in reserve and with the necessary supporting light craft, steamed towards the now open doors of the Dardanelles. (See map of the fighting area.)

It must have been an overpowering sight. The greatest battle which had ever taken place between floating ironclads and land batteries commenced. I will not attempt to describe it in detail. That has already been done by those competent to do so. The fighting, which began about 11 o'clock, developed along the main line in such a manner that first the six most modern fighting ships, the 1st Squadron, led the way, and in the neighbourhood of the Bay of Erenkoi discharged their mighty broadsides against the coast. A frightful booming noise – the land a belching crater.

Still not sufficient. Shortly after 11 o'clock de Robeck called the 2nd Squadron in support. The noise became a tornado – success appeared assured. Tchanak Kale burned, Killid Bahr burned, the batteries could not be seen.

As a courteous man accustomed to diplomatic procedure, de Robeck allowed the French the lead and the honour of the day. Admiral Guépratte received orders to carry through the crowning developments and advance to within 7,500 metres of the inner

Dardanelles circle of forts. About 1:30 the forts appeared to be totally reduced.

Minesweepers proceeded ahead, according to plan, to sweep a path 800 yards wide. De Robeck was satisfied. In spite of a certain amount of damage no ship had fallen out. All were still in good trim and only 40 men of the crews had been killed or wounded.

But here he had made a slight mistake. The brave defenders were still alive and knew how to use their guns. Owing to the necessity of digging out the guns covered in sand a result of the enormous masses of earth thrown up by the explosion of the large-calibre shells – and owing to the lack of ammunition, long pauses in the firing had occurred which had deceived the attackers.

As the French squadron advanced the forts again opened fire and this time with good success. *Bouvet* was hit about 1:50 direct hit with the 35cm from Fort Hamidié. The powder magazine exploded and the proud ship listed heavily on her side and sank like a stone in less than a minute and a half. Only a light green oily spot marked where *Bouvet* had just been fighting. *Gaulois* fell out of the line with a heavy leak to port, and in a sinking condition reached the base of the cliffs at the entrance, where she was run aground.

The reserve squadron was sent in to relieve the French. The clock was pointing towards 4 o'clock in the afternoon. *Irresistible*, which had struck a mine, turned on her side. *Ocean* came to her help with torpedo boats, but fate struck her also. On her beam ends she floated slowly in the current, where, deserted by her crew, she rapidly sank. *Inflexible* was similarly hit and had to quit the line and later was grounded at Tenedos. *Irresistible* ran aground about 7.30 in the evening on the Asiatic coast. *Agamemnon, Suffren, Lord Nelson* and *Albion* were all badly shot about. These were severe losses in such rapid succession. Robeck recognised that he would not get through. He gave the order to retreat, and by seven in the evening the proud fleet had left the Dardanelles under cover of its stern guns, the poorer by a mighty hope and several ironclads.

For the Turks and the Germans present it was truly an unforgettable day of glory, particularly when it is considered with what inferior material this victory was achieved. And, after the heroic defenders had cleaned the sand out of their eyes and the dust from their clothes, they found that their own losses in guns and material were very small, the damage to the forts easily repairable and the total losses of the forts not quite 150 men. 600 Frenchmen had sunk in the *Bouvet* alone. As I heard in Constantinople of this heroic fighting I felt I could not contain myself longer at my writing-table in the War Office. An official reason was easily found. The chief of the personnel section gave me certain Turkish decorations for Admirals von Usedom and Merten, Lt Col Wehrle and Lt Commander Schneider. I could scarcely go better prepared, so away for the Dardanelles.

As we reached Tchanak Kale, which clings friendlily to the shores of the small bay with tree-covered heights behind, there seemed to be no traces of the bombardment to be seen. Only the harbour left a dead impression. I was asked to lunch in the naval mess – a very pleasant house surrounded by gardens. The officers collected, we sat down to the table, the servants commenced serving. We had fillets and mashed potatoes just as we did in Germany in peace. Naval officers are always very courteous hosts, but only direct questioning from my side produced closer details of the great attack.

Then we visited the batteries under the guidance of the experts. The roads were completely empty – a few badly shelled houses, broken minarets – the latter painted in stripes to make them less observable. On the tower of the Kale Sultanié Castle which was built of enormous blocks, there was the direct hit of a 15-inch shell from the *Queen Elizabeth*. This had burst without doing any damage. These high, gloomy, mighty, colossal buildings of the Turks – I saw similar later in Sinope, but still more gloomy and crowded closer together, make a curious impression with their frowning mass. I felt what tremendous power this Sultan must have possessed. Kale Sultan has stood since 1463 and outlasted all earthquakes or bombardments, even that of the 1,600lbs heavy steel shells filled with high explosive which had been continuously fired against it. Around were modern buildings crumbled like rubbish.

A few steps round the corner and we stood in front of the most powerful Turkish work, Hamidié, which was entrusted to a German garrison. In the left background the tops of the white tents of the garrison could be seen on the right the open earthwork with guns on stone-built positions, old 35cm and 24cm ring guns from Krupps which still shot splendidly. Direct laying, over open sights by direction with the hand, without modern telescopes, orders given by word of mouth from the observation posts of the brave Commander Wossidlo, situated on the advanced right flank. When I was at the Military Academy in 1886 such works were already considered to be obsolete. The more astonishing the results obtained.

The destruction was very limited, only two guns out of action. Further rearward, in the court of the forts, we saw, however, most unbelievable shell craters from 38-inch shells. The craters were full of water so that a man could swim in them. The garrison were hard at work repairing the damage to the forts. They regarded fresh attacks with the utmost confidence. Still, there were only eight shells for each heavy gun and no possibility of fresh supplies. The position was similar in the other works.

I then visited the Commander of the Fort Tchanak Kale, General Djewat Pasha, who left a youthful, active impression, and who talked to me in fluent German of his sons who were cadets at Grosslichterfclde. He regarded the future with great confidence. When I asked him for horses the next day he very courteously placed one of his own at my disposal.

So the next morning on a splendid bay charger I rode along the Asiatic coast to visit Lt Col Wehrle, a good old friend of mine. Soon after we left the town my interpreter, Major Zia Bey, accompanied me with one or two servants we saw the wreck of the *Messudie* sticking her green-covered keel out of the Sari-Siglar Bay. An old warship, which had been used as a floating battery and which was sunk on 14 December 1914, by an English submarine. Then came Kefes Burnu and shortly after the battery Dardanos in sight, whose brave commander, Hassan Mewsuf Bey, had here died a hero's death on 18 March.

The road soon left the shore and led by a steep ascent to the village

MUSTAPHA KEMAL BEY, NOW PASHA AND PRESIDENT OF
THE TURKISH REPUBLIC

of Erenkoi, which lay shot to pieces. Only dogs and cats prowled around. Now, out of the first cellar a uniformed man arose and reported a telephone station. Here order ruled. Following this clear information Wehrle's quarters were soon discovered. A dug-out close to the battery position with a small garden. Even hens clucked around. Very comfortable. Our conversation naturally dealt almost entirely with the heavy fighting. The batteries were hidden in gulleys leading down to the Dardanelles and the positions were changed at night, consequently any aeroplane reports were already obsolete. Many dummy positions deceived the enemy. Shortly before 18 March the batteries had to approach one another more closely, so that the positions already indicated on the maps of the enemy were no longer accurate. This mistake could not be recognised in the extremely folded country. This is the only possible reason for the fact that in spite of the mad bombardment which tore up the whole area, the eight batteries of Wehrle only lost 3 dead and 11 wounded. But what ceaseless work day and night! What cuteness to continually find new positions! These were naturally only open field positions.

The batteries had scored 139 direct hits on different ships out of a total of 1,600 rounds fired. Wehrle said dryly: "We've been very lucky." The 15cm high explosive shells were useless against the armour, but there was a rich harvest waiting on the decks. Thus, for example, the battery Ali Bey tore open with a salvo the fore turret and deck of a ship of the *King Edward* type. Particularly good targets were offered to the howitzer shells by *Ocean* and *Irresistible* as they were forced to stop and order all hands to the boats. *Irresistible* lost in this way 168 men from one salvo, according to English reports.

I clambered about among the individual batteries so long as the light lasted. The view towards the Dardanelles, with the bare cliffs of Gallipoli and the islands in the back ground, was a beautiful scene from a military standpoint magnificently complete and encircling. I felt that I was looking from a protected box into the battle arena, only below a fire-belching merry-go-round. An extremely curious state of affairs in the world's history. When would the film operator arrive? Wehrle was quite enthusiastic over the efficient manner in which his officers and men had performed their duties, and at the splendid spirit prevailing among the troops. For instance, a badly wounded man, who was being carried from one of the batteries, shouted: "Let me just see one more ship go down," and another shouted as the hellish fire burst on them, "Comrades, now comes the hour for which our mothers bore us."

I also visited one of the many dummy positions. It lay close to an advanced wood on the road Tchanak Kale Erenkoi. Two brave Turks, a dug-out and an old boiler pipe. That was all. The boiler pipe pointed towards the sky. During the battle the Turks from time to time lit the fuse of a smoke cartridge, and retired rapidly under cover. This could be repeated as long as sufficient cartridges were available, or until a new battery position was ordered. The two Turks seemed particularly cunning, and quite content, and were very pleased at our generous praise. I had only one wish, that the whole army could be of the same spirit, then it would be hard for matters to go ill for us.

Wehrle and I also discussed the probable effect on its general War Policy of such an ignominious reverse to the sea power of England. We both unanimously concluded that the prestige of Proud Albion 'would not quietly accept the ignominy of this reverse. Too much was at stake quite apart from prestige.'

There were various possibilities open for further attack by the armed forces lying ready before the Dardanelles. Repeat the attempt to break through as a bull continuously lowers his horns and charges the closed door. This possibility became increasingly improbable with each succeeding day, because with such a decision the defenders would never have been given a moment's breathing space. Regardless of the possibility of fresh heavy losses, Robeck would have repeated his attack the following day. With their generally limited supply of munitions, the Turks would have been in an evil plight. Now the situation was daily improving.

It was still possible that the fleet would repeat its attempt to break through, but in that event troops would be landed on both sides of the Dardanelles to roll up the unpleasant batteries situated round the Bay of Erenkoi. Turkish coastal defence troops stood ready to repel such an attempt; whether they were numerically sufficient is another matter. However, if the English did not wish to again stake their naval forces only, they must consider landing a strong army under cover of the ships guns, to attain on foot what the ships had been unable to accomplish.

So the evening passed, and I curled up in my tent which had been pitched near Wehrle's, half hoping that something of a warlike nature would occur during the night. I had not yet received my baptism of fire. Unfortunately it was a very peaceful night. I did not grudge it to my comrades.

The warm rays of the March sun struck full on the side of my tent the next morning and woke me. Wehrle went to his work and I rode towards Troy, past the batteries at In Tepe, which were later to become so important on account of their flanking fire on to the southernmost point of Gallipoli.

I had to give up my intention to visit Kumkale, because lying close alongside like a watch-dog in the entrance was a
large English cruiser. It might have been possible on foot, but that would have taken too long. So we rode via Hissarlik, to the Ilion of the Ancients. The hill rose, unmistakable, out of the marshy mouths of the Skamander and Simoeis. I left the horses at Schliemannschuppen, and climbed the Hill of Ruins. I took out my Baedeker and tried to fix my position, sought to locate among the mass of ruins the differing layers marking eras. Impossible. Perhaps I lacked the devotion necessary for such work during such times.

I therefore contented myself with a general look round thought the yet recognisable living rooms miserably small and narrow, found several small silver coins among the debris and finally sat down on the outer wall of ruined Troy. A magnificent view of that battlefield of Homer, the Skamander, which divided Greek and Trojan, I saw the ford, which had to be crossed by wading before each attack, there where the gravestones of the Kumkoi cemetery rose sadly in the air, recognised the burial mounds of Achilles and Patroclus and saw in imagination the ships of the Achæans lying both sides of the mouth of the Skamander – all as a result of Baedeker. I had not brought it with me for nothing.

Suddenly a monstrous roar and crash. I still remember the stream of fire from the bow of the English cruiser – I heard later that it was the *Triumph* – and how the whole colossus seemed to quiver and apparently heave. A destructive stream of hate from a gigantic animal. The burst of the shell away in the direction of Gallipoli could not be seen, and quite an appreciable time passed before I heard the burst. Then all was peaceful again.

Zia Bey could not understand what kept me so long among the ancient ruins. In Constantinople there was quite enough to be seen. I finally climbed into my saddle and rejoined Wehrle in time for a most appetising meal. Parted from the courageous and experienced master of artillery science, assured that here the right man was in the right place.

I reached Tchanak Kale in the late afternoon, where the Marshal, who in the meantime had been appointed to command 5th Army, took me with him on his ship, a so-called Bosphorus-steamer, back to the town of Gallipoli. On my asking him not to forget me if the English later landed, the Marshal shook hands and said, "You shall be the first I send for." He kept his promise.

The following morning I rode across the Bulair lines to the front on the Gulf of Saros, unfortunately without seeing a single hostile ship. They had carried out an active bombardment here only a few hours previously. In the meantime a heavy southerly storm had broken which made the return journey to Constantinople somewhat questionable. So I thankfully accepted the courteous invitation of Essad Pasha, the General commanding the 3rd Army Corps, to wait with him. Essad Pasha was the famous defender of Janina in Albania during the Balkan War; he had served in a Strasbourg regiment and spoke excellent German. I had much to do with him later and always had complete confidence in his sustained and real kindness, his quick grasp of proposals, which, after calm, careful consideration, resulted in clear decisions.

That day I waited many hours in his office and as a result gained a most interesting insight into the work of a General commanding a

Turkish army. With us a commanding general had his regular reception hours, and only the most important matters which required immediate settlement could be brought to his notice outside these hours. The Chief of Staff knew his ideas, *minima non curat praetor*. He thus had time for his own brainwork, the working out of schemes, consideration of the situation with available maps, and the study of necessary documents.

Here, on the contrary, the door was continuously open, officers and civil servants came with documents for signature. The documents were explained, which I naturally did not understand, or on the order of the Pasha the documents were passed to others. The Chief of the Staff was called. By their uniforms I noticed that many civil servants dealt with their own matters directly, and each was treated individually. This continued for hours, and had not even finished by the common evening meal at which 35 to 40 officers and civil servants took part. The Pasha's desk was naturally empty, only pen and ink, because the continual disturbance rendered any real brain work impossible.

In a certain sense the Turk is, or rather is supposed to be, always on duty. I could now understand how a Major in Kerasun could be punished by an Army Inspector with 20 days' arrest, because he had been absent from afternoon duty in the barracks. I saw in the barracks in Kerasun a sentry with fixed bayonet standing in front of a door in the corridor. A Turkish officer replied to my question that he was on guard over his Commanding Officer for the above reason, and to my remark that a battalion commander could only rarely have duties which kept him in barracks in the afternoon, I received the astonished reply, "During parade hours every higher Commander must also be in barracks."

This is an appreciation of duty which we Germans fail to understand, because the value of work accomplished cannot be measured by the clock according to the time worked. The result of the continual presence of the higher commanders is a lack of independence, lack of initiative and capacity to take decisions. With such methods of training, 'independent' leaders must always be lacking in times of emergency. A very noticeable deficiency for an army it had already shown itself in critical positions with catastrophic results for the Turks. Everyone who has served with the Turkish Army can relate instances which occurred during his own period of service. The Military Mission was here confronted with a very difficult task, because it is quite impossible to dictate, "From tomorrow you will carry on independently – from tomorrow you will possess the spirit to carry responsibility."

Such qualities are the result of long systematic training, which continues through generations, but which is in itself dependent on the character of a race. I don't mean to say that all the officers were like this. There were quite a large number who were independent and acted independently, and who were full of initiative and ideas. Such thoughts were a result of my long visit to Essad Pasha.

During the late afternoon of the following day the *Mahmud Muktar Pasha*, with only a few guests on board, again approached Constantinople. In the evening light the town presented a magnificent spectacle. First appeared the minarets of Fatih Mosque, and the Seraker Tower of the War Office. It seemed to me that the ship itself was rising. The view became continuously more encircling, more and more mighty mosque cupolas, minaret points, massive blocks of buildings appeared until finally beyond the clear blue sea an endless sea of houses ringed the whole horizon from St Stefano past Jedi Kule (the seven towers), Stamboul, Selimi Barracks at Scutari, Kadikoi, Moda and as far as the Prince's Islands. Europe and Asia merged together. The Bosphorus was hidden by the Serail Point, white gulls flew clamorously towards us. Over the whole beautiful scene, the intensely blue eastern sky, gilded by the rays of the setting sun from behind us. This view is justly praised as one of the most beautiful in the world. It was a splendid conclusion to this interesting and informative journey. The journey had not been without result, as I had my diary full of notes and observations, and full of wishes and proposals for almost every department of the War Office. But I had not yet received my baptism of fire, and I still thought myself a second-class soldier.

CHAPTER VIII
Preparation By Fifth Army On Gallipoli

Following the unsuccessful effort of the English to break through with the fleet, and as they did not attempt to repeat this next day, the possibility of another such attack became less likely with each successive day. Had another attack with fresh units taken place immediately, regardless of consequences, it is possible that a portion of the battleships would have successfully broken through to reach the Sea of Marmora. But what would have happened then? Perhaps the history of Lord Duckworth would have repeated itself, who, on 20 February 1807, appeared before the walls of Constantinople with an English fleet, but after eight days and a loss of two corvettes considered himself lucky to be again at anchor in the road stead of Tenedos.

The Report of 12 February 1917, which contains the Report of the decision of the Parliamentary Committee of Enquiry on the Dardanelles action, shows clearly how the final decision was only reached after long deliberation. General Hamilton, who had reached Tenedos on 17 March, cabled Kitchener on 23 March 1915:

> Have just had a talk with the Admiral [Robeck]. Have both reached the same decision that an attack with all available land forces is necessary to render possible a passage by the fleet.

And on the same day Robeck spoke of the underestimated danger from mines which must be first removed. Actually the English overestimated the danger of mines. In particular, the Turks had thrown over no floating mines on 18 March. What actually happened was that *Ocean* and *Irresistible* on that day struck a hitherto unknown minefield which had been laid early on the morning of 8 March in the Bay of Erenkoi along the tideway. However, be the facts what they may, this uneasy feeling about mines considerably reduced the thirst for action of the English naval leaders.

The English Report which I have just mentioned states under date

26 March 1915,

Now two things were clear:
I. The Government was not prepared to give up an attack on the Dardanelles.
2. Should this be carried out as a combined action, with the help of powerful land forces?

The origin and the commencement of the Dardanelles campaign thus lie before us.

Kitchener, who originally had rather hesitatingly agreed to the employment of troops, now very correctly placed high value on an immediate start of the operations by land, and exerted pressure by telegram. Unforeseen trouble arose, however, in the preparation of the divisions on the islands lying before the Dardanelles, the greatest trouble being the almost unbelievable mistakes made during the loading of the troops on the transports in England.

There, the individual units had not been simultaneously loaded on the same ship with complete equipment ready to begin operations, so that they could go into action immediately on arrival; but the transports had been loaded in series with similar material, troops, wagons and et cetera, all horses, separately. This may be an excellent method looked at from a business point of view, but from a military standpoint it is, to put it mildly, not understandable. An unravelling of this puzzle was impossible in the limited space available on the islands. The ships were forced to go to Alexandria to tranship. Valuable time was lost, which was of the utmost assistance to us. Almost the whole of April was gone before Hamilton finally had his landing corps ready collected before the Dardanelles.

During the days following 18 March even the Turks were no longer in doubt as to the now threatening danger of a serious landing on Gallipoli in the near future. The time was passed for an academic discussion over the possibilities and probabilities of a landing. What was required was the taking of prompt, energetic and well conceived measures for the defence.

On 24 March 1915, orders were issued for the formation of a 5th Army for the protection of the Dardanelles, and the Marshal Liman von Sanders Pasha was entrusted with the command. The day following the Marshal with his small staff was already on his way to the peninsula. The immediate and main care was the securing of the coast. It was quite impossible to occupy the whole of the long coastal area which lay on both the European as well as the Asiatic side of the Dardanelles. The available forces, six divisions, were not sufficient for this. In addition, "He who covers all, covers nothing." So far the troops had been used on this ancient plan, and the troops of the available five divisions had been distributed along the coast like the Frontier Guards of the good old times. As a result of the length of this watching duty the troops had become completely benumbed. Energetic changes in the dispositions were here very necessary.

The chief issue was to so arrange matters as to be able to reach landing places with fighting forces as quickly as possible. The most suitable landing places on Gallipoli we are already familiar with, the upper Gulf of Saros, with Bulair, Suvla Bay, Gaba Tepe, and the whole of the southern point. Suvla Bay could be discarded for tactical reasons, because an attack here had no tactical objective sufficiently worthy of attack. As against this, however, the flat Asiatic coast, well suited for landings, with the large and small Besika Bays and the Island of Tenedos lying close to the shore, already occupied by the enemy, and the section as far as Kumkale needed special consideration.

Looking at the whole length of the coastal area requiring protection, two particular danger zones became apparent on the extreme wings, on the Gulf of Saros (Bulair) and on the Asiatic side. Certainly no pleasant position for the defender, who was forced to leave to the attacker an unlimited choice of landing points and complete liberty of movement. This last was increased in an almost ideal fashion by the speed of manoeuvre at sea of the transports carrying the attacking columns.

Of the threatened points on the wings I have already described the neck at Bulair. Success here would cut off the Gallipoli Peninsula completely, because the water route to Constantinople could easily be stopped. In such a case the communications rearward of 5th Army would be cut, and it must be starved out. It was quite impossible to transfer the base to Asia Minor and attempt to supply rations and munitions from there.

The other wing, on the Asiatic side, equally offered many advantages to the attacker apart from the favourable conditions on the coast. An attack must there be conducted over open, if partially boggy, land which was not so favourable to the defensive measures of the Turks as the many folds of the Gallipoli Peninsula. Once the low-lying land was crossed, particularly the Trojan Plain, the most important artillery positions of the enemy, those very unpleasant batteries of Wehrle and the heavy batteries at Tchanak Kale, could be easily attacked from flank and rear. The prize was worth the effort.

The French specially and repeatedly recommended that the main attack should be directed against the Asiatic coast. This did not take place, however, as Kitchener was against it.

During all preliminary negotiations over the Dardanelles question, and later during the course of the operations, the British War Office continually strove to limit to an absolute minimum the despatch of troops to the Dardanelles, or, in fact, to any destination far afield. Troops thus despatched were non-available for use on the near West Front or in Home Defence. For these reasons Kitchener did not wish to have English troops in the far-reaching plains of Asia Minor, as in such a case he feared the danger of continued demands for reinforcements. He preferred to use his troops in the limited area of the small peninsula.

The Marshal naturally could not know all these facts, and had to weigh up the actual conditions, or what he believed to be the actual position after a study of the many, often contradictory reports, and then decide on his line of action.

He accordingly cancelled the existing cordon system and divided his army into three groups:

5th and 7th Divisions (Col von Sodenstern and Lt Col Remsi Bey),

Saros Gulf by Bulair.

9th and 19th Divisions (Col Sami Bey and Lt Col Mustapha Kemal Bey), in the southern part of the peninsula in different groups, the 19th being near Maidos.

3rd and 11th Divisions (Cols Nicolai and Refet Bey), on the Asiatic side under command of General Weber.

The strength and composition of the Divisions varied considerably. A Turkish infantry division is generally made up of three infantry regiments, each of three battalions and one machine gun company, a field artillery regiment of two companies, one squadron of cavalry, a pioneer company, and a sanitary company, a total strength of about 10,000 to 12,000 men.

Apart from six such divisions with a total strength of about 60,000 men, 5th Army had nothing, absolutely nothing, neither heavy artillery, not aircraft, nor mechanical transport, and only the most parsimonious material for entrenching.

The guns of the Fort Tchanak Kale, built in to defend the waterway, could not assist because their limited traverse prevented them from covering this land area, and their scanty ammunition was unsuitable for land targets.

Apart from this, the fort of Tchanak Kale, and with it the waterway of the Dardanelles, was not under the command of 5th Army but under that of Marshal von Usedom, because of purely technical naval problems here requiring solution.

Every impartial observer who has heard of the defence of the Dardanelles by Marshal Liman von Sanders must naturally have taken for granted that this waterway, actually the main object of defence, was, as a matter of course, also under his command. This was not the case, however, and as 5th Army continually used the waterways, and the forts or rather the navy had to protect them from the land, this question of organisation contained the seeds of many possible conflicts. That such did not appear was due to comprehensive cooperation and certainly, in addition, to the successful course of the operations.

The divisions were ordered to keep concentrated as far as was possible and only despatch covering companies to the threatened points. These points were fortified as well as the scanty material available permitted with wire entanglements, pits, torpedo heads built in as land mines, and trip wires on the beaches under water, and well covered by flanking fire from machine and other guns. Major Effnert was responsible for the driving force behind all these works, particularly on the southern extremity where they were to prove of the utmost value.

The main factor, or rather a vital necessity, of such a form of organised defence is mobility and speed. All depended on timely recognition of the real attempt to land, as sham demonstrations would certainly take certain place, on quick, and accurate reports, and on the speedy despatch of troops to the right points.

Such a fluid condition of the reporting elements, and rapid mobility of the troops, could only be attained by constant practice. This required time. On 27 March, at Erenkoi, the Marshal, who was hurriedly surveying his whole zone shortly after assuming command, said to me, "If the English will only leave me alone for eight days." Actually four weeks passed, much against the will of the English, especially Lord Kitchener.

The land routes, which I have already described, were exceptionally ill-suited for the rapid movement of troops. An immediate improvement was rapidly effected by the use of labour battalions. These labour battalions were formed from the non-Mohammedan subjects, Greeks, Armenians and Jews. The basic plan on which these roads were made was to establish along the bank of the Dardanelles a covered route from the town of Gallipoli as far as the southern end of the peninsula, and from this main road to run side tracks from the individual sections to the sea coast; but this took many months to finally complete. The waterways of the Dardanelles were also intended to be used for moving troops, and transports were lying ready at

CLAY HUT—THE AUTHOR'S QUARTERS
From October, 1915, till January, 1916

CLAY HUTS AT 16TH ARMY CORPS HEADQUARTERS AT TURSCHUNKOI
15 October, 1915

the most important points.

All this work of preparation, regrouping, marching, shooting and battle practice was made particularly difficult for 5th Army by the ubiquitous cruisers who opened fire immediately at any available target, sometimes even on single riders or men on foot. The aviators were also most disturbing, as there was no defence against them. Most of the work had therefore to be done at night. How exceedingly successful this policy was, can be seen from Emil Daniels story of Admiral de Robeck's report to General Hamilton who had just arrived at the Dardanelles. De Robeck said:

> The Gallipoli Peninsula is being fortified in frantic haste. Thousands of Turks work all night like beavers, constructing trenches, redoubts and barbed wire entanglements. It is true we have never seen any of them, but every dawn brings fresh evidence of their nightly activities. All the landing places are now surrounded by trenches and effectively commanded, the Germans have obviously got the Turks well in hand, and all this work is being carried out famously by the Turks.

It is extremely pleasant to hear such remarks from the enemy. Certainly everything had been done on the Turkish side that it was possible to do, taking into account the lack of necessary materials and other disturbances.

5th Army now stood prepared and waited like a spider in its web.

All of us, who took part in the war, know how, after weeks of high tension and expectation, the final commencement of the attack was welcome as a kind of relief.

Such was the case here.

CHAPTER IX
The Landing

(Marked by letter 'L' on map of Fighting Areas)

At dawn on 25 April 1915, an enormous armada of 200 ships approached the Dardanelles from Lemnos.

Ahead, the battleships of the Allied fleet covered by torpedo boats and mine sweepers and followed by transports with lighters, boats and rafts in tow.

Seventy-seven thousand fighting men under the command of the English General Sir Ian Hamilton, including 17,000 French to land on the right flank as the *Corps Expéditionnaire d'Orient* under General d'Amade, the 29th English Division and the Australian and New Zealand Army Corps (ANZAC) under General Birdwood, with the Royal Naval Division in support.

A magnificent result of the many months' discussions of the War Councils in London, of the many opinions, commissions, reports and telegrams and, not least, the enormous amount of practical work.

Like a giant steel wave the armada clove the light morning mist of this Sunday with evil in its womb. It must have been a sight for the Gods. But Zeus sat no longer on Ida and Neptune no longer held aloft his trident on the neighbouring island of Samothrace.

The check of 18 March is to be wiped out today.

But the fleet did not enter the Dardanelles as on that 18 March, and it was apparently not to be a breakthrough in the centre this time. The ships encircled on a broad front the enemy coast, enclosing it in a warm embrace.

The French on the right wing, who were always for an attack on the Asiatic side, continued towards Asia, and they were covered by a squadron under Admiral Guépratte consisting of the ships of the line or cruisers, the *Jaureguiberry, Henri IV* (replacement for

Bouvet), *Jeanne d'Arc*, *Charlemagne*, *Ernst Renan*, *Ascold* (Russian), *Prince George* (English), and a number of torpedo and other covering boats, as well as five transports which headed for the Bay of Besika, and five transports which continued towards Kumkale.

The 29th Division was convoyed towards the southern extremity of Gallipoli. My observer counted there, in the early morning mist, 14 fighting ships, among them the *Queen Elizabeth, Agamemnon, Majestic, Triumph, Cornwallis, Vengeance, Cressy, Liverpool*, 9 destroyers and countless boats with 39 transports.

The left flank of the armada continued its progress further north in the direction of the Gulf of Saros. In the neighbourhood of the height of Kabatepe the Anzacs turned in towards the coast and seven transports with the Royal Naval Division on board, protected by a sufficient covering force, continued its approach towards the inner most portion of the Gulf of Saros.

A wonderful deployment centre by water.

And then, about 4 o'clock in the morning, began an awful cannonade against the coast. The guns were fired just as fast as they could be loaded. Those on the ships could work in absolute peace because they remained so far from the coast that no Turkish shell could reach their armour. The transports lay still further behind and continued slowly to approach the coast.

On the Turkish side everything seemed dead. Not a shot was heard and nothing was to be seen. The land was so shot about that no stone could remain on another. Everything was covered in thick, cloudy masses of smoke and dust – the whole a Devil's boiling cauldron in which it seemed impossible that anything could still live. The English rightly anticipated an easy landing. The battleships, firing continually, drew nearer the coast. Then they lowered launches, motor boats, pinnaces, lighters, in short, every form of boat transport, which were filled with troops and necessary equipment and supplies and formed into tows. They approached the coast under cover of the battleships fire, and still a deathly stillness reigned on shore.

The tow cast off, officers and men were obliged, in some cases, to spring into the water and wade ashore. In other cases the depth of the water permitted the boats to be brought directly alongside. Then the ships had to raise their fire inland in order not to endanger their own troops as the leading sections were already nearing the coast.

At that moment from the apparently dead ground a totally unexpected and intensely heavy fire from guns, rifles and flanking machine guns fell on the landing parties. The torpedo heads which had been buried as ground mines exploded. The men stumbled on barbed wire in the water. Shortly, let General Hamilton himself speak: "A merciless hail, a whirlwind of steel and fire covered the beach and fell on the approaching boats."

A terrible fight then began, man against man. The Englishman is a tough fellow, the Turk also. This the Turk had already shown by lying still under the hellish fire from the ships.

Thus began everywhere the battles for the beaches. Naturally the fighting for the individual landings differed according to local conditions, tactical aims and the conduct of the opposing forces.

If we follow the battles of the beaches individually from the right wing of the Entente forces, the warships approaching the large and small Besika Bay opened a heavy fire which lasted until 11 o'clock in the morning. The attempts to land which followed were easily beaten off by the 11th Division.

On Kumkale and its neighbourhood, from 5:45 a.m. a withering fire was opened by the French fleet encircling the point. The Turkish draft under Ali Effendi was very quickly totally destroyed.

Attempts at reinforcing from the east, over the marshy banks of the Menderes, were hindered from the start by the flanking fire of the battleships lying in the Dardanelles, which, from their high armoured decks, covered an unbelievably wide area of the Trojan Plain. The single bridge over the Menderes was shot to pieces. The Turks could only reach Kumkale from a southerly direction with the help of the sand dunes which reach to Jenischehir. This help arrived too late to prevent the unloading of the transports which arrived at 7:15, and which by 9:30 had already landed their first battalions of Senegalese and Foreign Legion. The fighting became more and more intense between the French and the 3rd Turkish Division who at first successfully confined the French to the fort and village of Kumkale. Every moment, however, greatly increased the numbers of the landing French.

In the meantime, Wehrle had sent as support his best howitzer battery commanded by Captain Ali Tewfik Effendi, with 200 rounds of shell. By 5 p.m. the battery was in a position to fire, and bombarded the growing masses of French troops which were drawn up ready for further advance. The 3rd Division were successful in at least maintaining Jenischehir and the cemetery. Col Nicholai had to wait for the darkness to drive the enemy back into the sea.

The hardest fighting took place round the southern point of Gallipoli. Apparently this was to be the main action. Hamilton's idea seemed to be to cut off this small piece of land which he could cover from three sides by fire from the ships, by landing simultaneously attacking columns at Eski Hissarlik, Morto Liman and various points on the extreme south and at the mouth of the Sigindere.

In this way the defending Turks were to be attacked from three sides at once. I was reminded of the finish of an athletic contest. From quite a number of landing places close to one another landing parties were to race to their goal. Nevertheless, these single battles had a close tactical relationship, as we shall see.

Hamilton began by attacking between Seddil Bahr and Cape Helles, that is at the extreme point, with the 88th Brigade.

Here the country is extremely difficult, scarcely welcoming for a landing party apart from the flat but narrow beach, because starting close to the massive old walls of the ancient Beach Fort a high cliff rises in a half circle from Cape Helles entirely shutting in the landing-place. Like the seats in an amphitheatre the cliffs rise to a height of 40 metres. Three companies of the Dublin Fusiliers approached the shores at 5:15 a.m., following closely on the cannonade which we have already described, but the top tiers of the amphitheatre were held by sections of the Turkish Infantry Regiment 26. Before the Fusiliers even reached land they suffered extraordinary heavy losses. Only a portion reached the small beach and found shelter at the foot of the high cliffs while another portion remained on the shore behind a sand bank 5ft high. Not a boat got back to the ships, the rowers being completely destroyed.

Then a large yellow transport approached and steamed at full speed towards the shore. It was the 8,000 ton collier *River Clyde*, with 2,000 men of the Dublin and Munster Fusiliers and two companies of the Hampshire Regiment – the whole commanded by General Napier. But what took place? The ship did not stop, but drove into the arena and crashed at full speed against the beach so that the bows crumpled. The propeller churned sand and water madly astern, forcing the ship still further ashore. The Turks looked on with astonishment.

The lighters towed by the *River Clyde* were now used to bridge the space between the ship and the land; an exceptionally audacious plan. In spite of the strong current, in spite of the hot fire to which Wehrle's batteries from Intepe added, the plan succeeded. The *River Clyde* began to empty itself. For this purpose, in the bow and waist openings had been prepared in the steel decks.

A company of Munster Fusiliers led the way, but only a few Fusiliers reached the shore. The Turkish fire shot them down mercilessly. A second company of the Munsters raced on to the bridge, which at this moment was torn away by the tide. Those whom the bullets missed sought to reach the shore by swimming, but the heavy equipment dragged them all down into the depths. Regardless of danger the English sailors pushed the lighter into position again and rebuilt the bridge, paying for the work with their lives like those who preceded them. A third company of the Munsters raced to the shore, but only a broken portion of them reached the covering shelter of the cliffs. A company of the Hampshire Regiment headed by Brigadier General Napier followed. At this moment the bridge broke again, but it was useless to seek shelter on the bottom of the lighter. Death again reaped a rich harvest, the General himself being caught by a bullet.

Up to this point 1,000 men had left the River Clyde, of which only a portion had reached the low shelter of the lower cliffs. A greater portion of the officers had been killed and wounded. The attempts to land were postponed for a while, leaving 1,000 men still sitting in the hull of the *River Clyde.*

At the beginning of this landing, *Agamemnon, Vengeance* and six destroyers left the rest of the fleet and proceeded, under heavy fire, towards the European shore of the Dardanelles. Wehrle's batteries drove them back. Six times they attempted to reach the land at full speed, under heavy fire. *Vengeance* alone fired more than 1,200 rounds. Then, about 6:30 in the morning, tows left the transports and with 12 boats approached Eski Hissarlik. Wehrle's batteries destroyed several boats and the rest retired. Here also the English showed extraordinary energy. The attempts to land were increased. They did not stop, but went so far up the Dardanelles as the mouth of the Kerevisdere, although at the fifth attempt a destroyer hit a mine and sank in 1½ minutes

The ammunition of the two splendid 12cm gun batteries on the Intepe ran short and from 12 noon onwards they could only shoot at long intervals. Wehrle sent 70 more shells, retaining 60 to meet the worst attack. He had to sorrowfully look on while the enemy drove forward afresh against Morto Liman, and landed. So the important height of Hissarlik was occupied by the English because of lack of ammunition on our side – the weak portion of the Turkish Infantry Regiment 26 being unable to resist the attacking troops.

The tactical envelopment had succeeded on the right wing. The immediate development of this shattered against the stubborn resistance of the Turks.

On the other side of the amphitheatre and Cape Helles the cliffs approach close to the shore, falling almost precipitously to a small sandy beach. On top, the country expands like a plateau with single, small hillocks. So the coast runs past Teke Burnu and Kumtepe till about halfway towards the mouth of the Sigindere. The Lancashire Fusiliers landed from boats at Teke Burnu (Cape Helles), the Royal Fusiliers and Marines at Kumtepe. The latter were particularly well supported by the *Implacable*, which owing to the depths stole close in shore and covered the landing at close range with her broadsides.

At the Lancashire landing the enemy were met by stubborn resistance from the brave Turkish Infantry Regiment 26, who coolly remained under the heaviest fire and prevented the Lancashire Fusiliers reaching the plateau at Teke Burnu. Thanks to the *Implacable*, the Royal Fusiliers successfully stormed the cliffs at Kumtepe.

Hill 40 now had to be taken, but always when the ships lengthened their fire to avoid hitting their own troops the Turks also got a breathing space and counter-attacked. These angry counter-attacks of the 26th held the Royal Fusiliers in check.

A moment of crisis now approached for the Turks on the southern point of the peninsula. The tactical envelopment by the English of the left flank could be developed. If this succeeded the Turks would be taken in the rear and the many battalions of the 29th Division hanging on the shore relieved. The King's Own Scottish Borderers and the Marine battalion 'Plymouth' were the troops selected for this attack which, if successful, would probably mean the fall of Krithia and Eltshitepe (Achi Baba) the same evening.

The landing-place of these two battalions was in the neighbourhood of the mouth of the Singindere (Gully Beach), only about 1km. from Hill 40, but direct north from it. Therein lay the great tactical value. As troops landed they were practically behind the rear of the enemy. A small sandy strip permitted a first landing from boats which were covered by the usual protecting fire from the cruisers *Goliath*, *Dublin*, *Amethyst* and *Sapphire*. The battalions first occupied a very well-placed cliff 80 metres high, covered with bushes. According to plan they now attempted to join up with the Royal Fusiliers at Kumtepe. The crowning success seemed to be near.

But a portion of the Turkish Infantry Regiment 26, which was literally everywhere, threw itself between the two English battalions which were striving to reach each other. The way lay only over their dead bodies. About noon, by forced marches, the excellent Lt Col Nail Bey arrived in support with two battalions of his Infantry Regiment 25 and some batteries of Field Artillery Regiment 9. The divisional commander, Col Sami Bey, had sent them just at the right moment. With the arrival of these reinforcements Hamilton's plan of encirclement was shattered. It is true that Col Koe made desperate attempts to break out of the valley of the Singindere, which cost him his life. The Scots made repeated bayonet attacks, but the Turks refused to break. Towards evening only half the Scots were left. Worn out with the heavy fighting and without prospect of reinforcement they were glad to retire on their transports under the covering fire of the Navy, sacrificing a small rearguard in their retreat.

Summing up, Hamilton had not succeeded in closing his small tactical forceps and thus cutting off the southern point of the peninsula, but nevertheless the English had succeeded in getting a firm foothold at several points on the peninsula by the evening of 25 April, even if only on the edge of the coast. (See Map a-a.) Of the 9,000 landing troops 3,000 had fallen out.

Hamilton had, however, a still longer forcep, which had as its aim the cutting off of the fortress of Killid Bahr. This was to be achieved by a landing at Kabatepe across the well known narrow portion of the peninsula to Maidos.

This landing, in contrast to the others, was to be a surprise landing without artillery covering fire, before daybreak. For this purpose it was proposed to land the Anzac troops on a lightly defended portion of the coast about an English mile north of Kabatepe.

Owing to the darkness and the strong current the boats were driven further to the northward, and landed at about 4:20 in the morning, under feeble fire from small posts, at the base of the high cliffs which overlooked a small beach. This receding cape, thus captured by chance, was known as Ariburnu (Cape of Bees) (Anzac), and afforded good cover against hostile artillery fire. However, the main objective, the road to Maidos, lay further off. Nevertheless it was hoped to reach this fairly soon, because it was believed that all available reserves would have been sent to the southern point and the four other Turkish divisions were known to be either in Asia or on the Gulf of Saros.

Against the limited enemy resistance the landing was accomplished without particularly heavy loss. In half an hour 4,000 men were on shore, about 7:30 a.m. about 8,000 and towards 2 o'clock 12,000 men with two mountain batteries.

General Birdwood pushed his Australians and New Zealanders forward with the greatest energy, and the Turkish Infantry Regiment 27 which was gradually arriving found it increasingly difficult to resist the attacks. The left flank of the English drew nearer to the Kojadere in a manner which caused us the greatest anxiety. The country here is very cut up. The steep hillocks and the deep valleys covered with bush allowed no observation of the enemy's movements. The mass of the Kodjadshemendagh (Sari Bair) does not lie far off, and the occupier of this is master of the whole surrounding country.

As luck would have it Mustapha Kemal Bey had decided to lead either his 19th Division, or a portion of it – I am not quite sure now – for exercises in this direction on that very day. He told me later how suddenly gendarmes, bare-headed and without weapons, and with every sign of excitement, came running in frantic haste. "What's up?" "They come, they come." Who comes" "Inglis, Inglis" A question to the Chief of Staff – "Have we ball cartridges?" "Yes." "All right. Forward." One regiment was sent at full speed to secure the important point of the Kodjadshemendagh and the rest of the division was sent forward in the direction of Kabatepe-Ariburnu. A highly welcome reinforcement to the heavily engaged Infantry Regiment 27, as with this extra assistance it became possible to recover the whole of Kabatepe, and the Anzac troops had the utmost difficulty in consolidating positions on the last cliffs of the Ariburmu, in the shape of a bridgehead.

By the evening the position appeared to be so critical for the English that it was earnestly debated whether the troops should not be re-embarked. As the English Admiral declared that this would take at least two days it was found to be possible to save the situation by heavy fire from the battleships and the landing of fresh reinforcements. On the Turkish side the situation was saved by the immediate and independent action of the 19th Division, which actually was not intended for use as coastal defence, but to be held intact in reserve in Maidos to be used either against attack from Kabatepe or, in case of need, in support on the Asiatic coast. In this case the commander had taken the right decision at the right moment, and success, which is the only real critic, crowned his decision,

We have now only one of the many landing columns to follow, that is, that on the extreme left where the Royal Naval Division was heading for the innermost portion of the Gulf of Saros. Here, at dawn, a withering fire was opened on the land.

Just in time to see this new play the Marshal arrived, who had established his headquarters in the town of Gallipoli, but on receipt of the first reports proceeded at once to the narrow neck of land known as Bulair, which permitted a wide field of view. The 5th and 7th Divisions were already in this area, ready for action. Essad Pasha, the General commanding 3rd Army Corps, was sent to take over command of the southern portion of the peninsula. On the Asiatic side the control was in the hands of the efficient General Weber.

The Marshal saw the 20 large ships in the northern portion of the Gulf of Saros which, although firing heavily, did not seem to be making any attempt to land, so he decided to remain at this point in person.

In the meantime the reports came in giving details of the different landings, and of the fighting whose course we have already followed till evening; but the news which reached the Marshal was not as clear as that which we have read, but a mixture partly correct and partly incorrect, confused and partially lacking, as is usually the case during critical moments, and more particularly so when dealing with old-fashioned methods of signalling and two languages.

During the day it became clear that landings had been effected by the French at Kumkale, and by the English on the southern point of

Gallipoli and at Ariburnu, even if their sphere of effective action was still somewhat limited. In the Besika Bay it would appear that only a false landing was being attempted. Here, however, in the Gulf of Saros 20 large ships still lay threateningly off the coast. It was impossible to see on board, owing to the thick brush work which had been placed round the decks. Boats were lowered and with 1,200 men approached the coast at three places in the neighbourhood of the island of Saros. Then it became dark. Essad Pasha requested urgently reinforcements for the southern portion of the peninsula.

The Marshal was now faced with an important decision.

Up to this time the dispositions which he had taken to meet probable attacks had admirably dealt with the actual attacks.

The time passed according to plan.

That is the beauty, I might almost say splendour, of a clear organisation which has anticipated the future—that in the moment of the greatest danger and confusion, at the highest point of the development of the attack, as in this moment of
the landings, further orders from headquarters are absolutely unnecessary.

As old Moltke said: "The quietest day of my life was the first day of mobilisation in 1879, as everything had been arranged for."

In this case, owing to a most careful and considered study of the map and personal reconnoitring of the territory, the probable landing places of the enemy had been correctly anticipated.

The moment had, however, arrived when the brave fighters of 9th Division could no longer hold their front with their own resources. The 19th Division also urgently required support. Perhaps it would be possible here to finally drive in one attack the Anzacs, who were clinging to the coast, back into the sea.

Where was he to take reinforcements from?

An army reserve was not available. All six divisions stood in the front line.

The Field Marshal had now to stand the test as to whether, from his own appreciation of the situation and from the confused reports that reached him, he could take the right decision. The success of the whole existence of the campaign, the whole Empire, hung upon his shoulders at that moment.

The Marshal decided, and ordered 5th and 7th Divisions and then 11th Division to Maidos, because he believed the decisive action would take place in the southern portion of the peninsula.

During the night the transport by ship commenced, all of which had to be hidden from the view of the enemy. Transports were available for 7th Division in the harbour of Gallipoli, for 5th Division, which was on the east border of the Gulf of Saros, in Sharkoi. The aim of all transports was Maidos, where they came under the further orders of Essad Pasha. This transport of troops took place during several nights. The cavalry and horsed arms travelled on foot along the new road from the town of Gallipoli which had just been completed, along the bank of the Dardanelles, out of sight of the enemy. To deceive the enemy a pioneer company and several labour battalions were left at Bulair with instructions to put up tents on the heights.

During the night the Marshal remained at Bulair to see what happened. A bombardment of the Gulf of Saros increased in strength towards evening. Troops appeared to have landed on the island of Xeros, as one saw fires burning in many places. As we now know, these fires had been lit by sections of marines for purposes of deception only, and towards midnight these were withdrawn.

The Marshal did not permit himself to be deceived. On the morning of 26 April he proceeded to the main scene of activity to join Essad Pasha at Maltepe.

It was a daring and responsible decision to remove the whole of his troops from the Gulf of Saros in the face of the many threatening

THE TRENCHES OF INFANTRY REGIMENT 125 (16TH DIVISION)

ships. But this cool decision was correct, as has been proved by the further course of events.

I have reported the events of 25 April so much in detail because they are in fact exceptionally interesting and, individually, curiously different.

Hamilton was right when he began his General Order for the troops on 21 April 1915, with the following words: "Soldiers of France and the King, before us lies an adventure without precedent in recent military history."

Whoever has followed with us the simultaneous battles at the 10 different points lying so close to one another, whoever has followed these with interest and on the map, must involuntarily pause here, for a moment, and once again review these events as one concerted whole.

Each individual landing truly bore in itself its own value as a coolly thought out and hardily carried through battle action, greatly to the renown of both adversaries. The real value and the underlying intentions can however first be recognised and understood if the individual landings are considered, in their inner connection, as equal links of the chain which Hamilton was attempting to throw round Gallipoli.

The individual incidents I have already touched on in the course of my story. Taken as a whole, we know that the Marshal had awaited the attacks on both extreme wings in the Bay of Besika and the Gulf of Saros with the greatest anxiety. These were not merely the extreme enveloping wings with the longest leverage which could snatch from the jaws of the defenders the southern peninsula and the fort of Tchanak Kale without fighting taking place at either of these spots, but they also bore in themselves the seeds of a strategic success for the enemy.

Hamilton did not, however, recognise these larger strategical claws. According to his ideas only false landings were to take place in the Gulf of Saros and the Bay of Besika. He was content with the smaller tactical jaws. These, as a hard-headed, pugnacious Englishman, he set at the extreme southern portion of the peninsula and closed them with enormous energy. He took the bull by the horns. He was in a position, as lord of enormous quantities of material, to use without undue anxiety as much munitions, material and soldiers as he considered necessary. England had the whole world as basis to draw upon.

It is certainly correct that the fleet could exercise a destructive fire across the whole southern portion of the peninsula, and yet on 25 April the results of this fire failed to come up to expectations as much as on 18 March. Churchill in particular was convinced of the enormous effect of the modern long-range artillery. He based his impression on the surprisingly rapid fall of Liège and Namur through the German 42's. The quick destruction of the outer forts of Kumkale and Seddil Bahr on 19 February seemed to prove his contention correct. That in spite of this the bombardment by the English fleet failed, in a certain sense, to come up to expectations is due to the essential difference between a short-barrelled land howitzer which, with shorter range, reaches its target by a high trajectory and falls directly on to the object, and the long-barrelled ships' guns – guns whose shells, built for the purpose of destroying armour, reach their target on a flat trajectory over enormous distances and approach from the front instead of dropping. The moral effect of these latter on the defenders is great, but the actual effect is not fully felt by entrenched troops, who as a target are lying below the trajectory of the guns.

This is the explanation of the almost laughably small losses on the Turkish side, in spite of the enormous preponderance of the Entente in ships' guns which far outranged the land artillery, besides being of heavier calibre. This is the main reason for the disappointment on the English side, which reason was later examined and confirmed by a Parliamentary Committee.

On the Turkish side the shrieking crash of such an armour-piercing shell from a 12-inch or 14-inch gun, which arrived like a volcanic upheaval, had always a great effect. If the shell was a bull's eye the Turks were blown up in a whole group, as happened to the courageous Infantry Regiment 26, at the south.

As time went on it was noticed, however, that the explosive effect of these enormous horrors mostly went through the base into the air, and after several seconds one heard the pieces of shell falling, without a tearing effect, flat to the earth. The Turkish soldiers named them "fountains" as they saw that they mostly escaped with a shock.

On the evening of 25 April Hamilton must certainly have remembered his first reconnoitring visit about five weeks previously, during which he sailed along the outer coast of Gallipoli. The whole outlook of this dour coast, the fortresses on which one could recognise the barbed wire had, as Daniels writes, greatly depressed his spirits. Even at that time he explained that Gallipoli appeared to be a nut which would be much harder to crack than he had believed when in Kitchener's room looking at it on the map.

Today, 25 April, he was, as certainly as all English men must have been, astonished anew by the stubborn energy, unexpected of the Turks, which showed itself in open counter-attacks the moment the heavy fire of the ships eased at all. In spite of this, as we have seen, the Turks in certain places only, drive the English back to their ships.,

The attacker in such cases must be always more stubborn if he has once been lucky enough to reach land. He has gladly left behind him a narrow, rocking boat which prevented him moving and on which he felt himself defenceless against the double death – the bullets of the enemy and the treacherous water. Once on land he again becomes active, can move and look for cover, and fight. Every step forward means more room for reinforcements. The defender, on the other hand, with every step he retreats draws nearer to his own reinforcements. Regarded from a purely psychological standpoint the attacker has therefore an advantage, and he will do everything that lies in his power to avoid being forced, probably under still more unfavourable conditions, to again enter this narrow, shifting boat. Whatever happens, no retreat. Hence the reason for the obstinacy and stubbornness of the landing parties.

For this reason the firing was continued all through the night of 26 April. Both parties began to get a clear appreciation of the main attacks and both parties strove to send reinforcements as rapidly as possible.

The 3rd Division had been successful in forcing its way, by murderous bayonet fighting during the night, into the streets of Kumkale, but they were forced to leave it again the next morning, as at dawn the ships opened a ruthless fire on the town which destroyed everything, including the larger portion of the Senegalese prisoners.

A French brigade had in the meantime landed and successfully occupied Jenischehir. There was nothing to do by day. The Turks tiredly sought cover and with the help of their field artillery, sent into position by their able and energetic commander, Lt Col Binhold, regardless of the cost, had to content themselves with defending their position against the French attack. But during the night Nicolai led his brave divisions again successfully forward and this time he was actually successful, during the night of 27 April, in driving the last French to their ships.

An important success which finally freed the Asiatic shore from the enemy. An excellent example of how to conduct a defensive division. This pleasant fact is not reduced in any way by the statement recently issued by the French that the landing on the Asiatic shore had from the first only been regarded as a temporary manoeuvre. This cost the French Eastern Corps 7 officers and 183 men dead, and 13 officers and 575 men wounded.

It is important to note that Hamilton wished to use French troops on 26 April at the southern point of the peninsula. Here the whole energy of the enemy was concentrated in collecting and uniting the forces which had landed at the various points on the previous day, forming one fighting line and pushing forward.

Under cover of night the rest of the troops on the *River Clyde* had quit the ship and landed at Seddil Bahr. In addition to the 29th Division, a portion of the Naval Division and of the French Orient

Corps landed, the first on the right flank and the latter at the mouth of the Singindere. There was a continual stream of troops from deck to land, which gathered and pushed forward against the Turks.

The Turks had also received their first reinforcements which, on arriving at Maidos, had already been sent forward to support the defence. Lt Col Remsi Bey led the first battalion of his 7th Division immediately to the storming of Hissarlik. The next battalion was sent towards Cape Helles.

The English ships again opened a heavy bombardment on this small portion of the peninsula. Both sides regarded their task as offensive, but in spite of the efforts of the Turks, the English were successful during the course of 26 April in forming a line on the heights to the north of Seddil Bahr. (See Map b--b.)

Behind them developed the picture of an enormously busy harbour – the continual coming and going of boats, lighters, pinnaces, launches between the shore and the regular forests of masts. Men, munitions, supplies, entrenching material, portable wire entanglements, steel loopholes and guns began to collect on the narrow beach. Through the steel body of the *River Clyde* one could safely approach the landing bridge as through a tunnel. Above everything, the continual wailing and whistling of the ships shells as they bombarded the Turkish lines. The Turks here saw for the first time the enemy's fire controlled by aeroplanes and captive balloons – something that was quite unknown to them.

The effect was such that Essad Pasha had to withdraw his troops on the evening of 27 April, as these had been broken through in the Sigindere, Kirthedere, Kanlidere. This did not mean that the offensive idea was given up, but in this shelter it would at least be possible to arrange to regroup the standard units, fill up with reinforcements and ammunition, and feed them.

Hamilton's whole idea was to concentrate as many troops as possible and then in one move to overrun the Turkish lines and storm the village of Krithia and Eltschitepe. These lay only 4,000 metres behind the enemy front.

By 29 April he believed he could do this. From the battles of the beaches emerged the first main battle on Gallipoli. De Robeck's ships for hours thundered heavily against the Turkish lines. For the first time field and heavy batteries were able to take part in this day's concerted attack. When the sun was so far overhead that it shone directly in the eyes of the Turks, shortly before noon, the English commenced their attack, four brigades strong, with two French brigades on their right flank.

At this moment the Marshal's daring decision of the evening of 25 April began to bear fruit. The heavily thinned line of the Turkish 9th Division was reinforced by practically the whole of the 7th Division, a portion of the 11th Division and several battalions of the 5th Division. Wehrle had also sent one of the howitzer batteries of his 1st Battalion to help on the eastern side.

Consequently, as the ships fire slackened and the Allied troops commenced their attack they did not find the shattered troops they had hoped but, on the contrary, after initial success, they were confronted by fresh Turkish reserves who first drove back General d'Amades' French battalions in heavy counter-attacks, with constantly increasing success, almost to the base of Hissarlik. No very pleasant position for the English, whose right flank now hung in the air. They also had to retreat and could only show, as the result of the day's fighting, a limited gain in territory in addition to the experience that the Turks are really very hardy fighters. How did this compare with their conduct in the Balkan War by Kirk Kilisse and Lule Burgas two years ago?

Kitchener was forced to send the 42nd Territorial Division and an Indian brigade from Egypt as reinforcements.

During this period heavy fighting had taken place at Ariburnu. Birdwood had become master of the situation which had looked so bad for him on the evening of 25 April. Increasing quantities of his Anzacs found footing on the heights of Ariburnu, but in spite of continual attacks under cover of heavy fire from the ships, he was not successful in smashing the narrow encircling front of Mustapha Kemal Bey. This latter also received a continual stream of reinforcements form Maidos, mostly from 5th Division,

So drew to a close the heavy days of the actual battles of the beaches which, in feverish excitement, had been conducted with a maximum of human effort and personal sacrifice on both sides. The fighting continued, however, with unprecedented severity, the English wanting at all costs Eltschitepe and Krithia as well as Maidos, and the Turks equally wishing to recover the sea coast.

The losses of the Allies give some idea of the heavy fighting at the battle of the beaches. The English had lost by 9 May, 683 officers and 16,000 men, the French up to 11 May, 246 officers and 12,632 men – a total of 29,561 in two or three weeks. The total losses of the English during the three years' South African war only reached 38,000 men.

In place of the many beaches there were now two clear fronts – the southern portion of the peninsula known as the 'Southern Group' and the Ariburnu, known as the 'Northern Group.' The Northern Command was taken over by Essad Pasha with headquarters at Kemalieri, scarcely anticipating that he would yet there experience snow, ice and winter storms. The Southern Group was taken over by Col von Sodenstern.

CHAPTER X
Over Ariburnu to The Southern Group

It was originally intended that in place of my old cadet comrade, Colonel von Sodenstern, I should take over command of the South Front, because on 28 April I received the following telegram whilst on duty in the War Office in Constantinople:

> To Enver Pasha.
> Please send Colonel Kannengeisser immediately to take over command of the southern portion of the Gallipoli Peninsula.
> Signed,
> Liman V. Sanders
> 26.4.15

Enver Pasha immediately gave me the required permission to travel, and I handed over with a glad heart my responsibilities as Director of the Army Department to my Second in Command, Lt Col Behidj Bey. I felt that I could not have wished for a more worthy successor.

Behidj Bey was the Turkish officer whom, as a result of many years working together, I felt I had learnt to know best. He was a wise, quick-thinking man, of thorough education, with a knowledge of the historical past, customs and usages of his country such as one seldom finds among the Turks. It was always a pleasure to converse with this intelligent man, even when off duty. His official accomplishments were first class, as with his great knowledge, quick appreciation and clear decision, combined with astonishing energy, he was able to accomplish an enormous amount of work. In addition to this he was a good comrade and well liked by all who knew him well. Those who did not know him were apt to be quickly turned away by his somewhat abrupt and curt manner of speech, quite the opposite of the usual polished, polite Oriental, who considers a direct "No" to be the reply of an uneducated person.

Whether below the surface he was actually a friend of Germany, I do not know. I believe that his was the standpoint of many of the higher Turkish officers, who, because the Turkish Army had,

unfortunately, neither the knowledge nor the power to carry out the urgently needed complete reorganisation, felt that a Military Mission was a necessary evil. They hoped in a few years to have accomplished sufficient to again be independent. The contract with the head of the German Military Mission was based on this premise. The fact that it should be a 'German' Military Mission was accepted by these officers as an accomplished fact. Many, particularly those who had trained with the French Army, would perhaps have preferred to see a French Mission. A considerably majority, and more particularly many officers who had learnt to know the German Army, and finally the High Directing Officers, amongst whom were Mahmud Schefket Pasha, Izzed Pasha and also Enver Pasha, were of the opinion that a reorganisation of the Turkish Army could only be effectively carried out if based on German plans and methods. I do not personally believe that Behidj Bey had accepted these opinions unconditionally – I worked with him, however, for four and a half years in splendid harmony throughout the period. We both had the same aim
– an active and efficient army for the good of the Turkish Fatherland. Thus I was able to contentedly leave my own sphere of work to this proved officer whom I greatly esteemed.

My bags had been packed for weeks, I only needed to close the lids. The afternoon of the same day I boarded the Plewena which lay alongside the Haidar Pasha, and which has already loaded with a machine gun company. It was 4 a.m. next day, however, before the three transports finally cleared the docks. A delay of only 12 hours is quite a good accomplishment for the Turks.

At 1 p.m. on 29 April, close to the Island of Marmora five torpedo boats took over the convoy of our ships. As we had to limit our speed to that of the slowest ship we crept very slowly forward.

About 2:30, I suddenly heard rifle shots, which I could not understand. I hurried to the bow of the ship and saw, close ahead and squarely crossing our bows, a bubbling line in the water – the track of a torpedo, the first I had seen in its own element. Ah! An English submarine!

Our torpedo boats drove round us like wild dogs, but there was nothing to see. The ships were now ordered to sail close to the shore so that the torpedo boats had only one side of the transports to protect. Three-quarters of an hour later I drew the attention of my interpreter, Major Zia Bey, to a four-cornered black flag which was apparent on the Asiatic shore, a fairly long way off in the direction of Kara Bigha. He had hardly the words out of his mouth, "the sails here look like that," when several shells exploded in the neighbourhood of the apparent sail, which was actually an submerged English submarine and which quickly submerged. It was a splendid sight for us to watch how the torpedo boats steamed at full speed towards the place where the submarine had been. Without success! We had, however, a comfortable and thankful feeling of safety.

At the entrance to the Dardanelles, our faithful torpedo boats, who had circled and looked after us like a sheep dog his flock of sheep, left us. Without them we should now certainly be lying at the bottom of the Sea of Marmora. As a land-lubber I had always thought that my first meeting with the enemy would be quite different.

Events always happen, however, quite differently to what one has anticipated. I was to almost immediately experience this again. Directly after we had made fast before the town of Gallipoli, I reported to the Marshal, who explained that I had to take over the 5th Division in place of Col von Sodenstern, who had already taken the position allotted to me as Commander of the South Front. It had taken me longer than G.H.Q. had expected to come from Constantinople, although I had lost no time.

I went rapidly on board again, and at half-past four we reached the burning town of Maidos, whose inhabitants we could see crawling along the coast, in miserable plight, with what few articles they had been able to save from the fire. A perfect picture of misery.

Our anchor had scarcely rattled into the harbour of Kilia when shells began to burst all round us. At first we thought these were the bombs of the aeroplanes circling overhead. It was soon clear to us, however, that these were only controlling the indirect fire of warships lying on the far side of the peninsula in the Aegean, who were thus greeting us in such a friendly fashion. The discharge of three large ships under these conditions promised to be very difficult.

However, anchor was raised almost immediately and we steamed up the Dardanelles again to unload at Akbasch – this time not discovered by the enemy. The Marshal had already landed troops here on 27 April.

Akbasch was not prepared at all for the unloading of transports. A peaceful bay, shores covered with scrub, no quay, no landing-stage, no roads to the inner portion of the peninsula, only three poor fisher huts. It was extraordinary to see how well the Turks accomplished their tasks under such primitive conditions. The *Plewna* was able to keep quite close to the shore. By spars, improvised landing gangways, jumping, climbing and sliding, they reached firm ground, myself amongst them. Then came the turn of the horses. The small Anatolian horses sprang like fleas from the high bulwarks to the land as if they were glad to reach firm ground. Whichever delayed was driven on from behind. I was somewhat anxious about my large Hungarian, but he got ashore all right, helped from behind.

Zia Bey and myself mounted immediately and rode to meet Esssad Pasha at Maltepe along roads which were no roads. I have already sketched his character above. He told me that I should probably meet the 14th Infantry Regiment of my Division and, for the rest Mustapha Kemal Bey would be able to give me information. This was not much information for a divisional commander who was afire to take over his troops and tackle the enemy.

We rode still further westward, and everywhere we met groups of marching or resting baggage wagons and supplies which were apparently looking for their own units. Nobody knew anything of the 5th Division. I finally found, west of the Kodjadere, a small clump of tents. This was the staff of the 5th Division, from now onwards my own Division. The chief Staff Officer was with Mustapha Kemal Bey. Where the troops were they did not know.

We climbed a steep cliff to Kemaliere, as this place was called, after Kemal Bey. He was extremely astonished when

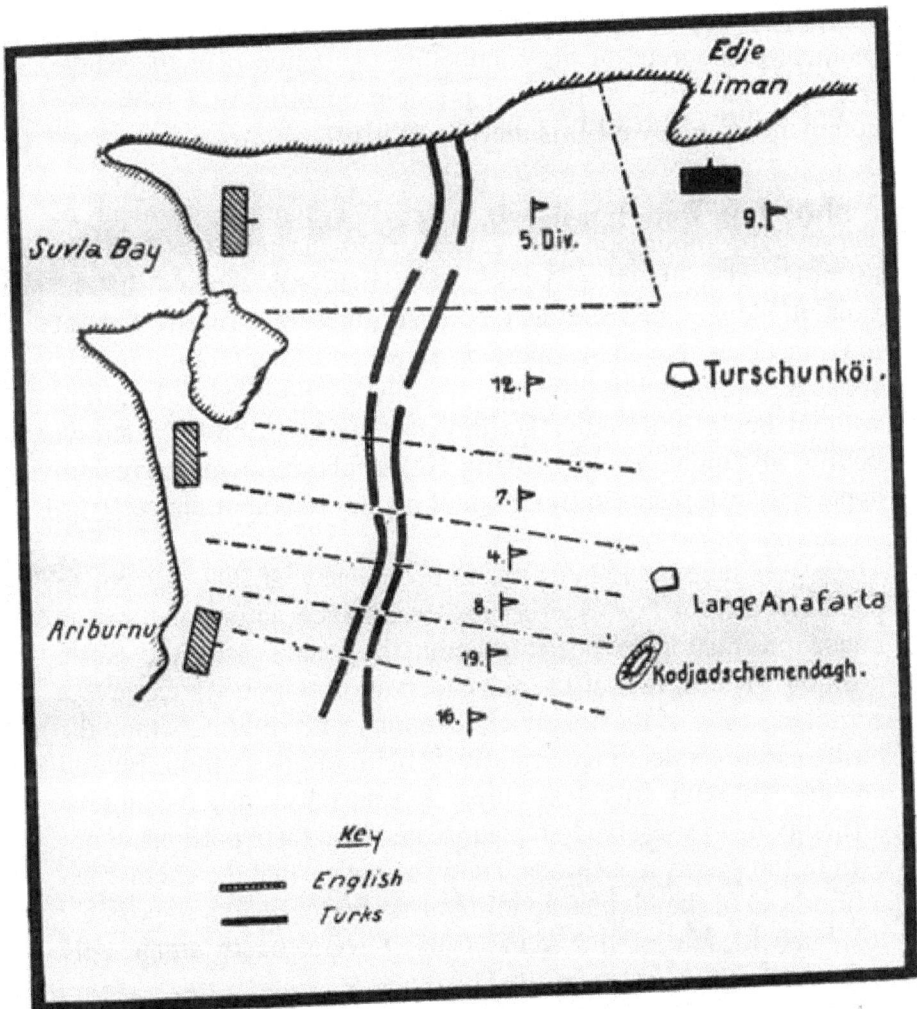

Edje
Liman

Suvla Bay

5. Div.

9.

12.

Turschunköi.

7.

4.

8.

Large Anafarta

Ariburnu

19.

Kodjadschemendagh.

16.

Key

English

Turks

SKETCH SHOWING THE DISTRIBUTION OF THE TURKISH DIVISIONS

I presented myself to him as Commander of the 5th Division and told him I intended to take over my own troops. "That's quite impossible," he told me, "as the 5th and 19th Divisions are completely mixed. I have arranged a big attack for tomorrow." I recognised that it was impossible to make any alterations at the moment and agreed to his conducting the action over the whole front provided that, at the first possible opportunity, I took over command of my own Division.

Mustapha Kemal Bey is the now world-famous President of Turkey. The impression that I gained of him during this period was that of a clear-thinking, active, quiet man who knew what he wanted. He weighed and decided everything for himself, without looking elsewhere for support or agreement to his opinions. He spoke accordingly but little, and was always reserved and retiring without being unfriendly. He did not appear to be very strong bodily, although extremely wiry. His stubborn energy gave him apparently complete control, both of his troops and of himself.

There was nothing left for me to do in view of this fact but to patiently control my eagerness to commence action and get as much information as possible about the country and the battle positions. I went forward to the observation station which gave a surprising view of the deeply cleft country of Ariburnu, which the bushy nature rendered particularly difficult of observation. Behind lay the sea with countless ships. It was only with the utmost difficulty that I was able to recognise here and there portions of our own or the enemy's positions. I saw, however, that the enemy had a firm hold of the high steep cliffs of Ariburnu. It was impossible to obtain a view of the whole front. Several badly aimed rifle bullets, most ricochets, whistled by our post.

I slept that night in a tent of my divisional staff and rode next morning at 5 o'clock – it was 1 May – again towards Kemaliere, in expectation of the ordered attack. During this climb my horse fell over backwards on me. I escaped with a bad bruising and scraping of my back, which was very painful and unfortunately hindered me considerably during the next few days. Mustapha Kemal Bey had thrown the whole of his troops into an attack to drive the Anzacs the short 800 to 1,200 metres back into the water. I saw the Turks in several places climbing the steep cliffs. Towards 8:30, information was received from the left flank that the enemy were giving way.

About 10:45 in the morning we intercepted a wireless call for help from Birdwood asking for the fleet to come out and shell the Turkish position. At the same time Mustapha Kemal Bey gave orders for a general attack. At 11:45, we received the news that the English fleet had answered, "We come in haste to Kabatepe." Kemal Bay continually urged the attack, but this did not really begin on the right flank until 4:30. Every attempt failed, and the whole of the attacks were smashed by the overwhelming superiority of the English fire.

Our troops were divided as follows:
Left flank, 11 battalions, made up from
        Infantry Regiment 72, 1st and 2nd battalions
        Infantry Regiment 13, 1st battalion
        Infantry Regiment 125, 1st and 2nd Battalion
        Infantry Regiment 33, 1st to 3rd Battalions
        Infantry Regiment 27, 1st to 3rd Battalions

In the centre, 6 battalions, as follows:
        Infantry Regiment 14, 1st to 3rd Battalions
        Infantry Regiment 15, 1st and 3rd Battalions
        Infantry Regiment 125, 3rd Battalion

Right flank, 7 battalions, namely:
        Infantry Regiment 72, 3rd Battalion
        Infantry Regiment 57, 1st to 3rd Battalions
        Infantry Regiment 64, 1st to 3rd Battalions

From four different Divisions.

THE TRENCHES OF THE
12TH DIVISION
20 October, 1915

DJEWAD PASHA
Commander of Tchanak Kale
1915

EDJE LIMAN
24 October, 1915

Here I must point out that a great portion of these battalions had been fighting steadily for six days and were only about half strength, with great gaps in officers and men. All the troops, owing to the fighting, were completely mixed. When I suggested to Kemal Bey that in order to better reorganise I should go to the troops myself, he strongly advised me not to, as in this deeply cleft country, where it was practically impossible to obtain a clear view, such an attempt would be absolutely useless.

I must say that the first general impression which I received of the conduct of the Turkish troops in battle was not particularly complimentary to them. Quite a number of battalions had failed during the attack.

It was particularly difficult for me to obtain a clear appreciation of the situation, because I only heard Turkish spoken, which I did not understand. My interpreter, Zia Bey, appeared to have little or no appreciation of the real tactical position. He was a Bosnian, no real 'Turk, and therefore did not speak good Turkish. His education was none too good, although he spoke bad German and French. He was a so-called regimental officer, that is risen from the troops without any special technical training. He was diligent and good-natured, and always took a lot of trouble to secure my personal comfort, for which I am indebted to him. As interpreter of my thoughts, my ideas and my wishes to the Turks he proved himself later to be ill-fitted for this very vital duty, because he often did not understand the inner meaning of my words. Educated Turks who listened to his translations often told me that. I therefore had but poor support from him in official matters, because, although he had the will, he had not the capacity. I can only say that I recognised with a shudder how frightfully difficult it was for a German to here fulfil the responsible position of a commander. The best will and the best ability in the world could not be used in action so long as it was impossible to converse directly with the non-commissioned officers and men, and reports and orders were received through the interpreter either incorrect, or badly translated.

Every soldier knows how, particularly at critical moments, success often depends on a single word, and what evil results follow misunderstanding. What could happen here? I found myself as a commander willing and able to carry out my duties, like a man who knows nothing and can say nothing, shortly, like a deaf and dumb person forced to depend solely on that most unsafe medium, the interpreter. I remembered the wording of the A.K.O. which had left us in Turkey: "Your difficult, often perhaps self-denying, but necessary work in Turkey." Yes, we often had to deny ourselves. It was very soon clear to me that I could only effectively fill the post of a 'Turkish Commander provided I had a general staff officer at my side with whom I could converse directly, and with whom I could work in complete accord and constant trust. Only when this officer possessed the necessary energy and oversight to watch the translation of orders into fact and see that these reached his own countrymen correctly, was success possible. Otherwise the best of orders were useless.

That evening Kemal Bey assembled all his regimental commanders around him in an empty tent. They all sat in rings on the ground, *à la turca*, with their legs crossed under them, the commander in the middle. I was also there and at first also tried to sit *à la turca*, but could not do so, so laid on the hard ground on my side. There were no chairs or tables – the Turks wrote with the paper laid flat on the palms of their hands. They do not like chairs to sit upon. As a result, and very welcome from the military point of view, he requires no more baggage than as a nomad. From the same source comes the custom of leaving the shoes outside to avoid dirtying the beautiful carpet, but of keeping the fez on the head as there are no pegs on the side of a tent to hang a hat upon. Maps were not used during the discussion, of which I naturally understood no word. I felt myself to be most unnecessary.

The afternoon of the next day I received orders to report myself immediately to the Marshal at Maltepe for use elsewhere. With very different feelings to those which had filled my mind during my ascent 48 hours previously, I again descended the steep path from Kemaliere.

Although personally I had accomplished nothing during this period, yet my desire for active occupation had received a severe check in view of the enormous difficulties which here confronted the employment of a German on active service.

Poorer in hopes but richer in experience I found myself facing the Marshal, who ordered me to proceed immediately to the Southern Group and place myself under the orders of Col von Sodenstern. The southern front was engaged in heavy fighting. The enemy was being continuously reinforced, had strongly occupied Hissarlik, and had landed wire, steel plates and similar material with the apparent intention of creating there a second Gibraltar. That had to be stopped, and the enemy forced by night attacks back into the sea. Reinforcements were already marching there. The Marshal placed his car at my disposal as far as Serafin Tschiflik, where horses were already awaiting me.

By 10 o'clock in the evening I rode out from Serafin Tschiflik, and my guide was the sky, reddened as from an enormous conflagration. I overtook battalions marching quietly and in good order, and supply columns with ammunitions and rations.

The closer I approached the battlefield the more powerful was the impression on eye and ear. I recognised the continuous flashes from the fleet which lay in a half circle round the peninsula and bombarded the land with a cease less fire, giving an impression of power and might which I can scarcely describe. A frightful thunderstorm which broke with elemental force and with never-ceasing thunder and lightning against the forces concentrated on that small portion of the peninsula. If the English ever give the figures for the ammunition consumed on one of those nights, one will easily be able to reckon how many pounds weight of steel fell per square yard of earth.

Even later, in August 1917, in the battles in Flanders I did not have the same overwhelming impression of concentrated shelling as during this period. Although in Flanders the effect of the individual shell was much more destructive, due to more sensitive fuses and methods of shell manufacture, yet the total moral effect was in this case much greater.

About 11:30 in the evening I reached the command post of Colonel von Sodenstern, which was situated in open country on a small hillock on the road to Seddil Bahr, Major Mühlmann was his Chief of Staff. Col von Sodenstern following careful personal reconnoitring, had already led his troops to attack during the night of 1–2 May. This was the second night of heavy, bitter fighting. The arriving reinforcements only just sufficed to cover the enormous losses. The troops attacked well, and some units were supposed to have reached the sea by Seddil Bahr during one night, but the strongly fortified Hissarlik could not be taken.

I quote here from the diary of a French Legionnaire, to illustrate with what stubborn energy the fighting was conducted. The man, a Swiss by birth, writes about this night, "The Turks were determined to drive us out of our positions at all costs. Three times they were successful in breaking through our wire and forcing their way into our trenches, where they were received with the butts of our rifles." These were the Turks of whom it had been said in Egypt and Lemnos that troops only needed to land on the peninsula to put them to flight. Now we were to see how these lowly esteemed Turks, having broken into the enemy trenches, drew their knives from their boots and girdles and set about them.

Soon after my arrival Naval Lieutenant Bolz reported with a landing party of marines, 8 machine guns and 32 men, a most heartily welcomed support. He was at once sent to the front line, where he did extremely well in spite of the difficult position, the pitch-black night, without knowledge of the country, in the midst of troops whose language he did not know and whose uniform he did not wear. The Turks naturally took the German sailors for the English, and a terrible catastrophe was only just prevented by the lucky arrival and intervention of Major Mühlmann. The original Turkish escort were all gone.

The news of the arrival of German machine guns in the front line gave new life to the defenders, and Bolz related how they had been able to drive the enemy back from the Kerevisdere to the shore and occupy the enemy trenches. Ultimately, however, the same picture. As soon as the light was sufficient to allow the ships to shoot at the Turkish line an attempt to stay forward was equivalent to suicide. They had therefore to withdraw and carefully dig in where they found themselves at dawn.

Any attempt at movement, any sign of life during the day was impossible, because whoever showed himself was immediately shelled from the ships. With frowning muzzles, the frightful armoured colossi surrounded the small, barren peninsula. Nothing could happen to them, just as little as to a sportsman out shooting.

As dawn came on 3 May it became still clearer to me how, in contradiction to the deeply cleft Ariburnu, everything here living which showed itself by day must be killed. The food supply, munitions, stretcher-bearers, reinforcements, and last but not least the attack, in short any movement could only be possible under the protecting mantle of night. Here I first properly recognised the enormous difficulty of this unbelievably unequal battle, and the bitter tough resistance shown by the Turkish troops fighting in this "Devil's cauldron." To stand this required a reserve of nervous power which European troops would not have been able to produce.

In the morning, at 5 o'clock, von Sodenstern and I met in the "Staff quarters" – a little clay house in the middle of a small bare spot called Salem Bey Tschiflik. The three canvas beds occupied the room. Instead of windows holes had been punched in the thatch of the sides. It was very cold.

I had scarcely gone to sleep – a man must do that sometimes – when we were attacked by aeroplanes. Sixteen bombs fell all round and quite close to our hut which began
to dance. Mud and earth fell on us, and yellow poisonous clouds drifted through the holes of the windows. The hut was not touched itself, probably because the airmen aimed at it. Quite superfluously the ships remembered us as well and shelled us, but nothing came nearer than 30 paces. Apparently the English had got to know that the hated German leaders were using this hut as their headquarters. We remained quietly in bed. As I have said, it was bitterly cold and one was bound to be killed in one way or another. The results of the shooting were one man and several horses killed. Whether we went to sleep again afterwards I cannot now remember.

During the day I began to look round. Our front was split into halves by the road Kirthe-Seddil Bahr, the right being commanded by Colonel Sami Bey, Commander of the 7th Division. A total of 24 battalions was engaged, mostly from the 7th and 9th Divisions with parts of the 3rd, 5th and 11th Divisions. Col von Sodenstern had no heavy artillery but he had sufficient field artillery, munitions for which were plentifully supplied in spite of all difficulties.

The 7tlh and 9th Divisions had their normal supplies. For the attached units which had been put in piecemeal, difficulties arose which Sodenstern settled out of hand by requisitioning herds of sheep which he discovered during his ride through the peninsula a few days previously, although such action was strictly forbidden. The troops received in this way at least meat and a little bread. I gratefully remember here a battery which lay close to Salim Bey Tschiflik which admirably looked after the rationing of the staff of von Sodenstern.

As a matter of fact, this staff was not particularly well off. There was actually nobody of any real account there in spite
of the fact that Sodenstern had more than an Army Corps under his command. The few men that he had, even including the able Major Mühlmann, could not possibly replace a properly constituted General Staff. There was not a single telephone line to any of the divisions and, added to this, there was the language complication, the extremely difficult tactical position where we were and the complete confusion existing among the troops. I must say that the tirelessly active Colonel von Sodenstern stood confronted by an insoluble problem, such as the unexpected, inexorable events of war sometimes furnish. I must further add that even my help under these conditions was necessarily limited.

Our right flank was faced by the 29th British Division, an old regular Division, and a portion of the Naval Division.

Joining them, and in front of our 7th Division, was the French Corps d'Orient, now completely in the line. General d'Amade, an imposing figure but little loved by his troops, had, so Kugler relates, put his colonial troops in on his left flank at the junction with the English – big, broad shouldered, thin-legged Senegalese, wild-looking negroes from Dahomey with their sharp cheeks, and intelligent, proud, almost light-brown negroes from the Soudan. In addition to these they had the Foreign Legion made up from men of all countries, the newly formed 175th French Regiment of the Line, and finally, on the extreme right wing, the 3rd and 4th Zouaves. These last were again a coloured mixture of North Africans, Europeans including many from Alsace, niggers and creoles from Martinique and Guadaloupe, who fancy themselves to be better than negroes from the Continent.

When one considers that Australians and New Zealanders fought at Ariburnu and later Indians had to send their sons
to Gallipoli, one can really say that seldom had so many countries of the world, races and nations sent their representatives to so small a place with the praiseworthy intention of killing one another.

Naturally, as happens in every war of coalitions, friction arose between the Allies. The French felt themselves injured, the English not sufficiently supported. The first real difference arose after the attacks of 29 April and 1 May. General d'Amade, who even his own people considered to be rather inefficient, was replaced by the able and well liked General Gouraud, who was badly wounded during the later fighting in June.

On the Turkish side during 2 May, the Commander of the 15th Division, Col Schükri Bey, arrived with five battalions, as reinforcements at Salem Bey Tschifik. He spoke very good German and impressed one as fresh and efficient. New hopes arose that during this night we should finally be successful. Schükri Bey attacked at dusk the stubbornly defended Hessarlik along the valley of the Kerevisdere. Sodenstern himself led his last battalion to attack under heavy fire. We were discovered by the searchlights of a warship shining on us from behind, and heavily shelled. How far forward we got could not be determined in the pitch-black night, but at dawn everybody was forced to retire in spite of partial success secured at enormous cost. During the confusion the Turks had fired on one another as well as on the German machine gunners. Attempts to bind white armbands on failed, because of lack of material, handkerchiefs were not available, shirts were no longer white.

I personally was forced to the conclusion that we dare not attempt further fighting of this description, and that it was my personal duty to report my conclusions to the Marshal. Following my return from the battlefield at dawn on 4 May, I asked by telephone for permission to report to the Marshal about the position of affairs. "Yes, a car would be sent to me to Serafin Tschiflik." At five in the morning I forced myself to mount my horse, and I can scarcely say what a wonderful feeling it was, after these heavy days, to sink into the soft cushions of the car at Serafin Tschiflik and be borne lightly and comfortably through the country.

I was somewhat in doubt as to how the Marshal would receive my report. He completely agreed with me, however, that it was useless to attack further and that we must prepare a defence. Replying to my proposal that General Weber should take over command of the Southern Group with his staff he replied, "He is already under way and should arrive here in a few hours' time."

At 10 o'clock in the evening General Weber arrived at Salem Bey Tschiflik and came to our poor mud hut. We were all of us very glad to see him present Col von Sodenstern with the Turkish medal for bravery (*Imtiaz*). He had honestly earned it.

The English then followed the Turks in attack. Two Australian brigades and a New Zealand brigade were brought round from Ariburnu. The English attacked from 6 to 8 May, but without great success, the most of their attempts being broken up by our artillery and machine gun fire. On 9 May Hamilton reported to London that without reinforcements he could not get further forward.

Thus the fighting on Gallipoli entered a new phase. Following the bloody battles of the beaches, the furious offensives of both sides – by day the English, by night the Turks commenced, on the Turkish side a defensive action, rightly based on the forces available and with the intention to resume the offensive as soon as their forces permitted.

Both sides had fought with a stubborn bravery as if each individual fighter was personally convinced of the world importance of these battles, where a successful breakthrough could have given the war a totally different complexion, because in addition to a new Russia fully equipped with material a powerful new front could have been constituted in the Balkans against the Central Powers.

CHAPTER XI
The Fighting For Krithia

On 7 May I received orders to join the staff of the 9th Division by Krithia, to act as adviser to the divisional commander, Colonel Sami Bey. I was very glad to at last have a definite field of action, even if it was not an independent one. The success of my activity would now largely depend on the personal relationship established between the divisional commander and myself. I did my utmost to establish as good relations as possible in order to assure that my intervention would be accepted without friction whenever this was necessary.

Sami Bey was a man of comfortable, passive nature, mostly to be found in his tent, which lay much too far backwards in the neighbourhood of the field hospital; who spoke a little German and showed himself at first to be not unapproachable although somewhat suspicious. His chief staff officer, Captain Hunussi Efendi, was hard-working, energetic and ambitious; he could also speak a little German.

Attached to the Division was the German General Staff officer, Captain Lange, who was naturally of great value to me, but who unfortunately broke down with heart trouble 10 days after my arrival and had to return to Germany.

In order to establish from the commencement a common method of giving orders, it was agreed by Sami Bey that all my orders should be accepted in the front line as coming from him, and that in the event of any heavy attack we should meet in the command post of the Division on Hill 150, north of Krithia.

I believe that Sami Bey was of the same opinion, as many Turkish officers in the field, "that the Germans having forced us into the war, they can now show us what they themselves can do." As a result he at first left me a fairly free hand, for which I was grateful. I relieved him of a large part of his work.

The first thing was to learn for myself the position and organisation of the front line. I went there the first night of my arrival, with

Lange. The men lay behind small, shallow trenches affording scanty shelter. The staff clustered in holes in the ground, in which it was impossible to stand upright, and which were particularly unpleasant for me with my bruised back and torn sinews.

Proper trenches for the men to stand in and shoot, with dug-outs for reserves and staff, must be built at once. This was actually fairly quickly accomplished.

The front line was fairly easily arrived at. Following the country, the divisional front was split into two portions each occupied by three battalions in the front line. The right half section received its name and approach from the deep valley of the Sigindere. Through this valley I could ride almost as far as the firing line. The left half section I reached through the completely destroyed village of Krithia, from which one could walk along the valley Krithedere and reach the front quite comfortably.

Every morning at dawn I went with Zia Bey to one of these sections. From 10 o'clock onwards, owing to the burning sun and the stench from the corpses, it was impossible for a European to remain. On 8 May the troops occupying the Sigindere section were Infantry Regiment 126, 1st Battalion, Infantry Regiment 21, 1st and 2nd Battalions commanded by Lt Col Ludwi Bey; in the Krithia section the 2nd Battalion of Infantry Regiment 31, 1st Battalion Infantry Regiment 32, 3rd Battalion of Infantry Regiment 126, under Lt Col Ali Bey. In reserve were the 1st Battalion of Infantry Regiment 127, 1st Battalion Infantry Regiment 38, 1st Battalion Infantry Regiment 26, 2nd Battalion Infantry Regiment 126. The battalions averaged 600 men strong. There were battalions from various divisions, of which only the 1st Battalion of Infantry Regiment 26 actually belonged to the 9th Division.

On one of the first days I discovered a small, very narrow valley north of Krithia which formed an admirable position for the staff of the Division. From this point the command post on Hill 150 could be easily reached by foot, from which I had good observation and telephone communication. That was the main thing. On 10 May I was successful in inducing Sami Bey to transfer his headquarters to this valley. We lay there for a whole month.

The field artillery consisted of 11 batteries cleverly concealed in the country round Krithia. From the observation post in particular one had an extraordinarily good view over the whole of the country in front, as far as the southern extremity. Practically all the battery commanders made an excellent impression and knew their country well.

I became convinced, however, that no clear plan existed regarding division of targets, and combinations to meet the various possibilities of attack. A common leader was lacking for the mass of batteries made up from various regiments. The very difficult problem of munitions supply needed a particularly well thought out organisation, if in spite of limited ammunition, we were to obtain the necessary effect at the decisive point. I had no time to attend to these things myself, nor could I spare time to follow them continuously. On the Asiatic side there was an exceptionally good field artilleryman, Lt Col Binhold, who was in addition a good friend and neighbour from Moda, who had already had considerable practical experience in the fighting for Kum Kale, and who was no longer absolutely necessary there. I therefore asked for him as artillery commander. He reached me on 9 May and I was able to hand over to him all my troubles regarding the artillery. Unfortunately, he joined the General Staff of the Southern Group on 25 May, but his successor, Assim Bey, took over a proper organisation which proved of great value.

I have pleasant recollections of my oft-repeated visits, sometimes of long duration, to the observation posts of the battery commanders. The battery commanders stood on an average considerably higher in education and intelligence than their comrades in the infantry. All were seriously worried by the very great scarcity of ammunition, which was only somewhat relieved by the arrival of the Pieper ammunition (see above). They clenched their fists, as I did, when they saw the most wonderful targets and dared not shoot. We daily saw the English riding their horses in the same place and in the same ménage. One actually recognised the colour of the single animals, and I myself remember a magnificent great chestnut, perhaps Hamilton's own charger. Thus a portion of the English life displayed itself openly before our eyes and we were forced to remain dumb onlookers. A typical scene was that of the many small clouds of smoke which climbed at dawn into the air from all parts of the line, showing where the enemy were preparing their early morning coffee.

When ammunition was allowed for a particular shoot it was regarded as a holiday, and it was heartily refreshing to see how direct hits on the target were applauded. We had naturally complaints from our infantry in the front line that they were being shelled by their own artillery. As an infantryman myself I could well understand this complaint, but I also saw how extremely difficult it was for the battery commanders to entirely avoid this evil in the unobservable and similar country. We were finally able to erect on the parados of our own trenches marks for our own artillery. Later many battery commanders had splendid sketches of the country and trenches in their own observation posts.

It was very curious to see how the Division was equipped with guns by both Krupps and the French Creuzot. At first the latter were preferred because, although heavier, they shot further and better. In the long run, however, they deteriorated quicker and began to shoot short, whereas the Krupp guns gave the same steady results.

In conclusion, I am bound to say that the field artillery made the best impression of the different branches of the Turkish army.

In the meantime, the front line was being built – the trenches were to be narrow and two metres deep. I carried with me a stick one metre long with which I measured. In spite of this order which ensured their own safety it took a long time before the required depth was reached. However, the troops only had their short infantry spades with, here and there, a pick to assist them. Sandbags came very sparingly from Constantinople, and those which arrived regularly disappeared, being mostly used to repair clothing.

We also received Verey lights, although not nearly as good as the English which floated over us for minutes at a time, lighting up the country like day. Loopholes were then built, not finished steel as with the English but quite primitive and packed by hand. They were small at the rear, widening out in front and forcing the shooter to

A DUG-OUT AT KANLI SIRT

aim horizontally because, particularly at night, the brave Turk generally fired into the air without aiming. It was a good thing that we always had plentiful supplies of infantry ammunition, thanks to the head of the Munitions Department, Col Schlee, and his organisation. A munitions reserve was always built in in each company section.Once the men in the front line had in this way a certain feeling of safety and certain limited mobility we began to improve the tactical position. On the right flank we had barren cliffs, on the left, flat plain covered with tough oaks and thorn scrub. These had to be burnt away from the front which was not everywhere successful. The single trees on the barren slopes behind us had to be cut down because they served the English, particularly the ships, as aiming points. This also took a very long time.

Where we had a bad field of fire in front of the trench, or it was possible to obtain a flanking effect, a sap was run out to a small hillock or a bush in front, or the whole position was advanced during the night. The front line was thus continually occupied in striving to improve its position. The digging of the communication trenches to the rear was greatly assisted by the two before-mentioned valleys. These provided good spots for aid posts and reserve trenches. The one disadvantage was the fact that in this way only one communication trench for each section opened into the front line, so that all reliefs, rations, et cetera, had to be borne the whole length of the trenches. This was, however, an advantage, because the brave Turk in front knew that to get out of the trench and run back was the equivalent of death, and he saw himself shut into his trench because a retreat to the side took too long and was controlled at too many points. In other words, he had to stick it out, and this he did bravely. I will not say only on these grounds.

To just read the story of the quantity of the excavations thus accomplished gives the impression that mere suggestions from my side would have easily sufficed. Actually it was a daily battle to force the Turks to do that which was necessary for their own protection. Those who know the Turkish ideas of comfort, their fatalism, their placidity, will understand. The reader must not, however, regard these qualities from the ordinary European standpoint and blame or disparage accordingly. They were much more a result of the Oriental psychology, or due to religion and climate and the low standard of education, because the ordinary Turkish soldier can neither read nor write. "If the English come we will deal with them all right. Why all this worry and oppression?" These were their thoughts, and often they expressed them quite openly.

During a period of many months of daily working with the Turks I learnt to know officers and men quite well, and the constant reliefs due to the heavy losses in battle brought me in touch with a large number of new regiments and battalions. At first they were pure Turkish-Mahommedan, Arabians came later on the peninsula. The Christians and the Jews, as I have already mentioned, were formed into labour battalions or used in other ways behind the front.

The Turkish soldier, the *Asker*, was the Anatolian and Thracian, slightly educated, brave, trustworthy, of whom a large majority were Anatolians. Content with little, it never entered into his mind to dispute the authority of those above him, He followed his leader without question even in attack in the face of the enemy. It is the will of Allah. He is deeply religious and regards this life as the first stage to a better. In the midst of shelling, shortly before the entry of the battalion into battle, the *Imam*, or the battalion priest, generally held a short address. The impression left on the onlooker was always curious, particularly when at those points in the address an *Inschallah* (we ask Allah to give it to us) rose over the thirsty plain in earnest but happy tones from hundreds of men's deep voices. One evening, as the jackals were already howling, the address appeared to me to last far too long. The battalion was urgently needed at the front, but nevertheless I did not dare to make a move. That would have been regarded by them as an evil action, coming from me as a Christian. The *Imams* were often splendid men with great and good influence on the soldiers, and in the event of all officers being killed they took control, sometimes taking control of the battalion.

The *Asker* bears the heaviest wound with wonderful stoicism. One only hears a small whimper, "*Aman, aman.*"

When troops fail it is generally traceable to the leaders. I often had in battle the feeling – the troops are all right, but we lack the leaders to give them their objective.

From this goodwill and unquestioning recognition of the authority of those above comes the extraordinarily great influence of a good energetic Turkish leader who knows his own mind on the troops under him (but he must be a Turk). The particular qualities of the leader show themselves much more in the Turkish troops than in the troops of European countries. The Turks are glad to feel an energetic leader's will, they feel supported in the consciousness that they are being led by a strong hand against a definite objective, and they are happy if under the iron hand they find a certain feeling for the personal welfare of the troops. I have learnt to know quite a number of such Turkish commanders, and in addition to Mustapha Kemal Bey, I call to mind the commanders of the 1st Division, Djaffer Tayer, the 11th Division, Refet Bey, the 8th Division, Nouri Bey, the 7th Division, Remsi Bey, against none of whom could any objection be raised as to their complete suitability to command. In addition I found here and there quite exceptionally good regimental commanders who were not, however, so well known.

This characteristic of the Turkish soldier which I might almost describe as "a definite need to lean on those above him," contained, however, a great danger which is always present with every mass concentration, and is the greater the worse the discipline of the troops, the lower their standard of education and training and the more limited the confidence in their leaders and comrades. That is the danger of panic, which, as we know, can have the most far-reaching consequences and during which the influence of any leader only reaches as far as his arm. Whoever has studied the history of the first Balkan War knows how this danger, due to the mentality of the Turkish troops, always slumbered under the surface, and as a result of their training and education, they lack the inner spirit to resist this danger.

Allah be praised, we did not have a panic in the Dardanelles! How close the danger was to us, however, in those critical days, I learnt from a leader of the Turkish troops. It was on 4 June, a day of very heavy fighting, as in reply to urgent calls for help from the Sigindere section I wanted to reverse a battalion sent forward from the Krithia section, to put it in on the right flank. "For God's sake, Colonel," said the Turkish regimental commander who was standing near me, don't order a single man to retire. If the others see that, they will all retire and run as far as Constantinople." I had learnt my lesson.

The brave Anatolian is therefore simply a flock in mass as other races are, but well trained and well led he is an ideal soldier. Moltke discovered this in 1835.

His demands for housing and feeding are remarkably small, if one can even use the word demand. He is accustomed from his youth up to sleep on a hard floor. The Turks don't know beds. The most they know are carpets and mattresses which are pulled out of a cupboard for the night and laid anywhere on the floor. Rice and flesh is a feast for them. Their iron rations, as and when available, consisted of a piece of bread and some olives, the latter generally wrapped in the corner of a more than doubtful looking handkerchief. In the morning a soup, towards evening a soup again, sometimes with meat in it and always prepared with oil. The main diet was *bulgur*, particularly when the rations were short owing to the English having seized several supply ships in the Sea of Marmora. *Bulgur* is rolled barley generally cooked in rancid oil and served cold.

Small donkeys with a panequin or old petrol tin right and left of their saddles, each tin covered with an old cloth to prevent spilling, brought this delicious meal to the trenches. Passing such a donkey column a European could easily be sick from the smell of old cart grease. But the men were always contented. "This is no real war," they said, "we get something to eat every day." Frightful memories of the Balkan War came to their minds, where they had actually had to fill their stomachs with grass and feared hunger more than the bullets of the enemy.

If I asked in my broken Turkish, "*Ejimi?*" (all content?) I was answered either by the individual or the whole troop in sonorous chorus "*Eji Bey*," or later "*Eji Pasha!*" (No complaint!)

It was quite a pleasure to see them at meals. Eight men sat round a tin tray having a common meal *a la turca*. Each threw a piece of bread into the soup and calmly and dignified, each without haste, recovered it with his spoon. I have never seen a battle for food, no matter how great the hunger.

At this point I want to include a report from the Quartermaster of 5th Army, the Prussian Quartermaster and Turkish Lt Col Burchardi, who placed this at my disposal, "The rationing of the 5th Army was entirely dependent on supplies, as there was practically nothing to be obtained from the Army area. Only those troops lying on the Asiatic side were partially able to subsist on the country."

The continually increasing strength of the army led to constantly increasing demand for rations, which finally reached 400 tons a day, and could only be supplied by water. In spite of hostile submarines all the transports reached their destinations, with the exception that in the harbours themselves in the course of a month a total of three steamers were sunk.

Owing to the lack of proper transport by land, the land columns could not properly cover the ration supply. The available land transport in the shape of camel columns and supply trains was only sufficient to carry supplies from the harbours to the divisions.

At the beginning of the fighting the main depot was with the Army Quartermaster in the town of Gallipoli, with forward depots at Maidos and Tschanak Kale.

With the exception of the Army Quartermaster the army supply organisation consisted of Turkish officers only, and the divisional quartermasters were all Turks. The three groups, formed later as the fighting developed, each had its own quartermaster. The supplies organisation was developed according to the German plan, which was accepted in full by the Turkish Quartermaster General, who assisted in its development to the utmost. The returns asked for were not only received punctually but were also correct. The regulations issued were correctly followed throughout.

Bombardment of the town of Gallipoli forced us to remove the supply depot to Lapsaki on the Asiatic shore. Later the harbour of Akbasch was equipped as the main supply depot and the Army Quartermaster took up his abode at this spot. The supplies to the troops were forwarded by columns from here.

Bread was baked in ovens built by the divisions themselves, and in the same way each battalion built its own cookhouse, which in the course of time were partially replaced by transportable field kitchens.

At the commencement stocks of supplies were plentiful and varied, but as time went on replacements could not keep pace with the consumption. We lacked ships and coal. The unloading in the harbour of Akbasch, owing to the lack of necessary equipment, could not be carried through sufficiently quickly. Soon we began to run short of sacks, as these were extraordinarily difficult to recover from the troops who used them for all sorts of purposes. As a result, the ships often arrived with supplies lying loosely in the hold, owing to lack of sacks, and this naturally still further hindered the unloading. In addition, we had to face almost daily attacks from the air and shelling from the ships, which, although they did little damage, still further hindered the work.

The stocks of supplies grew gradually less from day to day. Finally, even flour ran out and forced us to use maize flour for bread making. Similarly, variation in supply gradually ceased and the rationing steadily grew worse. In spite of this the Turkish Quartermaster General, Ismail Hacki Pasha – a particularly efficient, hard-working and clever man – deserved special recognition for the energy he had displayed in understanding how to tackle the supply problem of a land that during the time of the Dardanelles campaign was practically cut off from any appreciable import of supplies, and who made the best use of what was available for supplying 5th Army. It was interesting to read reports issued at the same date by the Entente regarding the question of Turkish supplies at the Dardanelles. On 3 September 1915, Emile Galli, a journalist who had fled from Constantinople, wrote in the *Gaulois* of the military organisation which the Turks, with the assistance of the Germans, had built up there, and attempts to explain through the press the secrets of the Turkish resistance to the Allies.

> Most attention and most time [states this article] has been spent in the organisation of the Quartermaster General's side, which did not formerly exist at all in Turkey, but is today a model of precision. During the Balkan War the Turks had not lacked troops, but the soldiers had no bread and still less ammunition. Today the soldiers at the Dardanelles lack nothing. Bread is baked on the spot. There is ample supply of flour. At many points on the Gallipoli Peninsula kitchens have been erected which supply the fighting soldier at regular intervals with plenty of warm food. They even supply them with coffee in the trenches. All the wounded who arrive in Constantinople are of good appearance. It was immediately obvious that they have been hygienically attended to as they all look so clean.

> The stubborn and continuous resistance of the Turks to all attacks is chiefly made possible by a magnificent supply service which the German-Turkish Quartermaster General's branch have understood how to organise.

Such is the report of Lt Col Burchardi in the *Gaulois*.

We will now return to the trenches in front of Krithia. The chief desire of the Turk is *tütün* (tobacco). I sometimes received from the Marshal whole parcels of cigarettes which I distributed in the front line only. It gave me particular pleasure, when in the trenches, to say to each man I found actively employed at his loop-hole, "Hold your left hand out behind you." I always put two cigarettes in his hand and it is seldom I received even a very soft *tesche kürderinn* (I thank you), but I felt how grateful they were, these brave *Askers*.

Sami Bey and perhaps other Turkish leaders were particularly annoyed at the way in which I looked after the men. Perhaps he thought I was trying to make myself popular with then in order to be able to turn them against their own leaders, which was naturally far from the thought of myself or any other of the Germans with me. Besides, we should always be for the Mussulman the *Giaur*, the unbeliever. We had been brought up in years of peaceful training to always regard the welfare of our troops as our first duty, and our chief aim was now to raise and maintain the power of resistance of the Turks by every means in our power. Our personalities certainly did not count.

Sami Bey sent me a request not to ask the men any more if they were content. I might find shameless fellows who would tell me the opposite, and that would be terrible. My reply that this was really the object of my question, to avoid misunderstanding and complaints, he did not understand. I simply continued my custom.

A very good example of the spirit ruling in the Anatolian *Asker* is the following incident which the Marshal related to me. One hot July day soldiers were announced to him.

Coming out of his tent the Marshal found six infantrymen in complete equipment, sweating and dusty, the oldest of whom said to him through the interpreter, "Pasha, our Company is at present on the upper Gulf of Saros where there is no fighting. Our brothers here, however, are fighting heavily. We have left our regiment to ask you that you will put us in here on the front." Their wish was granted and shortly three of them fell in battle.

A letter written by one of the survivors, which was placed at my disposal, I give as follows:

My Revered Father and Dear Mother

Mehmed Mustapha Tschausch, official letter writer, writes you this letter because he comes from our town.

He is to write that I am well and that I pray to Allah the all-powerful, that you, my highly revered parents, my brothers and sisters and our whole village are in good health and that you have been spared sickness and hunger.

I received your last letter in Der-es-Saadet and read with pride that two more of your sons, my brothers, have become soldiers.

We left Stamboul in the spring, and have now entered the Holy War and have been sent to the town of Gallipoli which lies on the sea.

As we lay in our tents at night we saw the flash of the enemy's guns, who had many great ships lying out sea, and whether by day or night we heard continuously the thunder of the cannons and the rattle of small arms and our hearts were very sad. Our officers told us, however, that we must remain in our positions, far behind the lines, to protect the backs of our fighting brothers. We dreamt, however, of fighting and war.

One hot summer evening a cavalryman came to our tent. He told us of the fame of our brothers and the heavy fighting for a castle named Sed-el-Bahr. He told us of the victories of ours and his, and as he left us we could not sleep.

Mehmed Tschausch, the man, greatly revered Father; who writes you this letter, jumped up and shouted: 'Truly my Mother did not bear me that I should die here in this tent while my comrades outside take part in the greatest blessing of Allah. Who is a man amongst you, follow me.' There was, however, in our circle a man who had learnt from the doctors how to bind up wounds. He had no weapon, but instead of a weapon he carried a haversack with white cloths and medicaments.

He was a trained man. A few days after this night I am writing about, during an attack on the English he, with his doctor, was killed. He was called Achmed and said: 'Mehmed Tschausch, how can you and these men go away without the permission of our officers?' He was a clever and trained man. 'Come with us,' said Mehmed Tschausch, 'we will not ask permission from our officers, but from the highest leader of all, the German Liman Pasha.'

He agreed to this suggestion and before the dawn broke we were marching with our weapons and our equipment in the direction from which stronger and stronger came the thunder of the cannon. So we marched for many hours along the road, and towards evening we came to a spring and slept there. As dawn broke came many men with camels, horses and mules, and we found one who was ready to show us the way to the tent of Liman Pasha. The march was heavier than the first day and we had no more bread or olives.

We found the Pasha, he was kind to us as a father, gave us food and said to us: 'You have behaved badly because you have left your company without permission of your officers, but you have behaved like brave soldiers Liman Pasha because you did not wish to remain idle while your brothers fought. Stay tonight by my tent and tomorrow I will send you against the enemy.'

So we came to a regiment and found that the most of our brothers came from the district of Konia. They were big, strong men, and although they talked our language it was hard for us to understand it. Still, they gave us all we needed and showed us the trenches with the barbed wire in front, but our wish to see the enemy was not fulfilled. And as we peered we saw and again the quick flash from similar trenches opposite us showing where the dogs lay who had dared to tread on the land of our Caliph without his permission.

Then came a night during which the earth trembled from the thunder of our rifles, and our holy *Hodja*, who had previously prayed with us, sprang from the trenches like a youngster although his hair was white, and he certainly was more than 100 years old, and we stormed forwards behind him swinging our rifle butts and what showed itself before us was killed without mercy.

Apart from this I can only write you, my highly revered Father and dear Mother, that all goes well with me. For many days I have lain with many of my brothers in a big room and nurses in white clothing, who look after us like mothers or sisters, walk between our beds and tend to our slightest wish.

I shall soon be with you again and help you to bring in the harvest, because the old doctor has decided that I am not to fight again this year as two fingers of my left hand have been shot away.

Mehmed Tschausch, who writes you this letter, sends you, most revered Father and dear Mother, his greetings. He was himself wounded, and when he recovers he will come to visit us in our village.

I kiss your hands and greet you, as well as my brothers and sisters.

    Your devoted son,
        ISMAIL

Those who so thought and carried out their duty from the best motives naturally belonged to the best elements. On Gallipoli these were at first in the ascendancy, but unfortunately the less worthy were later in the majority. The connection of the soldier with his home was not, as is usually the case, by exchange of letters through the post, but more often one of the older men decided to visit the troops in the field. He travelled around in his neighbourhood to collect messages from the parents or other relatives. Then he sought the troops in the field. After many months he found them and was able to exchange letters and news with the soldiers from his neighbourhood. Finally, after further months he arrived back home, eagerly awaited by everybody.

The Turkish soldiers' clothing was almost unbelievably bad, although we were only at the commencement of the war – summer and winter alike, torn and ragged. The covering for the feet differed widely, often only a piece of cloth tied round with a string. String was often used to replace leather in the equipment. Later I saw a good deal of English equipment and clothing used.

Now a word about those in authority. As I came in touch with them all, I got to know even the worst representatives, although the officers, when talking to a stranger, always emphasised the praiseworthy qualities of the Turkish men.

Non-commissioned officers, or *Kapitulanten*, of many years' service were seldom to be found in the Turkish Army. The *Tschausch* (non-commissioned officer) generally sprang from the ranks of the long-term service conscript. A big disadvantage for internal discipline.

Among the officers with the troops – I mention here only those whom I got to know in the Dardanelles, and not those of the higher staffs or the central organisation – the grade of training was generally very low. There were many who had been raised from the troops without having attended any training schools, and there were actually company commanders who could neither read nor write and were therefore not really *Effendis*. What value were, in such cases, the written reports and returns of the companies? I have also found company commanders who were negroes. Noticeably small was the number of officers who could read a map correctly. I remember in particular a company commander of the Pioneers who came to me from one of the higher staffs and could not show me on his map the communication trenches he had just been building. At the same time the Turks do not lack in intellect. The Oriental is seldom stupid, he is cunning. What he lacks are education and training, and that is the fault of the controlling classes.

Amongst these troops there were many who were efficient, active, and energetic, with a quick grasp of affairs, but unfortunately there were many more who were not so. These latter found the activity of us German officers particularly inconvenient and disturbing, and when we descended to the smaller details, as unpleasantly curious.

They received the tasks given to them without pleasure, had never any questions to put as to the method of carrying out their tasks, but simply laid their hands on their tunics, answered, *Pekki* (Yes, certainly) and went. Looking after them I was always in doubt whether they would do it or not, because I knew that the Turk is tireless in producing excuses as to why, in his particular case, the execution of this particular order was unfortunately impossible.

There were so many opportunities for misunderstanding, quite apart from the translation errors of the interpreters. Take, for instance, the particularly important matter of time: six o'clock in the morning is, *à la franca*, six o'clock in the morning, that is, six

BOMBING TRENCH AT KANLI SIRT
Three yards from the enemy

"KAPALI TSCHARSCHI"
Twelve yards from the enemy

hours after midnight whether it is dark or light, but six o'clock in the morning, *à la turca*, is six hours after the continually changing sunrise. The determination of the days is also different, because the Mahommedan calendar begins with the flight of the Prophet from Mecca to Medina, consequently as an example, our 8/5/1915 is in Turkish 20/2/1332. They have no fast figures. They like improvisation, and with their time and their calendar they could improvise wonderfully.

In addition to this the Turk has a particular regard for good form for the protection of his dignity, and a great shyness against scenes or actions likely to cause friction. It is particularly bad to do anything derogatory to good custom. It is uncivil to say "No." It is customary to say "Yes," but that does not at all imply that things will be done. Unpleasant matters are not reported to a superior for fear of angering him.

It is not good form to show outwardly internal thoughts. The Turk's expression always remains calm and unchanging, no matter how big a battle is going on inside. I have often envied the Turks their ability to do this, because with us Germans the expression on our faces and changing colour never fail to disclose our sensitiveness, and our treacherous eyes betray the slightest disturbance of mind.

This calmness, this immobility of feature, is based on the character of the Oriental and finds its typical expression in *Keff*, the prince of those who do nothing. It may be a result of religious fatalism, or again it may be the laming influence of the climate. Probably both have a basic share. I don't want to write a study on psychology, I am only trying to portray the chief characteristics of the people.

In any case there is one peculiarity of the Turk, based on his Oriental character, of which he is a real master – that is the art of passive resistance. He understands how to use this weapon extraordinarily cleverly and yet civilly.

This generally negative character of the Oriental in the most varying positions was faced by the positive character of the German. We German officers coming from the cold North, often trained in hard and difficult conditions, depended for salvation on a clear, far-seeing organisation and on previous preparation.

In the face of the enemy we were convinced of the truth of our field-service training that waiting was more of an evil than a mistake in the choice of means. "Haste comes from the Devil," said the Turks, whereas we Germans were often much inclined to feverish haste.

Here at the culminating point of our military training and under the very shells of the enemy, we Germans, instead of partners educated to the same level and of similar mind, met the Turk, whom we have already sketched. Quite, content to wait, always ready to remain in the background, reluctant to attempt any unnecessary work, and convinced that if things should actually happen he would find some means of extricating himself from the unpleasant position. He hoped for a last-minute chance and actually was often successful in his hopes.

When one clearly considers these basic divergences of character one can only anticipate, as a natural result, that during the critical time on Gallipoli both parties would come up against one another in the sharpest manner, and that they would not be able to stand the test of a common service, to the benefit of our enemy.

The opposite, however, proved to be the case. German-Turkish brotherhood in arms showed itself to be of the greatest value on Gallipoli and bore splendid fruit. Differences naturally arose. When is it not the case in the course of a campaign that ideas sharply conflict in moments of urgent action? Personally I believe that on Gallipoli there were fewer such moments than with armies having officers of the same race.

I must laugh, however, at the following extract from *The Daily Telegraph* which Prigge includes in his book, actually written under the guns of the Dardanelles. *The Daily Telegraph* on 16 August 1915, under the leader 'Mutiny of Officers,' writes:

> A mutiny of considerable importance broke out recently among the officers of one of the Turkish Army Corps on Gallipoli. A large number of officers were implicated. The

main reason for the mutiny was the increasingly haughty behaviour of their German comrades.

The mutiny was quickly put down by the arrest of a large number of mutinous officers, 45 of whom were sent to Constantinople in chains and thrown into the various prisons of the Capital.

Here naturally the wish was father to the thought. During a war such a form of lying can be explained by the psychology of war. It is, however curious to note that even today French literature uses such methods.

For instance, a novel appeared in the summer of 1926 in Paris written on the subject of the world war in Turkey. I refrain from mentioning either the author or the title. In addition to other hateful blackening of all Germans and the most grotesque ignorance of Turkish customs and manners it contains a fantastical picture of the Marshal complaining to the Grand Vizier, Talaat Pasha, about the disappearance of German officers in Constantinople. It is easy to see that the author thus aims at picturing the German officers as ruffians who pursued adventures in Constantinople and thus earned their wages while the Turks on Gallipoli were engaged in the heaviest combat. The Paris press naturally did not let this go unremarked, but drew the attention of their leaders to this as an historical document, in which in reality there was actually no word of truth.

No, between the German and the Turkish officers during the whole period there existed a very good feeling of comradeship supported by sacrifices on both sides. Perhaps, unknown to the other, each attempted to acquire the method of thinking and the ideas of the other.

Naturally the interpreter here played an extraordinarily important part. The *muavin* (helper) had more or less ceased to exist. The interpreter could be extraordinarily useful, but could also be most damaging. Here is an illustration:

A German captain who had been badly wounded and was unfit for service, but not unfit for the Tropics, was put in command of a Turkish regimental depot to improve the training. Full of energy he visited the living rooms the first day, also the kitchen and other parts of the barracks in Asia Minor where the depot was, and, accustomed to German conditions, he was naturally horrified. During a discussion with his company commanders he promised that all should be different, and in his eager discourse he used the word which is not exactly used in drawing-rooms, although often in Germany to describe such conditions, namely, *schweinerei* (piggery). For the Turks there is nothing more insulting than *domus* (pig). The interpreter either maliciously or unknowingly, I don't know which, translated the word in Turkish in such a manner that it appeared as if the Captain had meant it to cover the men of his regiment. As a result the German had lost the game from the first day. All his worry and trouble was without effect, without his knowing why. Even the civil population of this small town avoided him because he had called the Turks swine.

Those who have lived longer in Turkey know their many sensitive points and act accordingly, otherwise all their activities have no successes. The large number of Germans who entered Turkey during the war should have been properly instructed in these matters beforehand. As it was, they often damaged the work in hand and themselves, because in their impetuous eagerness they wrongly believed they could handle Turkish officers and men according to the German system. It is a very great mistake to consider that German system and German orders can simply be transferred to fit Turkish conditions.

Returning to our subject – the relations between the officers, particularly on Gallipoli, were everywhere good. The Turkish Corps of Officers, although not one body according to our peace time system, nevertheless contained in every grade of service, a large number of first class energetic, intelligent representatives, with whom we could work excellently.

I have attempted to paint for the reader a picture of the Turkish trenches on Gallipoli and of the customs and manners of its inhabitants, in the hope that the episodes of the war which follow will be more easily understandable. I further hope that the reader will now understand the extremely difficult position in which we Germans found ourselves in the middle of the Turkish troops. At the commencement we were only 20 officers; yet completely split up as we were, often completely misunderstood and distrusted in our eagerness, unable to explain our selves openly in the same language, under a burning sky, living on Turkish food cooked in oil, which a German stomach only accustomed itself to with difficulty, and generally without any appreciation of our work, worry and self-sacrifice, we had to carry out our duty.

At the same time it would be ungrateful not to recognise how the Turks nearly always tried to meet our personal wishes, and how, even in the extreme front trench, the well known Turkish hospitality was always in evidence. How often have I, tired by hours of walking through the narrow, hot trenches, refreshed myself at a battalion commander's by a cup of coffee, *à la turca*, which was always ready and always offered. Then a cigarette to drown the horrible, sickly smell of corpses and the walk could be continued. Here again one found the truth of Bismarck's words, "The Turk is the only gentleman in the Balkans."

I gratefully remember here the Turks who were attached to me personally: my interpreter, Major Zia Bey, as well as my brave Turkish servants Ali Effendi, a common writer from Smyrna, my orderly Arif Effendi, a teacher from the school of Galata Serail, who spoke a little French, Ali Tschausch my groom, Tahir, the cook from Boli, where all good cooks come from. They all looked after me continuously and were absolutely honest. I have never missed even so much as a cigarette from my tent.

After 4 May we had sunk our trenches deep into the earth near, and battle conditions in Gallipoli had settled down to the similar kind of trench warfare common everywhere in this world war, with desperate fighting for every yard of ground. For this reason one should not accept the positions marked on the map as a hard, firm front, but more as a snake which lies in a certain place with its coils winding here and there.

There was continuous movement in the front line as the result of the constant heavy fighting. Pieces of trench were taken from us and regained. There was practically unbroken fire, particularly at night, very often without rhyme or reason, which I tried in vain to prevent.

I shall not attempt to portray in detail all these battles, repetition would become merely tiring. I will only select one day of heavy fighting. Of these there were nine in May, five in June, due to the continually repeated attempts of Hamilton to smash through us and storm Krithia and Eltschitepe. With each attempt it became more difficult, because from the original simple trenches and dug-outs emerged a well thought out, well-organised fortress system in which those unacquainted with it would easily go astray. The material was taken from the destroyed villages and farms and the wood brought across from Asia Minor.

The Turks rapidly became accustomed to this method of defence. For each section commander I worked out written instructions which were handed over to the commander of the company relieving.

Little by little we received heavy artillery. We gratefully acknowledged help received from the Navy and the fort of Tschanak Kale. Even the Army Museum in Constantinople opened its doors. Old mortars, hundreds of years old, were built in to the front trenches for use as trench mortars. They hurt us, however, more than the enemy, because the thick white clouds of smoke coming from them immediately attracted the enemy's fire. Our request to have them replaced in the museum was granted.

An additional substitute for lack of heavy artillery was afforded by the ships *Haireddin Barbarossa* and *Torgut Reis*, the former German battleships *Weissenburg* and *Wörth*. They opened indirect fire on the ships lying off Ariburnu. Their fire control, owing to the lack of captive balloons, was on the Kodjadschemendagh.

The most direct help, however, came from the Navy with their machine gun sections. I was lucky enough to get for the 8th Division the brave Naval Lieut Bolz, who had done so well, during the first battles, with his section. The front line was very considerably strengthened by the eight machine guns built in there.

It was for me, personally, greatly reassuring to know that this splendid German Naval Section was helping in front. In addition I was sure of receiving from them explicit and accurate information regarding the position from the front line. In addition to the Naval Lieutenants Thomson and von Rabenau, I gratefully remember the following sailors: Boatswain Niemand, Schafföner and Leading Seaman Peters.

Even when I approached a German dug-out in the bare, primitive but generally clean Turkish front line, I felt at once a homely atmosphere. 'Bismarck Dug-out,' I noticed from a distance on a board. Inside, pictures, postcards, et cetera, as in non-commissioned officers' rooms in barracks.

The main thing, the machine guns, were taken care of like invalid children. They stood there clean and polished, thoroughly oiled, carefully covered against fine sand dust, with belts adjusted, ready for immediate use. Fresh, happy, concrete replies to my questions, from which one felt the acknowledgement of duty and manly steadiness combined with fresh sailor's humour and German comfort. Finally, German methods of cooking. How often has it reached my nose, and how willingly would I have eaten with them! Even pork and peas in this terrible heat. They still had a few of their own rations.

Apart from their commander, the German sailors in this front position had only been visited by their Field Padre, the excellent Graf Lüttichau, who was originally Minister to the Embassy at Constantinople and who had jumped into this war without a thought for himself. The brave Bolz conducted him. Bolz was not allowed to go into the dug-outs with the Minister, who did not like the presence of superiors when talking to the men. [If] the conversation lasted somewhat long, Bolz warned him to break off. It was the time when the English opposite had finished their tea and generally told us so by their bombardment. At last the Graf came out. Almost immediately commenced the bombardment of the trenches by shrapnel. The trenches, which lay under heavy fire, had to be taken by rushes. Finally, both reached me where I was awaiting them for afternoon coffee. "Can I now say that I have received my baptism of fire?" asked the Graf. "Certainly you can," I replied, and later he deservedly carried the Iron Cross.

This German cell in the front trenches acted like a firm anchorage on the whole position and gave all of us, Turks and Germans, moral support. If only we had had more of such cells!

During the month of May the German machine guns in the right section were put in fairly close to the Singindere. Recently a capable Turkish company commander had been successful in forcing forward the centre of our position between the Singindere and the Kirthidere, and as a result attaining an exceptionally fine flanking effect covering both wings of our position. I naturally put the German Naval Section in this important but heavily threatened advanced position. The whole position between the two streams was thus exceptionally strengthened. This happened on 1 June. Already on 4 June came the test, and we shall see later with what results.

Our position in the front was now fairly strong. A certain danger existed for the right flank resting solely on the sea, as they could be surprised by attacks from behind although the precipitous cliffs rendered such a possibility extremely difficult. In any case, to cover this possibility we had several battalions standing ready in the Saritepe.

I had visited these battalions on 25 May, and towards noon was returning to the staff of the 9th Division when I saw the English armoured cruiser *Triumph* lying close to the coast below. She was apparently quite comfortably making herself ready to shoot in the direction of Ariburnu. I had scarcely reached my tent when I heard, at roughly 12:30 p.m., a terrific explosion, and not long after my interpreter, Major Zia Bey, burst into my tent and announced that the *Triumph* had just been sunk.

This was the first success of Lieut Commander Hersing who, coming from Germany, passed Gibraltar in his U-boat 21, and had just left his first visiting card on the British Navy. Two days later followed the *Majestic*, which was lying at anchor off Seddil Bahr in the middle of many other ships, with no idea of the presence of U-boats. Through an opening between the ships Hersing was able to torpedo her.

These were hard blows for our enemies, the more so as on 13 May, Lieut Commander Firle successfully slipped out of the Dardanelles in the darkness of the night with the torpedo boat *Muavenet Millie*, Commander Ahmed Effendi, and sank the battleship *Goliath*.

The result showed itself in an astonishing manner. Next morning all the ships had disappeared as if God had taken a broom and swept the sea clear. They had all fled to the harbours of Imbros and Lemnos, no longer the port of Hamburg in front of us, no more ship-shelling of our trenches. The *Queen Elizabeth*, about which the British Admiralty were particularly anxious, was recalled to England.

The joy of the brave Turks can scarcely be described. They danced in their trenches and cried, *Allah büjük. Allemano büjük* (God is great and Germany is great). For us Germans in Gallipoli it was a pleasant feeling that we were able with such success to use the same weapon against the English submarines. In spite of the submarine nets at Nagara, Churchill writes that the English were continually successful in penetrating into the Sea of Marmora from a particular point, which only a few miles from the mouth of the Dardanelles led into a very deep canal more than two sea miles wide. The hostile submarines did a good deal of damage. On 9 August 1915, they sank the old battleship *Harieddin Barbarossa* and themselves got as far as Constantinople. Although they faced certain losses themselves and overcame the dangers they were not successful in entirely breaking the lines of communication by sea.

How often later have we wished for submarines as the English, with their floating batteries protected by torpedo and fishing boats in double rows, came out from Imbros for the bombardment.

It was no longer possible for our submarines to approach, owing to the excellent protective arrangements of the English.

The English Flying Corps were, like the English submarines, opposed by the same weapons, although not in equal numbers.

It was a joyful day for us as the first German aeroplane with the

Iron Cross on its wings appeared over our heads. This we owed to the Commander of the Turkish Field Flying Squadron, the exceptional Captain Serno. Up to this point the English had complete control of the air which had led them to unbelievable self-confidence, a sign showing how safe they felt themselves to be.

I remember one flyer in particular who flew just over our Divisional Headquarters, looping the loop many times. At the first loop the brave Turks believed him to be falling because all around me, as I stood alone on a small hill, to my astonishment I heard coming from the bushes and trenches loud laughter. I saw also at this moment how excellently well the brown-grey shade of the Turkish field uniform fitted the mud colour of Gallipoli. The plane, however, did not fall, but continued its antics in the air – apparently a trick flyer.

The reports received from the Southern Group told of a woman aviator. Our hopes of catching such booty were not fulfilled, however, but, one day, after a bombing attack, a message was dropped containing the following courteous words, "For your filthy heads – Henriette."

The planes with the silver gleaming bombs under the fuselage were most unpleasant. These fell with a shrill cry ending in a sudden burst, generally without result, but it was always a pleasant feeling when the look-out reported he had no more bombs left. At first they used arrows as well which, when dropped in flight, descended vertically. Oddly enough I only heard of foot wounds due to these arrows.

The English had received in the meantime the 42nd Division which had relieved the 29th. On their side they suffered much more than us from the terrible heat, the pestilential stench of the unburied bodies, the millions of flies and the terrible shortage of water. We read in the previously mentioned experiences of a Swiss, as a result of the great heat, much sickness and the merciless fighting, the spirit of the troops was not exactly the best.

And yet the enemy with their larger number of troops were able to arrange constant reliefs, so that the soldiers had only to spend a few days in the front line, then they came into the second line, reserves, beaches and the islands at regular intervals. Thanks to their better communications and larger quantities of material the enemy were able to make better arrangements for supplies and sanitation than we were.

There was a great lack of water on the side of the Allies as it all had to be brought in ships, 'we had to get through with the meagre contents of a water bottle which we were not allowed to drink till the evening,' writes an English soldier, in his letter, 'and during the day we used to take stones in our mouths to lessen the thirst.' Wine was also issued as rations, but at Ariburnu the English erected a pressure station to pump the water from the tank ships directly to the high-lying trenches.

The landing places and reserve trenches were being continually improved by the enemy. At Seddil Bahr a steamer of the Messageries Maritimes was sunk at right angles to the *River Clyde*, and an old French battleship run ashore in such a way as to form an artificial harbour which in November 1916 was still completely intact.

In one thing we were much better off than the enemy. In our higher ground, even in the hottest summer, we always had fresh, clear spring water in sufficient quantities, an advantage whose value cannot be put sufficiently high, because the Turk is not only a large water drinker, but he knows water and differentiates between different sorts as we do by wine.

It is doubtless owing to this lucky position that no epidemic broke out in 5th Army during the whole of the Gallipoli campaign. Actually a wonder, because the unfavourable climate and local conditions were made still worse by the complete indifference of the men to any hygienic methods of prevention. I have myself seen a man relieving himself into the water flowing through the Krithidere in May, from which the soldiers further down were forced to drink. The method of punishment which was used by the battalion commander leading them, whose attention I drew to this, I prefer not to relate. The Turk is unbelievably insensitive to corpses and their stench. I remember, for instance, two soldiers, who on the extreme right flank of the front line had laid three corpses one on another as cover from the sea. They sat on these and ate their bread and olives

Here was a further field of activity for the Turkish Army medical officers who, in the person of Army Doctor Professor Dr Mayer, had a very active and very energetic head. Among the Turkish medical officers some were good but many bad. The medical arrangements had been brought to a very high level considering the usual conditions ruling in Turkey. Nevertheless they were not sufficient, particularly when the losses in the main battle period increased so enormously. For this reason the help which came from Germany in the shape of doctors from the Red Cross and through special missions, such as that from the Graf Hochberg, Major von Truetzchler, et cetera, was very welcome, in fact we simply could not have done without it.

During the first days of June the enemy had been comparatively quiet. This was always a suspicious sign.

On Friday, 4 June, about 11 o'clock in the morning, a barrage suddenly descended on the front Turkish trenches from land batteries and from the cruisers and torpedo boats lying off the southern shores, which left nothing to be desired in accuracy or effect, although at this time the English carefully left their big battleships in the harbours which were protected against the U-boats.

There was no doubt that this bombardment was the preparation for a heavy enemy infantry attack. Churchill writes that on this date, 34,000 Allies attacked 25,000 Turks. I discussed with my staff officer, Hunussi Bey the advisability of bringing the reserves up to the north of Hill 145, and went myself with Captain von Westernhagen, as agreed with Sami Bey, to the command post of the Division on Hill 150.

From here one saw how accurately the English bombardment had come down on our front line. Crater lay alongside crater. A continual thick cloud of dust, which continuously blew into the air at various points like a volcano in eruption, marked our front line more clearly and accurately than I had ever seen it before. Shrapnel fire coming from the flank pierced the cloud of dust streaming upwards and raked along the trenches. "The poor fellows there forward," I thought. It was, however, impossible to help them; they must simply endure in their dug-outs directly behind the front line, ready to spring out and occupy immediately the trenches, or what was left of the trenches, the moment the artillery fire lifted and the enemy infantry began to storm.

We here in the rear received no shells, neither did the batteries around us. The whole artillery might of the enemy lay quite definitely on the front line trenches. From the command post of the Division I had a splendid view of what was happening. Only the divisional commander failed.

He had gradually withdrawn himself further and further from me until he had gone so far as to forbid his General Staff officer to keep me informed about the tactical position, reports received, et cetera. Naturally no official instructions, but in effect unmistakable. With this the boundary of a supportable working condition was crossed, and I was forced during the last days of May to report to the Commander of the Southern Group, General Weber, the insupportable situation which had arisen.

General Weber was a splendid man, equally liked by Germans and the Turks. Everybody had the greatest confidence for his quiet, clear-thinking personality, his imperturbable serenity and the clear, practical and accurate way in which he always gave his orders. As a pioneer he was particularly good in this trench warfare, as we Germans had been mainly trained for moving warfare with its constantly changing position. General Weber was successfully supported by his acting Chief of Staff, Major von Thauvenay.

General Weber completely understood my position, came the next day to the 9th Division and laid our personal relationships in so convincing a form before Sami Bey that the latter was forced to see that all our efforts should be directed towards doing the enemy as much damage as possible. Everything else must be subjected to this end.

Outwardly things improved, but internally the dislike of the unwelcome adviser continually increased. I portray this conflict to show what difficulties we Germans were faced with during out activities under Turkish conditions. Here we could depend on our German commander. Supposing he failed however.

It again required considerable self-sacrifice to accept responsibility for a very important part of the front without the necessary relationship between orders and fighting power. On the other hand, I willingly believe that it was not pleasant for Sami Bey to have such an adviser near him, but it was necessary. Actually I consider that everything happened correctly as far as tactics were concerned, and I did not take any notice of the remaining administrative matters of the division I was glad that I did not have it to do.

Such was our personal relationship as the enemy commenced to bombard our front line. I, waiting vainly for Sami Bey at the appointed place, knew that we were faced with heavy, anxious hours which could bring with them a total collapse of the whole Southern Group, if each did not give of his last and best, regardless of cost.

Finally, I sent Westernhagen to the divisional commander to advise him that I was waiting for him, as arranged. He first wished to eat his lunch and come later. There was nothing left for me to do but to return to Divisional Headquarters, as otherwise I should have no opportunity of intervening in the situation.

At 1 o'clock the enemy lifted his fire onto the rear trenches and commenced a general attack along the whole front. Sami Bey now agreed to come with me to Hill 150. I went in advance with Westernhagen, my faithful companion, now under heavy fire. A crossroads in particular lay under the continual shrapnel fire of the enemy, but the shrapnel was bursting too high and the bullets rattled harmlessly off our backs. We neither of us had even a bruise.

On Hill 150 the command post had in the meantime been completely destroyed and the telephone lines cut. With Sami Bey, who had in the meantime arrived, we sat behind a thin wooden shelter to give instructions to a commander of a regiment which had just arrived. It was impossible to understand one another in the

MAIN COMMUNICATION TRENCH LEADING TO 16TH DIVISION—THE RESULT
OF MONTHS OF WORK WITH PICKAXE AND SPADE

noise of the explosions of the lyddite shells with yellow fumes which drove down on us. I therefore proposed to move the control post of the Division to an open trench about 100 yards off. Agreed. I went ahead with Westernhagen, Sami Bey promising to follow. But he did not come. On the contrary, in a few minutes we saw the whole Staff in full gallop towards his tent, the sparks flying from their horses' hoofs. There was nothing left for me to do but follow. It was useless for me to stay on the barren hill.

In the front positions, completely smashed by shell fire, there was the fiercest fighting. Hamilton had attacked our line with the 42nd Division and the Manchester Brigade, while the French advanced against the neighbouring divisions. In the course of the afternoon the enemy succeeded in taking our trenches in the centre and on our left flank and consolidating them.

On the right flank, on the far side of the Sigindere, the first line was still in our hands. For some unexplained reason these trenches were left by the Turks without the English occupying them. Naval Lieut Bolz saw that in these empty trenches an undestroyed German machine gun had been left, the sailors dead behind it. Boatswain Schafföner volunteered to take over this gun, and later a second machine gun was brought into position. With this assistance the Turkish reserves, who had in the meantime arrived, were able to beat off four enemy attacks and maintain least this portion of our position.

Every attempt to recover our front position on the left of the Sigindere failed, in spite of the fact that the section commander there received continuous reinforcements. At this point, however, the main spirit of the resistance had already fallen at the commencement of the attack. Since 1 June, Naval Lieut von Rabenau, a fresh, efficient, brave man, with his machine guns had garrisoned this section of the advanced position.

In spite of the terrific heat and many casualties among his men through death and wounds, his machine guns sowed destruction among the storming English. None reached his trench. Rabenau, himself wounded, sent a sailor back to fetch fresh ammunition. This man, to his horror, met the English storming forwards from the rear. The Turks had left the flank trenches and the Germans, remaining fast, were surrounded. Neither pistol nor fist was of any use. The badly wounded Rabenau was carried back by two English and those sailors left alive sent back as prisoners. This was naturally a hard blow for us.

We had received continual support from the Southern Group owing to the many calls for help from both sections,. Each battalion that arrived had to be put in at once in small parties to prevent the worst. We were also able to supply the everlasting request for small arms ammunition and bombs. We were only able, however, to prevent a further retreat.

I felt that a further similar energetic attack of the English could have the worst results. It did not follow, however. As often previously, the English again failed to draw the utmost results from their success. Instead of that we were successful on our left flank under the leadership of Lt Col Kiasim Bey in regaining a portion of our trenches with part of Infantry Regiment 38.

It was impossible to tell the exact position of our front lines. To get some definite information, following a fairly quiet night, I sent the next morning Major Effnert, who had been lent me by the Southern Group, and Captain Von Westernhagen, from both the extreme wings along the front
Turkish line to reconnoitre and report. Partially creeping on hands and knees the officers carried out their reconnaissance magnificently and brought me a clear picture.

The lost trenches had to be recovered. I had arranged an attack for the afternoon when I was called to the Southern Group where General Weber placed five fresh battalions at my disposal including the 1st and 2nd Battalions of Infantry Regiment 5. I summoned all the commanding officers to Krithia and went with each of them individually the exact road which the battalion would have to take the following morning. Even if the shrapnel continually burst over the ruins of Krithia it was still a complete explanation of the ground such as one only experiences in peace time. Doubts about the approach, deployment, development, touch, direction could not exist and actually did not exist. At 1 o'clock on the morning of 6 June the troops began to enter Krithia and about 3:30 the deployed line began the attack without the enemy having noticed anything. The attack was completely successful. The excellent Bolz was the first to report, on a sheet torn from his notebook, that our old positions had been completely recaptured and the English had suffered prodigious losses. Seventeen English machine guns, a large number of rifles and ammunition as well as other booty had been captured.

This attack was the saving of a very brave man who was very near death. Amongst those taken prisoner with the Naval Lieut von Rabenau was Leading Seaman Peters. As he was being conducted to the rear he seized a favourable opportunity to knock his guard senseless. He then jumped down among the English in the trench who, in wild confusion, took him for one of themselves and wondered at his bravery as he suddenly jumped up and ran forward alone towards the Turks. But those, not recognising him, greeted him as an enemy. He had to throw himself into a shell hole where he lay for two days and two nights without food or water, with a constant hail of bullets overhead. Owing to the heat he was almost dead of thirst as the Turkish counter-attack of 6 June freed him, more dead than alive. When praised for his coolness and bravery Leading Seaman Peters merely answered, "I have only done my duty."

Due to the continual throwing in of new troops and due to the many commanders there was such confusion, both among the troops and the leaders in the far-reaching fortress net, that during the night of 7 June a portion of the trenches again fell into the hands of the enemy. Of the original 9th Division only shattered fragments remained, in addition to parts of the 2nd, 7th, 11th and 15th Divisions. I therefore rode next morning to General Weber and suggested that the whole section should be relieved by a fresh Division, the confused elements withdrawn into the valleys in the rear to be reorganised and put in elsewhere. My proposal was accepted and Colonel Schükri Bey indicated to me as the new commander of the section.

This was very pleasant news to me; then with this officer, who could talk good German and whom I had learnt to know during the battles of 3 and 4 May, I hoped o be able to work with confidence and trust on both sides.

As a matter of fact, however, he did not arrive, but in his place Lt Col Halil Bey arrived in the evening north of Krithia, with six fresh battalions. The relief of the troops took place without difficulty, the enemy remaining inactive. Halil Bey gave me the impression of an exceptionally fresh, clever and independent man. My proposal to advise him on the position he declined civilly but firmly, as he first wanted to look at the country himself. This he did, and this pleased me very well. Following his return he declared that he wished to withdraw the right flank to a position of better tactical importance. This I did not agree with, because I knew that we had to hold at all costs every foot of ground in front of Krithia. The distance to Krithia was far too small to permit of a selection between several positions. How the enemy would have triumphed and constructed a victory out of it! Halil Bey declined, however, to consider my ideas at all.

I had the impression that to remain longer in this position would be really useless, so I sent for my horse and reported to General Weber the intended retirement of the right flank, which was naturally immediately forbidden, and asked at the same time for employment for myself elsewhere.

The next day I received orders to follow the 9th Division which had retired to the neighbourhood of Maidos. Not a very attractive proposition, because I could not see any results coming from a renewed collaboration with Sami Bey.

CHAPTER XII
On Kajaltepe

On 9 June 1915, I left the tent headquarters, north of Krithia, which I had selected and in which I had spent many anxious hours.

In the course of the months life had gradually become more bearable on Gallipoli, the worst time being the first few days and weeks. We gradually became accustomed to the curious conditions. In addition to the normal Turkish ration we were able to obtain supplies from Constantinople and sometimes received presents of food, including beer and wine, and life generally became more pleasant.

Only the burning sun in the eternally blue sky remained unchanging. Not a shadow anywhere. We Germans had to fight with all our energy against the tropical heat which sapped our strength and threatened to render us as lazy as the local inhabitants. When the hot, dry south wind, so greatly feared by all, began to blow, the heat became almost insupportable, and those who had already experienced it felt its approach in their nervous system days ahead.

This same wind blew that day, occasionally developing into a sandstorm which enveloped us in thick clouds. The fine sand penetrated everywhere, our teeth ground and our eyes smarted. In my saddle wallets I had put against an emergency some chocolate and some soup tablets. In Serafin Tschiflik I met Captain Schroeder, who from this point under command of Col Bischof controlled the supply and munitions column, and as I went to take out these tablets to make myself some breakfast I found they had all melted and got mixed together as a hot, tough sticky mass. Nevertheless I was lucky that day, as I notice from my calendar which served me as a diary that Captain Schroeder provided me with five beautiful fresh eggs – a quite unaccustomed delicacy.

Then I rode on to Maidos where I found the 9th Division under canvas, close to the west side of the destroyed town. They had orders to protect the coast, from the mouth of the Asmakdere by Kabatepe as far as the Kundere, against any enemy landings. For this purpose a position close to Maidos was the worst possible choice, because it lay 73 kilometres marching distance from the nearest point on the coast. During the time necessary to march this a strong force of the enemy could land.

Perhaps Sami Bey had selected this point because the Marshal had ordered one of his divisions to concentrate there in April. Now, however, the coastal area to be protected was considerably smaller and the radius of action much more limited. The place for the Division was undoubtedly Kajaltepe, which was an ideal place for the concentration of reserves. I had now learnt to know quite a number of divisional commanders, and I believe that none of them would have thought of this solution.

My conversation with Sami Bey was without result, as during it he politely refused to have anything to do with me at all. I reported this impossible position to Army Headquarters and withdrew myself from contact with the division. For my part I rode through the divisional area and noted that it was splendidly laid out for coastal defence, provided one dug energetically. Unfortunately my Hungarian was wounded by a bomb splinter and I had to take a horse with a less comfortable pace.

On 12 June I was astonished to receive my appointment as Commander of the 9th Division. My farewell from Sami Bey, who wrongly believed that I had deliberately forced him out of his command, was not particularly pleasant. I did not at all want to take over the responsibility for the whole of the internal administration of the division. What interested me was the tactical leading of the troops in the face of the enemy. I actually had relations again with Sami Bey later in Constantinople, who showed himself to be loyal and energetic. Only here in the field he seemed to lack all initiative, and, contrary to many of his comrades of the same age, a lack of tactical ability and training. If he had only wished it we could have got on extremely well together.

The first thing I did as divisional commander was to summon the regimental commanders and, after giving them a short précis of the situation, ask them to immediately accompany me with their adjutants on a ride through the country. We quickly reached

Kajaltepe, where, from a stubble field south of Manol Tschiflik, I wanted to explain to them the country and the new grouping of the division.

I had scarcely begun when a shell from the heights of Ariburnu just missed our heads. It was so close we felt the wind. Like lightning the mounted group scattered, and riding away I saw the shell bursting on the cliffs behind us. To this day I am grateful to the English for this shot. Nothing could have illustrated better that the whole country to the coast was threatened from the right flank by the batteries from Ariburnu; nothing could have proved more forcibly to the whole of the regimental commanders that at least two-metre deep communication trenches to the coast were a vital necessity. The pleasant fields were no site for the Divisional Staff Headquarters or the reserves on Kaialtepe, and these had to be hidden in the valleys. For all this my grateful thanks are due to that warning shot, which did nobody any harm.

The coastal area was divided into three sections, each held by one battalion with the rest of the division in reserve on Kajaltepe. The next morning the division moved to its new position. Then I rose to report to Essad Pasha, at Kemalieri, who commanded the Northern Group to which I was now attached.

My main work was now the defence of the coast. The flat, sandy shore was about 10 to 12 metres wide and offered good facilities for landing, especially at the mouth of the Kumdere, on the left flank. Then the coast rose steeply 12 to 15 metres, covered with bushes, forming a continuous ridge about 750 metres distant from the shore, which was admirably adapted for a second line of defence.

The front line naturally lay near the shore and was simply ideally split up by the projecting Capes Palamukburnu, Semerliburnu and Tschamtepe. Deeply dug flanking works constructed on these capes would enfilade the whole of the coast with terrific fire at most effective ranges, whereas the fire from the trenches dug on the high ridge parallel to the beach would have direct field of fire. In addition hand grenades and bombs could be used most effectively from these higher trenches. It was a better example of the natural formation of a coast for defence than I had ever seen explained in the Military Academy by teachers of tactics.

The first and second lines were connected by communication trenches which permitted the isolation of the individual sections in case the enemy were successful in breaking in at any point.

The whole formation of the country was such as to force the main point of resistance close to the coast. A great advantage, because although we had to reckon with the destruction of the front trenches by the ships' guns, the occupying troops could, during this fire, obtain excellent shelter in the many small valleys and nullahs formed everywhere by the rainwater rushing to the sea.

Here, therefore, with greater possibility of success than at Seddil Bahr, we could catch the English at the moment of transfer from transports to land, i.e. in the boats, where they were themselves absolutely defenceless and at the moment when the covering artillery must raise its fire on to the interior.

The changes from one position or formation to another always carry with them moments of tactical weakness, as, for instance, when a column is splitting up for billets and putting out pickets, or the opposite, on the following morning, when the troops are again forming columns of route. Such a momentary weakness was to be found here during the transfer from ship to land in narrow boats. It is generally not possible for the defender to seize this moment in sufficient strength. Here we could seize it, however, because we had three regiments to cover a front of only four kilometres.

Nevertheless a good report system and secure communication trenches from Kajaltepe to the front were a first necessity. In addition to the telephone and mounted orderlies I arranged to use the old method of signalling by fire.

All along the coast, in each company section, a bonfire stood ready, with an enormous one on Kajaltepe, and sentries with matches in their pockets by each. The fires along the coast were also to serve to light up the water as far as possible as searchlights were unobtainable.

The road communications spread out in ray formation from Manol Tschifik to the north of Kajaltepe. Deep lying beds of small rivers were partially used for this purpose. Road A led in a curve to the right flank, Road B to the centre and Road C to the left flank. Road B was so wide and deep that a motor car could be driven unseen as far as Tschamtepe. A cross-country section along our position behind the already mentioned long high ridge was also prepared. In this way the great area which lay between Kajaltepe and the coast could be covered without observation by the enemy at Anzac (Ariburnu).

Nevertheless I later placed a regiment from the reserve behind the left flank because a false alarm had proved that it took too long before the supports came up. In addition, the area to be covered was extended to the Domuspazar.

The batteries were partially on the high ridge on the coast amongst them a 15cm gun battery which, to obtain maximum fire effect, was built in in sections. The Kajaltepe carried a heavy battery of, finally, 14 guns, which were under the special orders of the very efficient Major Emin Bey, who had been trained in Germany with the Field Artillery Regiment 15. The artillery fire effect was limited in so far that the boats approaching low under the coast came into dead ground for these batteries.

The building of our positions naturally proceeded slowly, under continuous control and encouragement on my part. I continuously drove into the workers my special theme: "Every drop of sweat now saves streams of blood later." I must in fairness say that now and again I was pleased by considerable progress. It depended entirely on the energy of the officers.

Parallel with this work, we developed other equally important recuperative training. The 9th Division, during a long period of unbroken fighting, had suffered exceptionally heavily, and was practically entirely made up of remnants. This was the reason why it had been sent to this comparatively quiet portion of the front. It was to be here reorganised and made into an instrument capable of fighting. On 19 June 1915, the divisional strength, in addition to

3,701 so-called trained troops, was only 440 trained and 2,734 untrained recruits.

As any day the division might find itself called into the fight, it was necessary that training should proceed at top speed. I was admirably supported in this work by the three excellent regimental commanders of the division. Infantry Regiment 25 was commanded by the gallant Lt Col Nail Bey, Infantry Regiment 26 by the clever Lt Col Cadri Bey, and Infantry Regiment 64 by the ever-fresh and energetic Lt Col Servet Bey. My General Staff officer, the ambitious Major Hunussi Bey, was also very active and energetic. Among my battalion commanders there was only one completely useless who had to find a job elsewhere.

There was ample time available for the training of the two regiments in reserve. They had to send reports in to the division each day, which sometimes contained unbelievable nonsense, as, for example, one battalion reported as their work for the whole day: 'sights correction and bayonet fighting', and another, 'Head right and left turn.' Shooting ranges were also prepared, and we actually found supplies of German ring targets with the head of a Prussian infantryman stuck on. The results were awful! A German range NCO would have had a stomach-ache, but finally the Turks shot quite well. When a bull's eye was reported I used to satisfy myself personally that the report was correct. I asked one company commander, "How many men have you who have not shot yet?" He replied, "I don't know. They have only just arrived." "When?" "A month ago."

I was forced to be continually on the go, either in front supervising work or else attending to the training of the troops. In addition I was able to watch from my tent on the heights the troops at work and on the exercise ground. There was no lack of goodwill but lack of ability. I saw that there was something to be made out of the troops if time and leadership and energy were available from the officers.

Unfortunately training was continually disturbed because I was forced to send battalions and regiments to the support of the still heavily battling southern front. For instance, on 29 and 30 June, I sat alone with my staff on the Kajaltepe, equally ready to leave at a moment's notice for the south front. Only the regiment on the coast and the artillery had remained in their positions.

Hamilton still tenaciously followed his plans to storm Eltschitepe and Krithia. The Krithia section, which was entrusted to myself, had a very heavy day on 29 and 30 June. The fleet had again regained confidence and appeared in large numbers from their hiding-places. A part of the front on both sides of the Sigindere remained in the hands of the enemy. The heavily shaken divisions of the south front had again to be relieved. The new divisions were taken from 2nd Army, and consequently Wehib Pasha took over the command of the South Group from General Weber. During this relief there was a fresh, large-scale attack on 13 July, by the enemy, this time on the left flank of the Southern Group, which left them with certain gains. Taken all round however, the Southern Group maintained their front splendidly even if, as already related, they lost portions here and there.

Now commenced the battle of the mines. This was an absolutely new development for the Turks. Up-to-date they had faced their numerous enemy only above ground. Up in the air, under the earth and in the water, this was too great a novelty for them.

In single troops, as civilians, a company of volunteer pioneers was brought from Germany. In the long run, however, they most of them succumbed to the murderous climate of Gallipoli. Only about 40 men were left, but these rendered excellent service as foremen in the mine warfare.

In the meantime we had, in comparison, peaceful days on the Kajaltepe. Only the hostile artillery and the 'planes took any notice of us. The aircraft emerged with especially large quantities of bombs on the days when great attacks on the north or south fronts were taking place, to prevent the sending of reserves.

We also received ample information regarding the bombardment of our positions by artillery. Directly above my tent I had a small observation post with an excellent field of view, which was continually occupied by a sentinel with a telescope. From this point we could look directly into the harbour of Imbros. Therefore I invariably received timely warning when the battleships came out to shoot. This was always immediately noticeable because a balloon ship followed them – unmistakable from the large captive balloon on the after-deck swaying to and fro in the wind.

Like a floating fort the squadron approached in a suspicious manner, protected by an inner ring of torpedo boats and an outer ring composed of fast-moving small boats, probably fishing craft. I continuously hoped, but in vain, for one of our U-boats. The English later brought out shallow draught monitors which were able to approach still closer to the coast. The guns of these stood openly on deck.

The first time that the approach of the ships was reported to me I naturally hurried immediately to the observation post to ascertain whether they would turn to the south, the north, or deal with us. I saw the ships approaching like the executioner to his victim, always in the afternoon as they then had the sun at their backs. On 25 June, a large cruiser of the *Nelson* class anchored almost in front of my coastal area. I hurried to my command post on the Kajaltepe and my batteries opened fire, but without disturbing the colossus in the least. Quite quietly Nelson got ready, the balloon went up. Finally came the flash of the first shot. Nothing to be seen. The same result with the second shot. Then it became clear to us that he was shooting over us at Tchanak Kale. Soon we saw thick clouds of smoke rising up from that spot. The firing of my batteries the enemy absolutely ignored. A somewhat contemptuous non-attention.

Three days later the same cruiser came again and this time honoured my battery on the Kajaltepe, but without any great result. *Nelson* was then relieved by a smaller cruiser of the *Liverpool* class, probably feeling herself too big to deal with my small coastal fire batteries. It did not open fire, however, apparently because the captive balloon swayed too much, so they again returned to the safe shelter of Imbros. After a time one became so accustomed to these ships' movements that I contented myself merely with reports as to results.

Much more unpleasant was the shelling of my coastal area at night by small cruisers and torpedo boats. The shelling was repeated then every two or three hours. Naturally everybody was alarmed and stood to in expectation of a landing. Further, a noticeable and steadily increasing aircraft activity was established over my area. These planes flew low over our positions, completely ignoring our fire, probably to take photographs. They must certainly have been amazed at the activity of my Division. There were, however, positions which they could not photograph as they could not see them.

In the meantime the July heat steadily increased. I had a roof of bushes built over my tent and on returning from my early morning ride wore only a thin white suit. It was lucky that sufficient fresh water was available so that I could sponge myself in a rubber bath. The nights were cool, with thunderstorms now and again, but as a result the heat during the day was so much the worse. The plague of flies was, under these conditions, insupportable. The walls of the tent inside were black. When eating, in spite of every precaution, there were always two or three flies on every mouthful. We bore the plague more willingly as we learnt from English papers that our enemy were suffering still more from it.

The health of the troops suffered severely in the continuous tropical heat. In three battalions scurvy broke out as a result of the unchanging rations and the lack of vitamins, as we know today. The Marshal sent me 50 Turkish pounds, about 1,000 marks, and I was able to buy some fresh vegetables in Asia for these suffering troops. This had a good effect, when added to the medical attention. Apart from this we remained free from epidemics.

Unfortunately another custom of the Turkish Army now began to take effect which did us enormous damage, which was continually combated by us Germans but which we were unable to overcome. That was the *teptil hawa*, or those ordered a change of climate, who were selected by the doctors from amongst the troops and then sent for months on leave to their homes. Earlier, during the reign of the suspicious Abdul Hamid, this system may have been justified, as it was an established custom during that period to send the new recruits to carry out their training period in the furthest parts of the

Empire. At that time, for instance, men came from the mountainous, healthy highland of Anatolia into the fever area round Salonica. Many became sick owing to the unaccustomed climate, particularly during the hot months. It was necessary to give them months of leave in their own homes to avoid heavy casualties. Today, however, recruits carried out their training in their own home areas as a matter of course. In spite of this, however, the doctors notified in increasing numbers the necessity of such a change of climate. Naturally these *teptil hawa* later attempted from their homes to obtain extensions of leave by lawful or unlawful methods. They never returned to their regiments at the right time, and often not at all. So the *teptil hawa* slid unnoticed into the class of deserters. The War Office had months previously issued orders prohibiting this custom, with what success was shown by the demands of the doctors which before me were laid.

In this connection I had had other curious experiences. At the beginning of the mobilisation in August 1914, the general officers commanding Districts had to render strength reports every 14 days to the War Office, which reports contained no less than 458 different columns to be filled in. This system was in force during the Balkan War and remained so. It was a truly monstrous list, fit only for a museum. After great effort I was successful in getting the consent of all departments of the War Office to a much smaller list which general officers commanding Districts were to submit quarterly instead of fortnightly. The necessary order with an accompanying form was sent to the army. How can I describe my astonishment when almost a year later, in a regiment of my Division, I found by chance a writer who had nothing else to do but fill up these 458 columns! Heads were shaken in disbelief when I suggested that this form had already been cancelled more than a year ago. Generally the methods of correspondence in the Turkish Army were most ceremonious. These were stubbornly maintained, as a form of heirloom, which was the pride of those actually concerned with it.

This little diversion has nothing to do with my activity at Kajaltepe, but it most illuminatingly illustrates the stubborn perseverance of the Turks with established customs. Whatever happens, no change! I had to constantly contend with this indolence. I was forced to

COMMANDER OF INFANTRY REGIMENT 125, WITH STAFF, INCLUDING THE MUFTI (PADRE), IN FRONT OF HIS DUG-OUT

OFFICERS OF INFANTRY REGIMENT 48 (16TH DIVISION)

always speak slowly and clearly so that I should be understood by the only two of those surrounding me who could possibly stand me – my General Staff officer and my interpreter. Their answers were made in such terribly broken German that I was forced to guess at least the half of what they meant. During this long period I, myself, missed the opportunity of expressing myself in fluent German. It was very pleasant for me, therefore, when Vice Sergeant Major Brandl of the Bavarian Light Cavalry was appointed to join me.

It was always a most refreshing change for me to be called on any official matter to Army Headquarters for discussion with the Marshal. A car was invariably sent for me, even if sometimes it was only a post wagon – a delivery van from Wertheim's in Berlin, which sometimes bumped so badly that I found myself sitting on the lap of the driver!

After the official matter had been discussed the Marshal kept me for a meal, or I joined the Staff table. This was always most refreshing to my mind as well as my body. I was able to converse again in my own language, heard something of what was happening in the world, and my own small personal wishes were readily complied with by the A.D.C., Major Prigge, and the officer in charge of Headquarters, Major von Frese. The Chief of Staff, Lt Col Kiazim Bey, made an excellent impression. In figure, small and active, calm and clear in his remarks, he had a good grip of the whole and at the same time an excellent knowledge of the smallest details. He was an indispensable support for the Marshal. I further remember the clever Turkish A.D.C.s, Lts Ekren Bey and Abdi Bey.

Generally speaking our General Headquarters always gave me an impression of a well-organised and harmoniously working High Army Command. During my earlier service, however, I had always conceived quite other ideas of the external appearance of Army Headquarters.

Even this high position bore the impression of the limited means available in Gallipoli. Everybody was under canvas. The dining table of the Staff was a shaky field-service table with old newspapers as tablecloths; the meals very plain but *à la franca*, and with an excellent spirit of comradeship between Turks and Germans.

Equally excellent was the manner in which the quite considerable numbers of Army Headquarters had been merged into the landscape. I could see nothing of this small settlement even when I was close to it. The car suddenly turned aside from the road Bighali-Jalowa, across the barren plateau and halted under the shade of bushes. A few steps led into a small valley which was almost hidden by the foliage of firs and other trees. The tents were pitched under these trees. The whole position had been selected in a masterly fashion. No stranger could possibly imagine that at this point were collected the many threads which controlled this mighty battle and which made possible a well-considered common leadership during a period of three-quarters of a year and on two continents.

The best evidence of this was that of the English flying officer who was taken prisoner towards the end of the campaign and brought to the spot. He could scarcely believe that he stood before the so long-sought-for quarters of the Marshal. This piece of country had actually lain in his observation area. How gladly would the English have concentrated the whole of their artillery on this point! Actually Headquarters was only now and again touched by a shot in the same way that practically no portion of the small peninsula escaped.

After such a refreshing visit I returned more content and internally strengthened to my Myrmidons under canvas.

I had in turn visitors on Kajaltepe, sometimes for myself sometimes for the position. On 24 July the tirelessly active Chaplain to the Forces, Count Lüttichau, again visited me. I wrote in my diary under this date. 'Count Lüttichau lunched with me. Pleasant conversation. As he rode off I felt a bit of home went with him.'

Some days later Faik Pasha, an efficient soldier, visited me by command of the Marshal. In the burning heat of the afternoon we rode forward to visit the coastal positions. I was greatly pleased to see how astonished Faik Pasha was at the work the Division had accomplished and how he continually turned to me and repeated, "*Je vous félicite, Je vous félicite.*"

On 5 August the Marshal came himself, but had only time to visit the battery on the Kajaltepe. However, he promised to come again.

The same day we received the news of the capture of Warsaw. It was astonishing to see the impression that this made on the Turks. They all beamed. The whole of the commands sent their congratulations and even my stout servant, Ali Effendi, ventured to express his good wishes. Russia was the long-feared hereditary enemy whom they now believed to be finally destroyed.

Towards the second half of July we began to notice signs that the Entente wished to finally roll us up on Gallipoli in order to be able to come to the help of the hard-pressed Russians. It is true that July passed comparatively peacefully on both battle fronts with only three heavy days fighting, but Hamilton appeared to be collecting his forces for a fresh heavy blow. The active interest for my position, which found expression in the many official visits from our side and the aircraft activity of the enemy between Kajaltepe and the seashore, led me to believe that the closed fist of Hamilton would descend on my division. The day of test appeared to be approaching, and I hoped that Faik Pasha would again be able to repeat his *Je vous félicite.* About the middle of July we knew on Gallipoli that reinforcements 50,000 strong had arrived on the islands and that more were expected. Where would Hamilton attack with these?

On the north and south fronts the enemy had bitten fast, like a dog. A regular fortress system of defence had been prepared. With map and protractor Hamilton could easily estimate how much more time he would need to capture Eltschitepe and Krithia at this rate. Both remained equally near and yet equally far and the war could end before they were reached. Russia, however, could not be left waiting much longer.

This was the period in Russia when, following the successful offensive of Mackensen which began with a breakthrough by Tarnow-Gorlitz, the attacks began in Kurland and Poland and the fortresses of the Vistula collapsed like packs of cards.

On 20 July the Russian General Bjalajew said to the French Ambassador, Paléologue, in St Petersburg:

> Can you imagine that in several infantry regiments which took part in the recent fighting at least a third of the men had no rifles? Those unfortunates waited patiently under the hail of shrapnel until one of their fighting comrades fell before their eyes and they could take his weapon in their turn. One of our army commanders wrote me recently, "Today, with their dumb artillery and infantry our army drowned in its own blood. We must have rifles at all costs I beseech you, Excellency, to throw all your weight in Paris on the side of assistance for us."

The many freighters which had long lain ready in the harbours of the Mediterranean were full of war material for Russia, only Hamilton had so far not been successful in opening the closed door of the Dardanelles. He now sought a new keyhole for the key which he believed he had in his hands.

Actually on the English side the pros and cons of a fresh attack had been carefully weighed at the commencement of June. Churchill had, by 11 June, already recommended an offensive on Bulair, and pointed out the advantages which would accrue by the cutting of the Turkish army lines of communication by land and sea at this point, and had further laid stress on the advantages of a direct base for the English submarines operating in the Sea of Marmora. An attack on the upper Gulf of Saros and Bulair from the direction of Enos was also considered. In London this operation was called 'a starving,' and was a starvation offensive as opposed to 'a storming' offensive.

The plan of an offensive at Bulair was finally abandoned, more particularly due to the doubts expressed by Admiral de Robeck. A storming offensive was therefore decided on, to be carried through in an extension from the Ariburnu front. It was certainly in the English interests to carry out this plan as quickly as possible. In London, however, a change in the Government had taken place, which consequently resulted in a new War Council. Much valuable time was lost by lengthy negotiations. The Parliamentary Committee of Enquiry estimates the time lost as six weeks. It was thus the commencement of August before the last of the newly granted divisions reached the islands.

The Marshal had naturally drawn his conclusions from the information that had reached him. An Army Order of 26 July opens with the words: 'A large-scale attack confronts us.' It was a similar position to that of April. It was possible to conclude that a simultaneous attack on the waterways of the Dardanelles would not again occur this time, because in such case the enemy landing army would have to do without the so welcome support of the ships' guns.

Possible, but scarcely probable, was the possibility of a fresh landing on the Asiatic side. Scarcely probable, because it was hardly likely that Hamilton would return to the earlier French plan. The Gulf of Saros and the Narrows by Bulair had lost nothing of their importance, and the Marshal therefore ordered the 9th and 12th Divisions into positions at these places.

The southern front of the enemy could not be extended as it was bounded on one side by the Aegean Sea and on the other by the Dardanelles. The enemy, however, south-west of Krithia had built two new landing stages which rendered possible a landing either in connection with the mouth of the Kumdere or still further northward. If these landings were to take place with powerful forces, the rear of the Southern Group would be seriously threatened and a direct breakthrough to Maidos not impossible. To hinder such an operation, I was already in position on Kajaltepe with the 9th Division. The Southern Group had also sent the 8th Division into this neighbourhood, south of the Kumdere. This rivulet formed the boundary between the Northern and the Southern Groups.

Such joints are always points of weakness. I had already discussed with the Commander of the 8th Division, on the spot, how to best combine our individual measures. On 5 August, the Marshal visited me and on the 6th Wehib Pasha sent his General Staff officer,

Major Mühlmann, to whom I personally showed the works on the Kumdere. The English would not have found it easy to make a landing here! The immense strength of the position lay in the excellent flanking effect obtainable.

We were thus prepared to receive the very possible landing between north and south front.

After considering the extension of the Ariburnu front in a southerly direction came the question of such a possibility to the north. Here Suvla Bay offered a splendid opportunity for landing, and the towering Kodjadschemendagh an alluring tactical aim. The circumspect and energetic Major Willmer was entrusted with the defence of the Anarfarta Plain which surrounded Suvla Bay, and three battalions, one squadron and four batteries were given him for this purpose. Somewhat little for the far-reaching plain, but 'only a knave gives more than he has.'

On 6 August the expected grand offensive opened. The large number of transports and warships left the harbour of Imbros in the morning. During the course of the afternoon the enemy attempted to chain our attention and our reserves. Both Northern and Southern Groups exploded with violent attacks.

The Gulf of Saros was also not forgotten. Transports, under the guns of the warships, proceeded towards Karatschali on the north bank of the Gulf of Saros, where boats were lowered. A Greek volunteer corps in *tirailleur* uniforms with black felt caps – very practical under this heat – and with a cross on them – a treacherous crew "the Swiss," Kugeler, called them – rowed ashore, but they certainly carried out their task badly when they quickly permitted themselves so be driven back by Turkish cavalry to their boats, leaving 21 dead behind them.

The battle alarm came more and more strongly from the left flank of the Northern Group. The 16th Division lost their trenches on the Kanlisirt. At 5 o'clock I had to send Infantry Regiment 64 to their help and an hour later followed with the rest of the Division. Only the coastal defence, Infantry Regiment 26, remained behind.

I must admit that I found it very difficult to carry out this order, because I definitely expected that the night would bring with it an attack on my position. My name was bound up with this position through almost two months of work. The coastal defence alone could not hold the position for any length of time.

CHAPTER XIII
Fresh Landings and the Fighting by Anafarta

Every soldier must obey, and that is a good principle. I again realised the truth of it in this case.

After I had started my troops marching in the late afternoon of 6 August, I rode ahead to the Commander of the 16th Division to obtain information regarding the battle zone. It was not a pleasant ride. The way lay over corpses. It was already dusk when I had to pass through the sunken road which led to the hill quarters of the 16th Division. This lay under the continuous fire of the English who always appeared to be excellently informed as to the whereabouts of our system of communication trenches or ways. My horse suddenly shied. There lay a brave lad whose company commander had given him a horse to fetch the rations up with. I often saw this picture of a personal servant fetching rations during my stay on Gallipoli. In this case horse and rider lay dead on the path, the rider still in the saddle holding in his right hand his ration bag, Conditions here were really awful, even to an already somewhat war-hardened soldier. I gave my horse the spur and my staff and I galloped untouched through this sunken road.

The Commander of the 16th Division told me that another Division had already been told off to recover the Kanlisirt. Shortly after Essad Pasha telephoned that the 9th Division were detailed for the moment as reserves for the Northern Group and I was to come to him to Kemalicri. I was unable to obtain any clearer appreciation about the battle front, Essad Pasha, courteous as ever, asked me to stay with him and await developments.

I met there Kiasim Bey, Chief of Staff of the 5th Army, who was unable to get back at the moment owing to the heavy barrage fire which shut off the Northern Group from their rear zones and which I and my staff had just ridden through. Both officers conversed in Turkish and I often heard my own name mentioned. I asked for information, because I always prefer to be able to consider quietly beforehand any task which they might be anticipating giving me, but Essad Pasha replied that the matter he had in mind was not yet ripe for discussion. I believe myself that at this moment it must have been shortly before midnight – the first reports were received which pointed to an extension of the Ariburnu front to the north.

I personally learnt nothing, and as a consequence naturally continued to worry about my position on the Kajaltepe. As this waiting appeared useless to me I asked Essad Pasha to allow me to withdraw to get what sleep I could, as the next day would certainly bring me fresh tasks to undertake. I went to my staff in the officers' mess room where my servant had already placed a thick wolf's skin on the table, as my bed. Unfortunately, the skin was so full of fleas that I had scarcely any sleep at all.

About 4:30 a.m. I was called to Essad Pasha, who informed me that the enemy had landed troops north of Ariburnu. Their aim was not yet clear. I was to occupy the Kodjadschemendagh-Djonk Bahir and wait there. My two infantry regiments, 25 and 64, with my battery, were at once given marching orders and I personally hurried ahead with my staff.

Stegenmann pictures very dramatically in his well known and first class book how 'with drawn sword, at the head of my Division, I threw myself on the enemy who were already entrenching on the Djonk Bahir.' I must say that it was unfortunately far from being as dramatic as he pictured it, or rather, Allah be praised! that it was not so, because actually I reached the top before the English, and that was the chief point at the moment.

From a deep valley I saw before me the steep side of the Djonk Babir whose high comb eventually merged in the near Kodiadschemendagh, we had to dismount from our horses and under the already burning rays of the sun (it was 6 a.m.) climb the sides of the Djonk Bahir, pulling ourselves slowly up by the help of small bushes and rough grass. On top was a long narrow plateau with an astonishingly far-reaching view over rough hilly country to the Aegean Sea.

Suvla Bay lay full of ships. We counted ten transports, six warships, and seven hospital ships. On land we saw a confused mass of troops like a disturbed anthill, and across the blinding white surface of the dried salt sea we saw a battery marching in a southerly direction. With our few revolvers we could do nothing against it.

All about us was peace and quiet – not a man to be seen and no enemy in front of us in the hills. With glasses I was able to pick up bit by bit Willmer's companies north of the Asmakdere on the east border of the flat country, and I saw English troops on the Lala Baba and, on the flat, in certain places, entrenching. Nowhere was there fighting in progress.

I now began a reconnaissance of the country so as to be able to receive the approaching regiments with final orders. This was a long, high ridge, which stretched from Abdurraham Bahir over Kodjadschemendagh-Djonk Bahir to the Dustepe, and to which the English gave the group name Sari Bahir. My two regiments would be simply lost in this immense position if the enemy commenced the steep ascent from the valley immediately. A very limited field of fire. In front of us a confusion of valleys, nullahs and heights. It was impossible to find a post properly controlling the massive position as it was very broken up and covered with bush. Very unpleasant for us was the Schahintepe which lay in front of the Djonk Bahir, somewhat to the south-west. This ought necessarily to have been included in the defence line if I had had time to make proper preparations.

It was only now possible to occupy the Djonk Bahir, as the key point of our position, with the reserves close behind, as the position had no depth. Additionally unpleasant was the fact that both wings were without support and I had no troops to protect them. It was also impossible for the moment to find touch with the neighbouring 19th Division.

During this reconnaissance we found a Turkish battery whose battery commander I had to awaken, as he had no idea of the altered battle front. He opened fire on the troops crossing the dried salt sea, but could only reach with high explosive. I also found a platoon of infantry of roughly 20 men covering the battery, which was at least something.

While I now dictated reports and orders to Hunussi Bey, who had first to translate these into Turkish, Zia Bey continually swept the country in front of us with my glasses, as it was essential to keep the English as far as possible away from us.

Suddenly the enemy infantry actually appeared in front of us at about 500 yards range. The English approached slowly, in single file, splendidly equipped and with white bands on their left arms, apparently very tired, and were crossing a hill-side to our flank, emerging in continually increasing numbers from the valley below. I immediately sent an order to my infantry – this was the 20 man strong artillery covering platoon – instantly to open fire. I received this answer. 'We can only commence to fire when we receive the order of our battalion commander.' This was too much for me altogether. I ran to the spot and threw myself among the troops who were lying in a small trench. What I said I cannot recollect, but they began to open fire and almost immediately the English lay down without answering our fire or apparently moving in any other way. They gave me the impression that they were glad to be spared further climbing.

Now I received unexpected reinforcement. From the direction of Dustepe I suddenly saw a Turkish column coming which was about to descend rearwards in the deep valley. It was two companies of the Infantry Regiment 72. My orders to halt immediately and come under my command had to be urgently repeated before they obeyed. At the same time the Commander of the 1st Battalion of Infantry Regiment 14 reached the Kodjadschemendagh, and I took him with his companies under my orders.

Thus I was slowly able to establish a small firing front which I grouped in two wings, as the commanders of the Infantry Regiments 25 and 64 reported to me that their battalions would shortly be arriving. I had been successful in keeping this exceptionally important height in our hand and bringing the forward progress of the enemy to a halt. Stegemann very justly says, "Whoever first reaches the base of the Kodjadschemendagh, whoever first succeeds in climbing and establishing themselves on the crest is the winner in the battle. The Briton had the advantage as the attacker and is there before us. We, however, got there before him. Now everything depended on our holding the heights."

How was it that the English did not make full use of their advantage? The enemy who had appeared before me had not landed in Suvla Bay, but had very correctly taken the much shorter way from the northern corner of his Ariburnu front. During the last eight nights the English had continuously landed reinforcements without our knowledge, so that General Birdwood commanded a total of 37,000 men and 72 guns. At dusk on 6 August he started two columns each of 8,000 men along the shore of the sea in a northern direction. The left column, 4 Australian Brigade, was to reach the heights of Kodjadschemendagh from the Agildere Valley, the 29th Indian Brigade the Djonk Bahir from the Tschailakdere (see the road marked on the map). The enemy hoped by dawn to have these decisive heights in their hands, which, according to their air force information, were unoccupied and unfortified.

The distance would take two hours to cover under normal conditions. Six hours were allowed for it. That ought to have been sufficient. The advance guard, the 4th Battalion of the South Wales Borderers under Lt Col Gale-Spy, was successful in throwing back the Turkish posts on the sea shore, and shortly after midnight were in full possession of Damakdjilik Bahir which they occupied and held as a flank guard.

Under this protection the 4th Australian Brigade crossed at 12.30 in the morning the Tschailakdere, entered the Agildere, surprising in this valley the Turkish outposts, took two hurriedly clad officers prisoners and then split into two sections to climb to their final objective, the Kodjadschenendagh.

During this period the right column, the 29th Brigade, had accomplished the climb from the valley of the Tschailakdere and split themselves to the north-west of the Schahintepe in the same way. The Otago Battalion, as left column, reached the source of the Tschailakdere and the Canterbury Battalion were successful in reaching the source of the Saslidere, south of the Schahintepe. Here, at five o'clock in the morning, the Indian Brigade deployed.

It was seven o'clock in the morning before these troops,

THE AUTHOR IN THE IBRIDJE VALLEY, NEAR LITTLE ANAFARTA
25 December, 1915

GERMAN HOSPITAL AT BIGHALI, WITH MALTEPE IN THE BACKGROUND
Autumn, 1915

168

dead beat from the exertions of the night march in the difficult valleys and partially held up by our coastal defences, first reached the source of the three, many times mentioned, brooks just below the heights, while at the same time I had already been successful in organising up on top of the heights a defence, although a very thin line. Actually the careful calculation of six hours had not proved to be sufficient.

An attack by the 5th and 6th Gurkha Battalions (it was probably these battalions which, with my 20 infantry, I had opened fire on) failed. Nevertheless these Gurkhas succeeded in bringing a machine gun into action on the Schahintepe which took the narrow ridge of Djonk Bahir under flanking fire. It was a very thin fire which did not disturb us much. Nevertheless I wanted to prevent my regiments, which were due to arrive at any moment, from being caught by this fire during their deployment. I therefore went over to the battery and ordered them to open fire with both guns of the left section on this machine gun.

As I was starting back towards the left wing, which I considered endangered and which had still not found touch with the 19th Division – it was about 8 o'clock in the morning – I received from this machine gun a shot through the breast. This was most annoying. Up-to-date I had escaped from many other worse positions without a scratch. Now I was forced to leave my brave Division just in
this most critical moment. Zia Bey and Brandl sprang to my help immediately, but had to leave me lying as the machine gun kept this point under continuous fire. After some time the fire slackened and both carried me behind the near protecting cliff. Brandl, who had studied medicine for six terms in Munich, found a bullet wound in the middle of the breast, close to the heart, and tied me up with a field dressing.

I did not remain there much longer. I sent for my General Staff officer, Major Hunussi Bey, who was thoroughly acquainted with my plans for carrying on the defensive as much as possible in an offensive fashion, and told him that I considered it necessary that he should provisionally take over command. Lt Cols Nail Bey, Servet Bey and the Commander of the Artillery, Lt Col Asmi Bey declared themselves in agreement.

They laid me on a stretcher, already thoroughly soaked in Turkish blood, and carried me down the steep hill, where I soon met the leading sections of my Division coming up. Below in the valley the Divisional Surgeon, Lt Col Nevres Bey, bandaged me up extremely well and I was then taken in a motor ambulance and put on board the *Ac Denis* at Akbasth. On the way I halted at the Army Headquarters so that I could report to the Marshal on the critical position on the Kodjadschemendagh.

Unfortunately I had to remain four days in Akbash, in considerable pain and under continuous fire from ships guns and aeroplane bombs. On 11 August at about 4 a.m. the *Gülnehal*, to which I had in the meantime been transferred with 3,000 seriously wounded, finally left for Constantinople. In view of the heat and the stench I had my stretcher carried up on deck, where I was continuously stared at by curious Turks. En route we met in the Dardanelles a German U-boat, and not very much later, near the Island of Marmora, an English submarine on the surface, which passed us at about 200 yards distance with the crew on deck. We looked at one another without a word but with great curiosity. They left us in peace, although they often stopped the hospital ships travelling towards the Dardanelles under the protection of the Red Crescent and searched them for ammunition, war material or provisions.

At 5 in the afternoon we entered the Golden Horn. I was immediately placed in an ambulance car and taken to the German Hospital, where I was well and carefully looked after by the German nursing sisters and my wife. I also remember with gratitude the services of the splendid doctor in charge, Dr Orchan Bey.

What I was completely unable to understand and what considerably disturbed me, was that during my journey through Galata and Pera I saw everybody in the streets extremely joyful shouting, dancing, music, everywhere a happy throng – quite the opposite of conditions on the not far distant Gallipoli where, at the same moment, the heaviest fighting with serious losses was taking place, and thousands falling or receiving wounds or mutilation for just this so heavily threatened town. In the morning still under enemy fire, now, in the afternoon, in this triumphal town. An extraordinary contrast which one was quite unable to grasp. Beiram was being celebrated, the great feast of the Mahommedans of three days' duration, following the four weeks' fast during the month of Ramadan, that is to say, one fasts during the day, and during the night, with general rejoicing, consumes considerably more than usual.

I preferred to return to Gallipoli where my thoughts dwelt continuously.

There, on the Kodjadschemendagh on 7 August, about 9 in the morning, the enemy had gathered for a general assault which, however, was beaten back by the 9th Division. The Schahintepe, however, remained in the hands of the enemy and an attempt by Nail Bey to regain it failed. About noon Hunussi Bey was able to report that an attempt of the enemy to occupy the summit had been prevented with heavy loss to the enemy. About 1:30 in the afternoon Lt Col Djemil Bey, with the 4th Division, reached Kodjadschemendagh and took over the command.

With this ended for the moment the crisis which had taken the form of a conflict for this commanding height, and to which Hamilton in his report of 15 December 1915, gives the descriptive title, 'A quarter of a mile from victory.' The unmistakable sign of an approaching new attack was the heavy artillery fire which now commenced to break and from the ships' guns on our positions on the heights, which reached such an intensity in the early morning of 8 August that an attack was momentarily expected. On the Turkish side everything was fully prepared. The enemy had in the meantime rested and fed, had received reinforcements and organised a continuous strong attacking front.

The right column under General Johnston, composed of a New Zealand brigade, the Auckland Mounted Rifles, two battalions of the 13th Division, the Monoy Section and the 26th Indian Mountain Battery were to take Djonk Bahir, while the middle and left columns under General Baldwin, composed of the 4th Australian Brigade, the 39th Infantry Brigade and the 29th Indian Infantry

Brigade, the 6th Battalion South Lancashire Regiment and the 21st Indian Mountain Battery were to storm the Kodjadschemendagh. Apart from the overpowering artillery bombardment from the ships' guns, at 5:15 in the morning 20 English battalions attacked 17½ Turkish.

In spite of this the attack failed with extremely heavy losses on both sides. On our side we lost the splendid Lt Col Nail Bey and Major Mehmet Bey from Infantry Regiment 25, and Hunussi Bey was wounded in the head from a bomb. It is true that the English were successful in actually reaching the summit, but they were thrown back again by gallant counter-attacks.

Very interesting and instructive from a military point of view is a report from the commander of the 6th Gurkha Battalion, Major Cecil Allinson, which I give in extracts as follows:

> Until 5:15 in the morning the ships were to bombard the heights. At 5:15 our attack was to commence. I had split up two companies of the 6th South Lancashire Battalion amongst my own men, I had never seen such an artillery preparation. The accuracy of the shooting was astonishing, the Turkish trenches were smashed to pieces. I had my watch in my hand. It was 5:15. It was 5:18. Was my watch wrong? At 5:20 the firing died down. I waited three minutes longer to be quite safe, then we jumped up and went forward, all hand in hand. On the top we met the Turks. A bitter hand-to-hand fight began. Captain le Marchand fell with a bayonet through his heart. I received a bayonet wound in the leg. At last the Turks began to run, we after them. I was proud. The key to the whole peninsula was in our hands. Below me I saw the Dardanelles, active movement of ships and the roads which led towards the Eltschitepe (Achi Baba). We streamed forward in the direction of Maidos, but had hardly gone 100 paces forward as a salvo from one of our own ships fell right in our ranks. It was a frightful disaster. We lost about 150 men and had to retire to our starting positions. Between 5 and 7 in the afternoon the Turks began a counter-attack. Later I reported to the General, who told me that the attack had failed along the whole line and we must await the dawn on the lower

heights.

So this attack on the decisive commanding position merged into the frame of the developing battles by Anafarta, and from now onwards its further course must be considered with that of the whole battlefield.

The English had the initiative, the Turks were therefore forced to take their steps accordingly. To understand the position the English plan of attack must now be studied. This had, as its chief aim (I follow here the authoritative English sources), the capture of the commanding heights of Kodjadschemendagh, called by the English *Sari Bahir*, so as to be able to take the peninsula by the neck along the line Kabatepe-Maidos. To attain this end the following movements were planned:

1. A surprise attack from the Anzac front to cut the land communications of the Turkish Army with Constantinople.

2. This cutting of communications to be completed at sea and in Asia by artillery fire from selected positions.

3. To form a winter camp in Suvla Bay.

In accordance with the above the detailed operation orders were worked out during July as follows:

1. A limited offensive under General Davis on the south front with two new divisions as a containing attack to hold the available reserves, 35,000 men.

2. A main attack under General Birdwood in the Sari Bahir with the 2nd Australian Division strengthened by the 13th Division of the New Army, with a British and an Indian brigade, 37,000 men.

3. A landing of the 10th and 11th Divisions as the 9th Army Corps under General Stopford in the Suvla Bay, to occupy the heights north and west of Anafarta, 25,000 men.

On the islands were the 53rd and 54th Territorial Divisions as reserve, 25,000 men.

The English strove to make particularly safe the success of these very well-prepared operations by two factors, the factor of deception and that of surprise. The attention of the Turkish North Group was to be drawn to their left flank by the attack on Kanlisirt, while at dusk the main attack followed on the opposite right flank. How this did not succeed I have already described. The crisis here, the first during the course of these battles, was past.

We must now return to the landing in the Suvla Bay.

The period of the new moon had been selected, and under cover of darkness, at 10 o'clock in the evening of 6 August 1915, the three brigades of the 11th New Army Division, commanded by General Hammersley, landed in Suvla Bay, actually on the two ribs which run out into the sea as hilly tongues of land and form Suvla Bay- the 34th Brigade at Large Kemikli and the 32nd and 33rd Brigades at Small Kemikli (See Map L). *Kemikli* means rib in Turkish.

It appeared that the English had learnt their lesson from the experiences of 25 April, and with a view to facilitating the landing had sent new steel bulletproof motor lighters which took 500 men, travelled about five knots and carried landing bridges in the bows. In addition, the usual landing in boats from destroyers, lighters, transports, under the protection of the guns of the fleet, just as I saw it some hours later from Djonk Bahir. In spite of the Turkish fire, the explosion of land mines and the loss of some of the new special boats, the landing was completed in three hours without any great loss.

The 34th Brigade had orders to take the Softatepe, called by the English, Hill 10, as well as the heights ascending towards the Kiretschtepe, and the two other brigades were to occupy Lala Baba. This was to be followed by a joint attack on the Punartepe-Mestantepe – the latter called the 'Chocolate Hill' by the English – and the Ismailtepe lying behind it. It was hoped that at dawn by the latest all these positions would be taken. The factor of surprise was to be used to the utmost.

These hidden aims were absolutely in accord with the tactical position which demanded a ruthless attack. Energetically conducted they were also obtainable, the more so as the estimated Turkish resistance did not consist of 4,000 men but only of 1,800. Major Wilmer, who commanded the defences in the Plain of Anafarta, had at his disposal only the *Gendarmerie* Battalions Gallipoli and Brussa, one battalion of Infantry Regiment 33, one squadron of cavalry and 4 batteries for the whole portion stretching as far as Kiretschtepe. These troops, however, magnificently carried out their task, in the beginning the two companies splendidly held Lala Baba until 2 in the morning in itself an almost incomprehensible accomplishment in the face of the two landing brigades, which was only explainable by the fact that the dried-out salt sea made their retreat possible.

On the left flank, by Large Kemikli, the 34th Brigade incorrectly took a nearer sand hill for Hill 10 (Softatepe), so that this itself had at dawn to be taken from the Turks. At the same time the Turkish batteries opened a very well aimed fire, as the rising sun disclosed the English measures.

Under this fire the landing was completed by the 10th Division under General Hill. A total of 20,000 men of the 9th Army Corps landed during the course of 7 August, and opposed to them was only the small, already heavily battered handful of Turks.

It was already evening on this day before the 33rd Brigade succeeded in taking the Mestantepe which they should have taken in the morning. The Isnailtepe, however, was stubbornly held by a company of the *Gendarmerie* Battalion Brussa and the 2nd Battalion of the General Infantry Regiment 33. General Stopford had lost most favourable opportunities,

The English ascribe this incomprehensible inactivity to the youth of Kitchener's Army, unused to war, and to the fact that the generals did not dare to try them too hard in the great heat, in view of the lack of water. Well, they would have been able to obtain water enough for themselves on the heights which the Turks held fast.

During the night it was expected that reinforcements would reach the Turks. They did not come, however. The reason was as follows:

The Marshal, during the course of the evening of 6 August, had gained the impression that the already long expected main attack of Hamilton in the extension of the Anzac front to the north, with all the possibilities likely to arise from it, had begun. He immediately took the necessary counter-measures.

The 16th Army Corps, consisting of the 7th and 12th Divisions commanded by Col Fehsi Bey, watching the Gulf of Saros, received orders the same evening to march by Usun-Hisirli into the neighbourhood east of Big Anafarta. The reserves of the Southern Group, the 4th Division, commanded by Lt Col Djemil Bey, were moved on the morning of 7 August to the Djonk Bahir front. In spite of his
own needs Wehib Pasha strengthened this 4th Division with every available spare unit. The one brother helped the other. Mehmet Ali Pasha was ordered to send immediately from the Asiatic side all troops not actually in the front line. We raked together everything that was available.

At noon on 7 August, as I was passing through the Army Headquarters I saw the Marshal who was in quite a confident mood. He assured me that the Kodjadschemen Dagh-Djonk Bahir would be held and the two divisions from Bulair would that day reach Big Anafarta by forced marches.

I have already described Djcmil's Bey's part in the attack on Djonk Bahir. The Marshal personally gave orders to the commanding general, Col Fehsi Bey, when he reported, to attack the enemy who was advancing from Suvla Bay on both sides of the Asmakdere, on the morning of 8 August with both his Divisions.

The enemy appeared to be continuously extending his line more towards the north. This offered opportunity for immediate attack. In the morning of 8 August the Marshal himself rode into the assembly place of the 16th Army Corps and sought vainly for the troops. He found, however, only the General Staff Officer of the 7th Division, who was looking for an advance guard position, and learnt, contrary to his expectations, that the greater part of both divisions were still far behind and these were only just beginning to deploy. These circumstances forced the Marshal to postpone the commencement of the attack to the evening of 8 August, which in itself gave a certain advantage as the ships' guns of the enemy were then unable to find any targets. However, that evening the commanding general, Col Fehsi Bey, declared that he could not attack with his tired troops. He reported himself sick.

The Marshal sent for Mustapha Kemal Bay, the well known Commander of the 19th Division, from the near Ariburnu front who had in the meantime been promoted to Colonel, and placed him in command of the whole troops in the Anafarta area. But 24 costly hours were lost. For more than two days the weak forces of Willmer had alone faced the overpoweringly superior forces of Stopford.

During the whole of 8 August the Goddess of Victory held the door to success wide open for Stopford, but he would not enter. He personally remained on 8 August, as on 7 August, on board the *Jonguil*, because of the wireless and other signal communications, and only paid a visit to land in the afternoon.

There everybody was busily employed. Baggage and rations for the troops were unloaded. Order was restored amongst the troops, trenches were dug, the men cooked and smoked and, as Churchill relates, bathed in the beautiful cool sea. They awaited the still missing artillery whose arrival had been delayed owing to the necessity of landing water, as thirst was heavy in the heat of those cloudless August days. But nobody advanced. In short, a peaceful picture almost like a boy scout's field day.

At the same time under this same sun on the other side the panting troops of the 7th and 12th Divisions were straining forward over the hills from Bulair; from the Asiatic side along the shadeless Sultan's Way; over Erenkoi the Turkish battalions and batteries were pressing towards the embarkation stations in Tchanak Kale. Will they arrive in time? This thought feverishly occupied the mind, not only of the Marshal who waited there by Anafarta.

His opponent, Sir Ian Hamilton, was in an equal position of anxiety on 8 August, on the Island of Imbros, his headquarters. The awaited reports from Suvla Bay did not arrive. This energetic man could not stand it any longer on the island and hurried on the Admiral's speedy yacht *Triad* to Suvla Bay, which he reached at six o'clock in the evening. The idyll there was rudely disturbed. With Stopford's greeting, 'everything was quite all right and going well,' Hamilton was not at all in agreement. Fruitless explanations. Hamilton landed to personally obtain information from the divisional commanders, and ordered General Hammersley to attack the same evening with one brigade in the direction of the heights north of Small Anarfarta. Unfortunately, the divisional commander, who was very badly informed regarding his front, ordered troops to do this who had already occupied, on their own initiative, the Jussuftepe and Ibridje. These important positions were vacated, but the ordered attack could not be carried through owing to the fall of darkness. As if this was not sufficient, this unexpected movement threw into confusion the whole of the general attack ordered for the next morning.

So 8 August passed bloodlessly at Suvla Bay on both sides, only a commanding general superseded, as Stopford was also recalled by telegram with two other generals to London on Hamilton's report. Kitchener, according to Daniels, aptly commented, 'This is a young man's war.'

Not for nothing on 8 August did the two Commanders-in-Chief, who certainly never before during the course of this war had been so close to one another, throw the whole of their personal influence into the scales directly behind the front. The next morning both sides commenced a general attack, each hoping for a decisive success.

Leaving the important and bloody opening scenes on the Djonk Bahir, the Battle of Anafarta now first opened. From both sides the waves of troops drove against one another, but the Turk had now grown equal to the English.

The Turks had to thank Mustaph Kemal Bey's energetic intervention that on the morning of 9 August the 12th Division under Col Salaheddin Bey finally commenced to more on the important positions of Jusuftepe–Ismailtepe, north of the Asmakdcre, while south of this stream Halil Bey with the 7th Division attacked the Damakdjilik Bahir This division found little resistance, and had by 1 o'clock forced the enemy back to close on the coast. The 12th Division met with stronger resistance, as the 9th English Army Corps, strengthened by some battalions of the 53rd Territorial Division which had in the meantime landed, was in full advance towards the same line.

The 31st English Brigade had instructions to retake Jussuftepe which they had left the evening before as the result of the unfortunate instructions. But now this was occupied by Salaheddin's brave troops, and further north the 32nd Brigade was unable to advance in the direction of
Baka Baba, and in the same way the 11th Division failed in its attacks on the Ismailtepe.

By the evening it was clear that the Turks had everywhere brought the English to a complete halt, successfully surmounting the second crisis in the course of these operations.

The English had learnt the bitter truth of the old proverb 'Opportunities once missed can never be regained.' On the heights of Kiretschepe also, the brave *Gendarmerie* Battalion Gallipoli under Kadri Bey had, with the assistance of a battalion of the 12th Division sent to its help, gallantly maintained its position.

On 10 August with a fresh attack the English, strengthened by the rest of the 53rd Territorial Division, stormed Jussuftepe and Ismailtepe, but their joy was of short duration. With a furious counter-attack the Turks retook the heights and from then on never again lost them.

Mustapha Kemal Bey made his principal operations for the day on his left wing. He endeavoured to clear up the position in the commanding mountainous positions on the Kodjadschemendagh, where a narrow portion of the ridge still remained in the hands of the English just about sufficient for cover for 1,000 rifles.

This narrow position had been taken over on the morning of

10 August by two new battalions, the 6th North Lancashires and the 5th Wiltshires, when they were heavily shelled by the Turkish artillery. Mustapha Kemal Bey attacked with the 8th Division which had arrived from Asia, and personally took command, as the attack was held up his watch was destroyed by a bullet during this period –and he was finally successful in clearing the Djonk Bahir, but he could not take the Schahintepe. He had to rest content. The Lancashire battalion was for the greater part, and the Wiltshire battalion almost entirely cut up.

A similar fate now threatened the Turks who followed after the enemy across the heights into the valley. Under the annihilating fire of the ships' guns and land batteries only a small portion of the Turks regained the high ridge. This was, however, from then on firmly held. Already the future line of trench warfare from Dustepe over Djonk Bahir, Kodjadschemendagh to Ismailtepe and Jussuftepe began to show itself. Only the north wing was still in movement; and the attention of the English Commander in-Chief, poring over his maps, was turned to this point.

Now the third perilous crisis of those burning August days approached for the Turks. Kadri Bey, with the *Gendarmerie* Battalion Gallipoli and only two guns, had so far gallantly held the Kiretschepe. The country must be known for it to be understood how, in this huge area of hilly country, regiments could not entirely disappear unseen. Close to the far distant coast lay the English warships covering the long high ridge with their flanking fire. Shortly, it was a very dangerous point, but strategically of great importance, because whoever entirely occupied the Kiretschepe could easily descend into the broad valley which runs across the peninsula from Edje Liman over Turschunkoi to Akbash.

The Marshal had not lost sight of the importance of Kiretschepe. Although the enemy had so far not seriously attacked it, the Marshal had, on 10 August, already sent what troops he had of the 5th Division with other small units from coastal defence under the command of Major Willmer. This rapidly paid for itself, because in the meantime the enemy had received the additional reinforcement of the 54th Territorial Division; and on 15 and 16 August, this division, supported by two brigades of the 10th

Division under General Mahon, attacked along the high ridge of the Kiretschtepe. Those were again days of the heaviest fighting

on which the balance of success seemed to tremble, swaying to and fro. The Marshal was again personally on the spot. Reinforcements received from Asia laid their packs at the foot of the heights and scrambled rapidly up to help their comrades. By the evening of 10 August the Turks had succeeded in driving the enemy back to the middle of the high ground, and so the third and last crisis of the Battle of Anafarta closed happily for them. Kadri Bey found his grave there on the heights.

Now both parties were forced to take a few days' breathing space.

The clever, continually active A.D.C. of the Marshal, Major Prigge, who was always ready to help anybody, wrote to me as follows on 19 August, knowing that I was lying in the German Hospital in Constantinople, longingly awaiting news from the front:

> Since the 7th His Excellency has been literally day and night en route, and only by the most extreme effort have we succeeded in preventing a successful advance by the enemy, who landed four to five divisions. The situation is today as follows: (Sketch facing page 126.)
>
> The sketch shows the distribution of the Turkish divisions. The chief danger lies at present on our right wing by Edje Liman. For the moment it has become quieter. The English have this time suffered enormous losses and the battles were far more bitter than any we have had so far.

In the meantime Hamilton had once again scraped together all his forces in a last large attack. From the south front the trusty 29th Field Division which, on 25 April, had so expeditiously carried through the landing on the south point, and from Egypt the dismounted Yeomanry Division were sent to Suvla Bay. General de Lisle, the successor to Stopford, had now six divisions under his command and, in addition, strengthened forces of the Anzac Corps attacked on the Anzac front under General Cox. A heavy superiority as against the diminished strength of the Turkish

VIEW OF SMALL KEMIKLI, AS LEFT BY THE ENGLISH
20 December, 1915

ENGLISH LANDING BRIDGES AT SMALL KEMIKLI
20 December, 1915

EXTREME POINT OF LARGE KEMIKLI
25 December, 1915

divisions. But the Turks stood ready, fully entrenched and well organised.

On 21 August, following two hours of artillery preparation, the English commenced their general attack. Everywhere the heaviest fighting with quite exceptionally heavy losses. The Turks held an unbroken front, having drawn their last man into the trenches. It is true that the Jussuftepe was lost by the first attack, but the Turks quickly counter-attacked and retook it.

For that particular neighbourhood it was misty day, and the mist clouds were continuously thickened by the smoke from the burning bush. As the sun sank blood red, behind the Gulf of Saros on the Thracian horizon, the Turks stood everywhere victorious, masters of the heights, admittedly under heavy losses – 26,000 wounded alone were brought to Constantinople from 22 to 26 August by water (the total losses I don't know) – but the English lost 45,000 men, their losses being particularly heavy in the 29th and Yeomanry Divisions.

That was the last big-scale attack by the English. The front now resolved itself into trench warfare, consisting here of the many-lined fortress system of the Anarfarta Group commanded by Mustapha Kemal Bey. The protection of the upper Gulf of Saros, which during the present fighting had been almost entirely denuded of troops, was now taken over by the 1st Army under Field Marshal von der Goltz.

Practically, the English had not succeeded in accomplishing anything other than an extension of their front. A kind of race to the north along the sea coast had taken place similar to what had taken place in France on a larger scale in the late autumn of 1914. The Marshal points out in his book, *Five Years in Turkey*, that the English would have had more chance of success if they had begun their operations on the outer instead of the inner wing.

The English press was very indignant, the more so as the public had several times had its attention drawn to an approaching happy end of the Dardanelles programme, and particularly so by one speech of Churchill's. *The Daily News* complained on 24 August that 'No certain information comes from the Dardanelles, only a continuously increasing stream of casualties.'

But the Battle of Anarfarta remains a glorious page in the history of the Turkish Army.

CHAPTER XIV
At Turschunkoi

My wound had in the meantime considerably healed, and as I could get any necessary bandaging done just as well in the field, on 7 September, at 8:30 in the evening, I joined Binhold, who had himself been sick, on a torpedo boat travelling back to Gallipoli.

It was a cold and stormy night that we spent together on the narrow deck, as we had given up the small cabin to two Swedish officers. The commander of the torpedo boat was considerably frightened of English submarines, although we travelled with all lights out and through a considerable sea in the blackest night, and from time to time he made matters still more unpleasant for us by a zigzag course. Completely frozen and shaken we landed on 8 September at 7:30 in the morning in Akbash, from which spot a car bore the Swedish officers and myself to Army Headquarters

The Marshal informed me that I was to take the place of the sick General Trommer, commanding 14th Army Corps on the southern front. After lunch I pursued my way in a shaky post wagon towards the southern front, over the finally completed new road along the Dardanelles, through
Maidos to the mouth of the Soanlidere, and then up this in the direction of Krithia. After a considerable amount of searching I found my headquarters and rode the same evening to report to the Commander of the Southern Group, General Wchib Pasha, at Salim Bey Tschiflik. Wehib Pasha, a typical Turk, with a full beard, was a brother of Essad Pasha, equally clever and energetic but otherwise not a bit like him.

I naturally spent the first few days in relearning this area which had been entrusted to me during the May-June battles, and which now as the result of human activity was scarcely recognisable. A far-reaching fortress system with many lines and particularly strengthened strong points had been created with extraordinary diligence and dexterity.

The Krithia section was now held by two instead of one Division; the 1st, commanded by Col Djaffer Tayar Bey, and alongside the

10th Division under Lt Col Salaheddin Bey, the two comprising 14th Army Corps, while the left section was held by 5th Army Corps under General Fehsi Pasha, with the 13th and 14 Divisions. My headquarters were well established. Chief of Staff was Major Scheffket Bey, who spoke very good German. I was able to greet as Commander of the Artillery Lt Col Assim Bey, whom I had met previously.

Djaffer Tayar was an excellent divisional commander, but extremely sensitive. He had so far taken the place of General Trommer and felt himself slighted by my appearance and wanted to send in his resignation. The regiments of the 1st Division and their commanding officers were splendid. As I went through the trenches, particularly those of the 1st Division, they looked spick and span. Once looking round the corner I saw a brave *Asker* with a straw broom, who had been sweeping our path, rapidly disappear.

The actual front line trenches lay fairly close together. Tunnelling operations were in full swing. Each time mines were blown there was a fight for the rearrangement of the front line. Apart from this the battle front was comparatively quiet. Each of the opponents was certainly convinced that he could not be thrown out of his position, but on the other hand he could not achieve this with his enemy.

I had just reached the front trenches of the 1st Division on 22 September as the enemy sprang a mine and immediately commenced a heavy artillery bombardment. This could be the start of a general attack, to meet which I ought to have been at my command post to be able to overlook the position and give the necessary instructions to my corps. It was a fresh example to me that a Commander once in the front line is no more effective than the individual fighter. On the other hand, I was able to quickly convince myself how excellently the enemy had registered and how his flanking shrapnel fire, with low bursts, swept the trenches. The fire after a time gradually died away. Two days later my staff quarters were heavily shelled, but only the Corps Veterinary Officer was wounded.

On the evening of 27 September there was again a short burst of fire, but only from rifles, followed by a "Hurrah" which ran along the whole of the enemy line. Then a number of jam tins were thrown into our front line trenches with paper bands round them on which was written in Turkish: 'The Allies have taken 32km on the West Front from the Germans, with 27 guns and 20,000 prisoners.' This, then, was merely the loud and warlike expression of overflowing joy on the part of the enemy. This dealt with the initial success of the great battle in the Champagne on 25 September, but by 27 September this tremendous breakthrough – the world to date had not seen the like – had in the main failed, although the fighting raged furiously for a considerable period longer.

We were not in a position to advise the enemy in a similar manner of the victories of the Central Powers. We had to go carefully with our ammunition, and we simply had not sufficient jam tins to cover all the victories which during these months followed one another in a manner seldom previously seen as the result of the breakthrough of Mackensen by Tarnau-Gorlitz, and Hindenburg's attack in Poland, the collapsing Russian fortresses falling one after another like the pearls from a necklace. There were further victories to follow which would be of still closer interest to the enemy opposite.

So as September drew near to its close, it was known that the enemy was continually withdrawing forces from the peninsula and collecting them on the islands. Further arrivals of reinforcements from home seemed probable. Where would the enemy use them? The possibility of a fresh landing again demanded careful attention. Wehib Pasha was worried about his right flank. My old Kajaltepe position again became important. So a third Corps front was formed there and, with the consent of the Marshal, Wehib Pasha, on 2 October, in a very courteous letter, entrusted me with this command. I cannot suppress the thought that Wehib Pasha wished in this way to again make
Djafer Tayar Bey Deputy Commander-in-Chief of 14th Army Corps. All the same, the possibility of another landing was at that time an actual fact, as is known from the plans of the enemy which are now available.

Following the unsuccessful Suvla landing Sir Ian Hamilton had asked for reinforcements of about 100,000 men, which at first was refused. Nevertheless the Gallipoli campaign was to be carried on with all possible energy. For this reason England at first voted against the French idea of an autumn offensive in 1915 in Champagne. She had only given way unwillingly, because she feared this would be to the detriment of the Gallipoli campaign. The English were, therefore, pleasantly astonished when the French, in the early days of September, came forward with a plan to send an independent French Army of six divisions to the Dardanelles, which, under General Sarrail the successor to Gouraud, should, as an independent undertaking, land in October 1915 on the Asiatic coast and attack Tschanak Kale. The English would simultaneously attack on all the fronts in Gallipoli. A magnificent plan!

Two new English Divisions were immediately promised to relieve the French fighting at the southern extremity of Gallipoli, but Joffre, the French Commander-in-Chief, wished to await the results of the battle in Champagne, which was to him of first importance, and indicated 10 October as the embarkation date for the four French divisions destined for the Dardanelles. Including the two English Divisions, the task of transporting these troops from Marseilles to Lemnos would last until about the middle of November. By the end of November, at the latest, the new French Army would certainly be ready to attack the Asiatic coast.

But this brought the autumn of 1915 and with it a number of crises and surprises which rendered useless most calculations.

The results of the Battle of Anafarta had not been without effect on the Balkan States. Bulgaria, as the result of the Turks making a heavy sacrifice and assigning to her the railway to Dedeagatsch, including the railway station of Adrianople, mobilised on 22 September and declared herself ready to enter the war on the side of the Central Powers. Bulgaria was to attack Serbia at the moment when General Field Marshal von Mackensen with his army group from southern Hungary had, at the commencement of October, crossed the Danube and fallen on Serbia. This actually took place, but naturally the setting in motion of such masses of troops could not be hidden. Serbia felt the evil coming and reminded Greece, at the end of September, of her alliance against

Bulgaria and demanded from the Entente 150,000 reinforcements, which were to be landed at Salonica.

At this particular moment the great autumn offensive commenced on the Western Front in Champagne and at Loos. Germany had anticipated it, had everything ready in the west and did not allow anything to disturb her final preparations for her attack in the east on Serbia. Bound up with the final defeat of Serbia was the reopening of direct communication with Turkey and the ability to come to her assistance in her heavy struggles on the Dardanelles.

The Entente had to do something for Serbia. On the French battlefields every available man was being used. There was nothing left but to instruct Hamilton to withdraw a French and an English Division from the Dardanelles front and send them to Salonica. As a result of this Greece was terribly disappointed, because she saw in these measures the first steps towards the withdrawal from the whole Dardanelles campaign. So far Athens had still considered the entry into Constantinople as not impossible. Now, however, Greece broke her alliance, as Serbia was not only attacked by Bulgaria but also by other Great Powers. Venizelos was dismissed. The Entente could not, however, leave Serbia in the lurch.

This led to a conflict between the Allies, France wished to use the six divisions destined for the Dardanelles at Salonica. England was against this, because she saw her Dardanelles adventure coming to a halt. General Joffre himself visited London on 10 October and threw his personality and his position into the scales. England gave way. The first step towards the coming retirement from Gallipoli was completed.

The waves created in Europe by the discussions and troop movements which I have described reached as far as Wehib Pasha's tent in Gallipoli, and caused my previously described despatch to the Kajaltepe where the English were expected to make a new landing.

I revisited my old position with the greatest interest. Practically nothing new had been done. I pitched my tent in my old place. Following some very cold days we again had an almost tropical heat. I was not left long in this position, because six days later I received my appointment as Deputy Commander of 16th Army Corps with the Anafarta Group in Turschunkoi.

At 7:30 on 9 October with Major Welsch, who from now onwards till the close was my faithful attendant, I rode over the well known route past Kemalieri to Essad Pasha, and from there past the Large Anafarta to Mustapha Kemal Bey, my new Group Commander. He very kindly placed his car at my disposal so that I quickly arrived at my new headquarters, west of Turschunkoi, and as a result met my predecessor, Colonel Nicolai, who had gone sick.

As during the past months I had had many opportunities of getting to know the north and south fronts, it was particularly instructive to me to now be actively employed in the extreme north of the Anafarta Group.

The Corps had three divisions in the front line. On the right flank was the 11th Division (Infantry Regiments 33, 126, 122) holding the Kiretsclhtepe, under the tried Lt Col Willmer. With great effort trenches had been carved out of the rocky ground on this mountainous position. They suffered much from wind and the weather and often from the fire of the ships guns from the Gulf of Saros.

The centre of the Corps front held by 12th Division (Infantry Regiments 34, 35, 36), first under Col Heuck and later under Lt Col Remsi Bey, occupied an exceptionally low-lying position in the Anafarta Plain. From the heights of the Kavaktepe or Teketepe, I descended by narrow, deep trenches or winding paths which were concealed by camouflage from the enemy's view into the front line of the 12th Division.

The left flank was formed by my old 9th Division (Infantry Regiments 25, 27, 64), under Lt Col Sabri Bey, and held the important heights of Jussuftepe and Ismailtepe. As the hinterland could be seen from everywhere the divisional staffs and reserves lay fairly close behind the front line, under continual fire from the English. The zone of the 9th Division was very difficult to reach from the rear. During my first visit to my old battle comrades I unfortunately found that as a result of the extraordinarily heavy losses on Djonk Bahir only Lt Col Servet Bey of the commanders, and very few officers were left.

On the exposed right flank the Army Corps had only one danger point, which was the small but very protected bay of Edje Liman. This was defended by the two *Gendarmerie* Battalions Brussa and Gallipoli under command of Major Tachsim Bey who, on 7 and 8 August, had so heroically held the Ismailtepe. In addition the Navy had laid a number of fished up Russian mines in the entrance to Edje Liman.

The Corps staff quarters lay in a valley west of Turschunkoi, at first in tents with the command post on Teketepe. One by one, we built small clay huts in the sides of the valley which made the Marshal exclaim during his first visit, "In what kind of gipsy camp are you living here, then?" Perhaps it did not look very well, but it was extremely practicable, because in spite of the many bomb attacks we had not been disturbed, although a labour company lying close to us, which in spite of oft-repeated orders had failed to hide itself, lost 13 dead and 43 wounded on the evening of 17 December. I had obtained as my Chief of Staff my trusty Major Hunussi Bey.

The tactical position of 16th Army Corps was characteristically defined by the mighty, fortress-like heights, which we held everywhere in a firm grip, while the
English, deep below us, occupied the far-reaching flat plain and the shores of the Salt Sea or Suvla Bay. With a glass every movement on the English side was easily recognisable. The many scattered trees on the plains only in very few places hindered our view. This gave the hill a feeling of safety.

This feeling was considerably increased by the presence of the well-organised heavy artillery which, allied to the field artillery, gave this position, so powerful in itself, a still firmer backbone. On 13 October the energetic Major Senftleben arrived as commander of the heavy artillery, with a number of German officers.

The right half section was covered by the 1st Battalion of heavy artillery commanded by Captain Haehnert, with five batteries (two

12cm howitzer batteries, one 15cm battery, one 12cm Mauser battery and one 88cm battery). Captain Knab held the left section with his 2nd Battalion, consisting of two 12cm howitzer batteries, one 12cm gun battery, one long 24cm gun battery and one 21cm Mauser battery. Almost all these batteries had German commanders and if, with the exception of the 8.8cm gun battery under Captain Volmer, they were not modern and they had to carefully husband their scanty ammunition, it was still quite another form of fighting as compared with the months of April to June on the southern portion of Gallipoli, when, with doubtful hearts, we clung to the ground without any firm support. If we had only had modern guns and sufficient ammunition it would have been quite impossible for the English to remain in occupation of their low-lying positions.

I still have the scheme for one of the few large trench raids which were to be prepared by a heavy artillery bombardment. For these operations each field battery was allowed 80 shells, each howitzer battery 20 shells, and the batteries of field artillery on the flank were allowed four rounds each. Those who are accustomed to the modern mass consumption of the world war in the west will laugh at these figures.

The bringing of the heavy guns into positions on the heights proved extraordinarily difficult owing to the bad roads. 24 buffaloes were insufficient, because they did not pull equally. Hundreds of soldiers had to accomplish this, with long ropes.

The whole artillery of 5th Army was under the command of General Gressman, an officer who had been tried out on the Western Front and who handled his artillery in the most modern manner. The famous Colonel Wehrle was commander of the heavy artillery of 5th Army. On the staffs of the group commanders and army corps efficient artillerymen were employed, whose names have gained particular fame on Gallipoli; for instance, in addition to my Major Senftleben, Majors Lierau, Fensky, Vonberg, Schmidt-Kolbow and Lieutenants Klein, Diesinger and others. In all 500 Germans were now deployed on Gallipoli.

Thus we were able to dispose of our time in a somewhat more

generous fashion. This was also apparent from the general daily dispositions. If Hamilton had so far swung the hammer and we formed the anvil, the hammer was now slowly passing over into the hands of the Marshal.

A large-scale offensive with the assistance of gas was in course of preparation. German experts arrived. Behind the front the troops were trained as storm troops. Marching exercises were again begun. Storming materials prepared and the very wasted teams of the field artillery were well fed, and brought into condition. Shortly, there now blew another wind for us, which became still stronger when, as the result of the splendid Serbian campaign, the long-desired direct communication between Turkey and Germany was reopened and the Balkan trains travelled undisturbed from Berlin to Constantinople. In November the eagerly awaited ammunition arrived, and from Austria a splendid 24cm motor howitzer battery which was used on Ismailtepe, and in December a 15cm howitzer battery which was sent to the Southern Group.

About this time the English Army command on Gallipoli issued an instruction about the Turkish Army which was later found in a battalion dug-out. This proved to be fairly accurate as far as the distribution of the forces was concerned but stated that the morale of the Turkish troops had sunk very low, that the increased artillery activity was only intended to raise the spirits of the troops in the trenches, and that for the same reason the fable had been circulated about the arrival of new guns from Germany.

This instruction continued: 'Turkish soldiers see in the arrival of these guns a mixed blessing, as they believe that their arrival will coincide with a large-scale attack on our position, which they regard with very little pleasure.' This last sentence is perhaps true of many Turkish soldiers. It illustrates, however, the manner in which the Entente attempted to raise the good spirits of their troops by casting doubt upon those of ours.

The month of November was not very pleasant on Gallipoli. A storm raged for four days over the peninsula. The few old Turks who had remained in the village of Turschunkoi declared that they had never lived through a similar. Cloudbursts which ended in snowstorms filled the trenches full of water, burst into the shelters and flooded the whole peninsula. The 12th Division occupying the low-lying plain was particularly badly hit. Such masses of water streamed like cascades down the steep communication trenches leading to the heights that the troops hurrying up were carried away, were unable to save themselves and part of them drowned. As if this were not sufficient, almost immediately after this flood a heavy frost commenced, which again carried off a large number of victims. As a result of their soaked clothes the 12th Division lost 90 men during this inclement weather and the 11th Division also suffered heavy losses.

The English, however, on the plains were in a much worse plight, as all the water from the heights and cliffs bore down on them, 280 men were drowned in the trenches on the Anafarta Plain, and 16,000 men with frozen feet had to be taken on the ships.

The activity of the enemy infantry limited itself during these last few months of 1915 to patrol activity and occasional bursts of fire. No large-scale attacks took place. The activity of the land and ships' guns continually increased, and enemy aircraft were particularly active.

This severe weather demanded increased care for the troops. The 26th Division lying behind the front, commanded by Col Essad Bey who, like myself, had been director of a department in the War Office and with whom I had always worked in the best harmony, sent me regimental reliefs who, unfortunately, were quite untrustworthy Arabs.

Nevertheless, as a result of this help, I was able to arrange that each of the three front divisions always had one regiment behind the lines, for the purpose of resting and training in attack. For the latter purpose an exercise ground was prepared by *Turschunkoi*, with trenches and wire entanglements in the English fashion.

We also issued clothing of every kind, such as fur waist coats, fur coats (for the sentries), scarves, sabots, waterproof coats, and, finally, civilian trousers for lack of others. Our supplies were not nearly sufficient and a just distribution

CAMP ABANDONED BY THE ENGLISH AT SMALL KEMIKLI
20 December, 1915

AT ARI BURNU—GUNS LEFT BEHIND BY THE ENGLISH

was very difficult. It seemed that the Quartermaster General must have requisitioned anything and everything from textile and shoe shops in Constantinople, because we received the most wonderful kinds of underclothes and shoes which may have admirably suited the Pera Quarter in Constantinople but which were absolutely unusable for war purposes on the cliffs and in the miry soil of Gallipoli.

The health of the troops needed the most continuously careful watching, as well as their protection from the weather, which in summer had given us no cause for anxiety.

A characteristic picture in this connection is given by a report of losses of the 16th Army Corps, at the same time an indication of what the Turkish War Office were continuously called upon to send as reinforcements to the Gallipoli front. Between 14 October and 9 December 1915, the losses of 16th Army Corps were 509 killed, 2,158 wounded, 3,386 sick and 2,159 having a change of climate (as described in a previous chapter), making a total loss of 8,212 men during a period of two months, from an Army Corps of three divisions approximately 12,000 strong. In considering these figures it must be taken into account that the bodily resistance of the Turk is generally much less than that of the European. The reasons for this, apart from climatic reasons, are insufficient nourishment and care of the body, the lack of any kind of hygienic arrangements and the terrible amount of vermin. In peace time a sick list of 15 percent of the strength is quite normal.

We now experienced continuously wet, cold, unfriendly weather. I also fell a victim and had to be sent for a few weeks with para-typhoid to Constantinople, in spite of the sacrificing attention of the very energetic and circumspect Dr Baader, who was attached to my staff.

This was a period extremely full of work, as the settlement of many questions demanded my presence in the front line, which took a great deal of time on account of the distances and changes in altitude. The training of the troops behind the line needed continual watching and spurring on, and in the office I was awaited with questions and proposals.

It was always refreshing for me to join the common German mess *à la franca*, which had been made possible by the efforts of the war volunteer Mors. Even a common Christmas festival with a candle-lit Christmas tree – it was a sort of fir bush which grew in this part – was possible with Majors Welsch, Senftleben, Fenski, Lt Orthmann, Drs Baader and Mors, whom we naturally called *Mors Imperator*.

While we were occupied during these last months of 1915 in steady, careful work, overcoming all difficulties and tying to prepare, with German and Austrian help, the Turkish troops for an attack which was to drive the Entente from the peninsula, our enemy at the same moment were carefully weighing measures which would then have interested us still more than they do today.

As I have already stated, Joffre had visited London on 10 October 1915, and obtained the consent of England to the despatch of considerable forces to Salonica to the assistance of Serbia. The very next day Kitchener tried to obtain from Hamilton an estimate of what losses must be anticipated in a retirement from the Gallipoli Peninsula by the Entente. Hamilton considered such a proposition to be unthinkable. It would cost at least the half of men, horses, guns, stores, et cetera.

Three days later the meritorious Sir Ian Hamilton was recalled. General Munro, who up to that date had commanded an army in France, was sent out in his place with instructions to report in his turn on the future of the Gallipoli campaign. He decided on a complete retirement from the campaign, the liquidation of which would cost from 30 to 40 percent loss. His estimate was thus considerably lower.

After a certain amount of struggling Kitchener definitely accepted the thought of an evacuation. Before he reached a final decision, however, he was torn by conflicting emotions, which is quite understandable. It was a difficult birth with great pain, because the bitter recognition of the necessity of an evacuation was a painful matter

The fleet assembled before the Dardanelles. Not under the command of the leader, Admiral de Robeck, but under his Chief of Staff, Admiral Keyes, by agreement with Vice Admiral Wemyss. Keyes had, during the summer, worked out a far-reaching plan, complete to the smallest detail for a fresh breakthrough the Dardanelles with the fleet. He guaranteed the success and was prepared himself to head the leading squadron.

The idea was shortly as follows: A squadron of eight old battleships, with the necessary covering ships, was shortly before dawn to sail into the Narrows and as soon as daylight broke steam at full speed up the waterway. With the help of smoke screens, minesweepers, et cetera, it was estimated that at least half of the ships would reach Nagara and so take the batteries at Tchanak Kale in the rear. A squadron of modern battleships and battlecruisers were to simultaneously attack the fort from the front while a third squadron of cruisers was to keep them under indirect fire from across the peninsula. Each phase of the attack was accurately worked out. The battle was to be preceded by a simultaneous attack by the troops on land on all fronts, which was to be continued two or three days before the battleships and battlecruisers received the order for the final attack.

On 28 October, Keyes reached London, with de Robeck's consent, to personally explain there his plan. On 2 November a new War Council was formed there to take over supreme command of the Army and the Fleet. This reached no decision but decided to send Kitchener to the Dardanelles. He arrived there on 9 November and reached the conviction – contrary to the accepted opinion in Germany that the land army could further maintain its positions on Gallipoli, but that the powerful fleet attack was no good. He proposed a further new landing in the Bay of Alexandretta. The War Council, for very understandable reasons, was not in agreement with this. On the contrary, it decided in principle to accept the evacuation of Gallipoli. De Robeck, however, urged that at least the southern front should be maintained in the interests of the fleet. He went on leave and Wemyss took over the command of the fleet. Wemyss tried by every means in his power at least obtain permission for the fleet attack alone.

Even at the conference with the French on 8 December, where the final decision was taken to evacuate the Dardanelles in favour of Salonica, Wemyss with Keyes still supported and insisted on the fleet attack, so much so that Monro, who was in favour of the evacuation, forbade his commanding generals to even discuss this question with the admirals without his consent.

All struggles were thus unavailing. The decision to evacuate was firmly established, including the southern front, as without the Eltschitepe (Achi Baba) could not be held in the long run. It had not been found possible to storm this hill.

CHAPTER XV
The Entente Evacuate Gallipoli

Rumours and suggestions that the enemy were going to evacuate Gallipoli naturally swarmed round us on Gallipoli. I, personally, did not believe in such a possibility because, taking into account the English character, I considered it out of the question that they would give up such a hostage of their own free will and without a fight. However, I was mistaken.

On 19 December, a powerful attack was made on our Southern Group, which was completely repulsed. Opposite us there was peace with the exception of the usual fire from the enemy. About 11 o'clock in the morning our howitzer battery on Ismailtepe, with a field battery, had shelled Lala Baba, as a result of which Ismailtepe was immediately shelled by several enemy batteries. The usual picture.

That evening Major Senftleben, commander of the heavy artillery of the Army Corps, visited me to report. I asked him whether he had noticed any diminution in the enemy artillery fire. He immediately produced his fire records and proved to me that the enemy land batteries had maintained their accustomed rate of fire on our positions throughout 18 and 19 December. In addition the infantry fire from the trenches was as usual. The enemy, during the last few days, had worked hard to improve his position Lala Baba-Softatepe-Karakoldah. That appeared to indicate the intention of a stubborn resistance.

The only exceptional item of interest was the large number of ships lying in Imbros harbour, still this we had often seen before.

On the night of 20 December, about 3 a.m., Hunussi Bey came to me with a report from the 9th Division that the commander of Infantry Regiment 25 had seen from his observation post that the enemy had lit two great lanterns on the coast – or so he expressed himself in his broken German – one in the neighbourhood of the Salt Sea, the other at the mouth of the Asmakdere. In actual fact, as we later ascertained, these were two dumps which had been set on fire. Between the two lanterns lay, parallel with the coast, eight cruisers or battleships with many small warships, and behind these many transports between which and the coast an active traffic with lighters and boats of all sorts was taking place.

That must either indicate the commencement of the English retirement, or we had to expect a large-scale attack tomorrow. The immediate thing to do was to see whether the transports were being loaded or unloaded. An immediate enquiry from the 9th Division led to the reply that they were not yet able to ascertain in which direction the boats full of troops were rowing and they could not establish how deeply the ships were loaded.

Simultaneously with asking this question the alarm was sent to all the divisions, the reserves brought close up and orders issued to immediately send out strong officer patrols to approach the enemy trenches to establish whether they were occupied and report forthwith any evacuation by signal. It was urgently necessary to establish the enemy's intention, and in the case of evacuation to immediately drive forward with all available forces to the seashore. The artillery was to open fire on the coastal area and the landing stages. It was impossible to do more at the moment. A clearing of the position depended on the resolution with which the patrols advanced towards the enemy lines. Yes, this was the only possible way of clearing up the position, because about 3 in the morning a steadily increasing mist commenced rising which hid the full moon which so far shone, and clouded the English activities in a curtain which we were neither able to pierce nor penetrate. God had been stronger than Allah! I awaited with impatience the results of the advancing officers' patrols.

In the meantime I received continual reports from the divisions which, as is usually the case, were so conflicting that I could not obtain any clear picture.

The 9th Division reported that the two great lanterns had now disappeared, but in their place fires could be seen at other spots and light signals were apparent in the enemy's lines. An evacuation by the English appeared to me to be more and more probable. I therefore ordered a strong patrol of pioneers to follow the officers' patrol, with instructions to render useless enemy mines.

In the meantime the patrols had reached the enemy's front line on both the mountainous wings of Kiretschtepe and Mestantepe, where they were received with heavy fire. We heard the sounds of battle. Only in the centre, in front of the 12th Division, calm reigned.

Advanced Group Headquarters, which Fehsi Pasha had a short while previously taken over from Mustapha Kemal Bey, now began to get active. There, acting on the conviction that the enemy were bringing new troops ashore, instructions were issued for the defence of the front line reserves to strengthen them and, at 5:20 in the morning,
large patrols were ordered forward to test the enemy's front line. I had long ago done all that. Ten minutes following the
receipt of the last group orders I was able to report that in front of the 12th Division Lt Mehmed Effendi had already reached the English reserve line of trenches, which lay close behind the front line. There was now no longer any doubt that the enemy was actually evacuating. I ordered the infantry of the 3rd Division to advance and the field artillery to follow up.

Then – about 6 in the morning – I rode myself to the corps battle command post on Teketepe, so that with the approaching dawn I could immediately see for myself what the exact position was. On the way there, the usual picture of stubborn resistance. I heard from both wings, continually clearer, the noise of battle and met many wounded on their way to the dressing stations and field hospitals. They told of stubborn enemy resistance. Was it true that the enemy was not evacuating without a fight, and was the more cautious conclusion of the group justified? Did the enemy wish to draw the 12th Division into the low-lying ground, into a trap, in order to overwhelm them during their advance from both commanding flanks and destroy them, and then to storm forward themselves through the opened breach and take our splendid high positions from the rear? Shortly before I left I had spoken to the Commander of the 11th Division on the telephone, who advised me of unaltered, stubborn machine gun fire on the Kiretschtepe, and with the 9th Division, who reported that on the Mestantepe the enemy had only just attempted to repair their barbed wire, which we had destroyed, but they had been driven back by bombs. This did not look like evacuation.

All my doubt, however, disappeared as with the growing dawn from the command post I recognised through the mist fires burning on the enemy's side. That could only be his depots and material which he grudged us. Then I saw the infantry of the 9th Division quite clearly, climbing the Mestantepe. The beggars are actually evacuating! Now forward, after them. Catch them before they are all on their ships. I telephoned urgent commands in this sense to all points. Perhaps the enemy still held his second line Lala Baba-Softatepe-Karakoldagh.

I issued the necessary orders to carry through on the divisional fronts to the coast with the artillery in close support; the many mines to be rendered useless, the English trenches to be consolidated facing the sea; divided the routes forward and ordered new telephone wires be laid down. Then it was a wonderful feeling of freedom to be able to walk out into the open, and undisturbed by enemy fire, have a clear view of the situation. The horses were brought up, and across the open, as if we were at peace, we rode forward by Baka Baba, Jussuftepe, in the direction of Mestantepe, Lala Baba. We crossed our front line trenches and there we stood in 'no-man's-land' between the opposing front lines.

Mines continually detonated around us and still cost many unnecessary lives. I took with me five Arabs and sent them ahead to look for mines. My staff had never remained so respectfully behind me! We passed one small bush which apparently had been the aim of many nightly patrols since we had become anchored here several months before.

The dead lay thickly round this bush in all stages of putrefaction, as nobody had been able to fetch them away. I still remember one Englishman with a skull and large typically long protruding teeth. He had tried to be very clever and had pushed a big sandbag in front of him with his hands, as shelter. There he lay with a round hole in the middle of his forehead, the bony fingers still holding the sandbag on which the skull was resting. Jackals, birds and the merciless sun of Gallipoli had quite cleaned his bones. Close to him, but already stripped, lay a still fresh corpse – a stupid Turk who, as I was told, had tried to desert the previous evening, but a following bullet had reached him in this hedge.

From Ismailtepe towards the Mestantepe ran a communication trench, a relic of the August battles, which lay between the two front lines. It was often used during the night for crawling towards the enemy positions. A Turk and an Englishman must have suddenly met one another there, and in the hand-to-hand fighting the Englishman had driven his knife into the back of the Turk from above, while the Turk had simultaneously driven his dagger into his enemy's vitals. There we found the two skeletons, locked together, lying against the side of the trench – a typical picture of the stubborn fighting on Gallipoli.

Today, however, we met no enemy. The retreat was entirely successful, even if considerably assisted by night and mist. On the other hand, the Turks, in spite of every effort, could not be driven forward. The officers' patrols sent forward during the night would, with a little more initiative, certainly have been able at some point or another to break through into the English trenches considerably earlier, and this would have rendered possible the capture from the flank of the still covering machine guns. I had the impression that unuttered, the following opinion reigned: 'Why unnecessary losses? The English are going away on their own.' As I have already said, the Turks are masters of passive resistance, and their failure as soldiers lies in their passive acceptance of anything that comes along rather than in initiative to overcome it. As a result of this we did not capture a single Englishman.

They were forced, however, to leave us their works, their material, and their stores, as the result of their secret flight. I was very astonished at the condition of the English front line. All sorts of waste, jam tins, paper, cake boxes, et cetera, were either thrown over the parapet or lay about inside. It is true that certain extremely necessary hygienic arrangements stood in the trenches in the shape of large tins. I had always thought that the English would have been more hygienic. On the Turkish side things were much cleaner. For particular purposes special side trenches were built. It is true that the Turks had neither jam tins, nor cake boxes, nor papers, to throw around.

From the tactical point of view the English trenches were admirably sited, with splendid flanking effects. Millions of sandbags had been used in their construction. The battery positions were excellently sited. The more I penetrated into the rear positions and saw the depots and stores on the coast, the greater was my astonishment at this superfluity of material, this well-organised control, suitable grouping and extreme tidiness.

They had a very good communicating system with well known English names, such as Oxford Street, Common Street, Piccadilly, or indicating names such as Dump Street, Well Way, with directing signs and warning signs and traverses if they lay under our fire. In addition, magnificent telephone communications with exchanges like those in a large town. On the shore, numerous landing stages and light railways. I saw all this with envy.

As I reached the strongly fortified Lala Baba, on the shores of the sea, I looked backwards at our positions on the other side of the hills. I readily realised that even if they were less comfortable, from a tactical point of view they appeared to be almost untakable, and formed a wide and threatening bow round the flat shore. How grateful we should be to the Marshal, who, grasping the situation, had thrown all his energy into seizing all and any available troops from the whole peninsula and getting them here in time, and also to the brave *Askers* who had defended them.

Today the thoughts of the *Askers* certainly ran in quite other directions. The hungry Turks swarmed out of their narrow trenches and flowed like locusts across the English trenches, depots, and stores. As was their custom they received everything quietly, calmly, without any expression of joy; still, they were not now to be held either by the orders of their officers, or by exploding mines, or by the broadsides from English warships which fired wherever they saw troops congregate. Cakes, jam, corned beef, biscuits! These were unthought-of delicacies, and here they were laying freely all around. This was something quite different from the eternal *bulgar*, or *bakla*, or *fasulia* (beans). In addition, woollen and rubber covers, coats, boots, puttees, et cetera. What more could they wish for? I allowed them free liberty that day. They had richly earned it.

Corps orders were issued about 10 o'clock from Lala Baba, giving the tactical and administrative instructions covering the new situation, and I specially included an instruction to each division to immediately appoint a special booty commissioner. I did this because the booty was simply prodigious, and I saw that only the closest attention and clear organisation would save those enormous quantities of such necessary stocks for the common good and protect them from senseless destruction. The settlement of this booty question caused me a great deal of trouble and considerable annoyance. At that time everybody regarded the enormous masses of booty lying around in the same light as a child who is confronted with a heaped-up Christmas tree.

The English had left everything as it was, because a removal under our eyes was simply not possible. Speaking roughly, the booty in my Corps area alone between Kiretschtepe and Asmakdere consisted of 300km of telephone wire, 180km of barbed wire, millions of sandbags, 300 splendid double-walled tents lined internally with yellow, guns, weapons, munitions, clothing, entrenching materials, food supplies, sanitary, telephone, light railway and ship building material. Two mules were the only living things left.

Stocks of tinned food, house high, had been drenched with petrol and fired. Stocks of flour had had hydrochloric acid poured over them. We succeeded in putting out the fires and saving a large quantity in spite of the English warships which patrolled up and down the coast like watchdogs and sought to hinder this work with their fire.

I will only just mention the enormous amount of splendid sides of bacon, each beautifully packed in a clean white bag. The Turks greatly detest anything to do with the *domus* (pig), so that the Germans received untouched the whole of these supplies. Two days later I was able to despatch two wagons loaded with bacon to the Germans in the Southern Group.

The letters and writings left in the dug-outs were also very interesting. The attempt to destroy everything was easily recognisable, but it had not everywhere succeeded. A certain amount had still escaped destruction. In this way I found Operation Order no.15 of the 32nd Infantry Brigade dated 17 December 1915, which gave a good picture of the evacuation by the infantry, even if it was difficult to understand it on account of the many curiously chosen English names for local places. The greater part of the troops of the 9th English Army Corps had apparently already been taken off in the preceding nights. Under command of the divisional commander of the 111th Infantry Division, the 88th Infantry Brigade – originally belonging to the 29th Infantry Division – and the 32nd and 33rd Brigades were detailed to act as a rearguard on the night of the 19–20 December, to cover the retirement. The strength of these brigades, or in any case the 32nd, consisted on that particular night of only 1,500 men with a sanitary and pioneer detachment in addition. Extremely accurate, and, in our opinion, too accurate orders and timetables, controlled the retirement by sections from the four defence lines lying one behind the other

The last English must have left the peninsula about 8 o'clock in the morning from the landing places, of which two lay to the north and south of Large Kemikli, and one north of Small Kemikli. (See E. on the map.)

Detailed orders controlled the laying of minefields and mines. They were for the greater part between the parapet and the barbed wire entanglements as well as in the paths left through the entanglements, and had already been prepared for action during the night of 18–19 December. In addition, following the departure of the last troops, all the crossroads as far as the coast were protected with contact mines, as were the ammunition rooms and the water tanks.

A descriptive picture of the manner in which the retreat was conducted is provided by the last defence of Kiretschtepe. Here, right up to the last moment, we were received with machine gun fire, and this spot must have been held by particularly selected volunteers. At the last moment they threw their machine guns into the grave which had been dug alongside, hurled sandbags on top of them and rapidly retired to the coast. They could not lose their way in the darkness because thick chalk lines right and left marked the road. Any possible side alleys were barred with barbed wire. In spite of the very difficult mountain paths across the Karakoldagh – I went over them next morning – the last defenders of the front line, rapidly retiring between these two white lines, reached with safety the torpedo boats awaiting them.

Close in the neighbourhood of the embarkation point was the headquarters of my special colleague, the general commanding the English 9th Army Corps. No larger than my mud hut by Turschunkoi, but being blown out of the side of the hill it was absolutely shellproof, discreetly withdrawn from the noise of the depot, and with a magnificent view across the steep, high, deeply cleft coast to the Aegean Sea, and the snow peak of the Island of Samothrace. Now he was on his road with his men to Salonica to try and lend the Russians a helping hand from this point – again in vain.

I must admit that the English had splendidly prepared and very cleverly carried out their retreat, even if, as the opponent, I found their success rather painful. The English had simultaneously retired from the Ariburnu position, as I soon learnt on my ride to the coast. They had commenced their retirement by the exploding of an enormous mine under the front Turkish line. This scarcely friendly farewell card cost us 60 dead. The road to the coast here was very much shorter, but led, in the black night, across steep barren hilly country, while the few roads to the coast were blocked with mines. So the enemy here also had disappeared by the time the Turks reached the narrow beach, where they were immediately received by fire from the ships' guns.

Now came a period of well-earned peace, must be the thought of every reader, but exactly the opposite occurred. Our work increased steadily. The enemy was still in position on the southern front. We heard that this was to be continually occupied by the Entente as a second Gibraltar.
Quite possible, but we had other ideas about it.

Under the mighty impulse of Liman's energy, the work of the 5th

Army was now directed towards preparing a powerful attack on the enemy on the southern front. For this purpose rich supplies of war material of all sorts from the splendid booty was sent to the Southern Group, as well as special troops consisting of the best bomb throwers and men trained as patrols. In addition, by 22 December 1915, the 12th Division and the bulk of the heavy artillery were withdrawn from the front of my Army Corps, and sent to the Southern Group. This, in conjunction with the new tasks for the coastal defence, necessitated a rearrangement of the Army Corps. The Anarfarta Group wound up and the 16th Army Corps placed direct under Army Headquarters. In addition to my own divisions, the Marshal entrusted mc with the training of the 6th and 8th Divisions in methods of attack. The last-mentioned Division made a quite excellent impression.

In addition to the exercise grounds at Turschunkoi, a second was built by Large Anarfarta. Workshops for storming materials had to be built, and every day instructions and discussions over the best methods of attack took place shortly, everything was being done at top speed to prepare the necessary troops and material for the attack.

A letter from Major Senftleben, my former artillery commander, written to me on 4 January 1916, from Salim Bev Tschiflik, is descriptive of the spirit and the conception of the position prevailing among the Southern Group. He wrote:

> I am now commander of the heavy artillery of the southern portion from Kirthedere to the shores of the Dardanelles, and have two old and 10 new batteries under my command, among which is the Austrian 24cm howitzer battery with 1,200 rounds. I also have ample ammunition for the other batteries, so that we are shooting from early till late and somewhat facilitating with German shells the retreat of the enemy. The many Red Cross cars which we see on the enemy's side are not only carrying ammunition! In order to stir things up a bit I have brought my 15cm quick-firing howitzer battery so far forward that from early morn we can also treat Seddil Bahir to some of our good ammunition. I await each dawn with impatience to be able to reopen firing,

and you, Colonel, can very easily imagine what joy such artillery activity with such good observation affords us, and with what zest we sit from 7 in the morning till dusk in our observation posts but in my opinion the enemy is withdrawing slowly but certainly. I deduce that from the daily reports of the batteries and from my own observation. Many batteries are now only firing with one or two guns. I personally believe that in 8–14 days the enemy will have retired, if not earlier, but I am satisfied that this time he will not get away quite undisturbed or undamaged. Unfortunately the infantry cannot be induced to attack

On 7 January 1916, the 12th Division attacked an advanced section of the enemy front on our extreme right wing, to improve the position there before the intended main attack. The strong resistance of the enemy was here particularly noticeable. In spite of this he had already commenced his retirement. On 26 December, the War Office in London had already issued orders that the southern front was to be evacuated before 10 January. During the night of 8–9 January these orders were carried out. Thus Gallipoli was finally given up by the Entente.

The enemy, to speed up his embarkation, had embarked at various points along the west coast as well as at the southern extremity. Our artillery was still able to sink one loaded transport. Although the Turks storming after were held up by mines and ships' fire, they reached the coast before daybreak. Everywhere the usual picture. The booty was here perhaps still greater than with us, as the embarkation had been more hurried. Here, for instance, lay hundreds of horses in long rows in their lines, poisoned or shot.

For me personally, it was especially interesting to visit the Southern Group on 11 January, and follow the route in the Sigindere valley, which I had so often followed in summer, right across the English positions as far as the sea, and then across the southern corner of the Gallipoli Peninsula, as far as the mighty beach castle at Seddil Bahr. Everywhere heaps of booty, and everywhere masses of wandering, plundering Turks. In addition, plenty of shells from the English ships, so that finally Major Welsch, who was walking close

CAMP OF CLAY HUTS OF INFANTRY REGIMENT 25, NEAR PALAMUTLUK
4 October, 1915

BIRD'S-EYE VIEW OF KIRETSCHTEPE
Taken from an aeroplane, 25 October, 1915

to me, was wounded by a splinter from a bursting shell which exploded close behind us. In the air, a battle between 'planes which ended in the destruction of the English. We saw the body of the aviator fall like a doll, with outstretched arms and legs, into the sea, the aeroplane fluttering behind. Torpedo boats hastened up, sought vainly for the aviator and took the 'plane in tow. That was my final war picture on Gallipoli.

A few figures which have since been published will indicate the stubbornness of the fighting on the small peninsula. The total numbers engaged on both sides were:

The Entente: 539,000 men.
The Turks: 310,000 men
Totalling: 849,000 men

Of this quantity fell, were wounded or missing:
On the side of the Entente 180,282 men, including officers.
On the side of the Turks 165,371 men, including officers.

In addition to these were the losses as the result of sickness, which reached, on the Turkish side, a figure of 85,938 men, but I do not know the figures for the Entente.

On 12th January instructions were received for the transfer of the main portion of the 5th Army to Thracia. I was ordered to proceed with the 16th Army Corps (11th and 12th Divisions) to Adrianople.

The next day I left Gallipoli, to proceed, via Constantinople, to Adrianople, while the divisions commenced their march on foot by Keschan and Usunköprü. I only commanded the Corps for a short time longer, as I had to again resume my former position as departmental director in the War Office.

For the moment there did not seem to be any immediate prospect for the further use of 5th Army, although, in my opinion, one lay very close to us. Now that the greater part of the Anglo-French Dardanelles army had joined the new Salonica expedition, it seemed to me that we ought to have followed our former foes to that spot. The Turkish attack could very well have taken this army in the right flank and the rear, and, in combination with the German Bulgarian army, smoked out this nest. The German High Command refused, however, to consider such a proposal.

A Bulgarian officer told me that in the autumn of 1916 on Gallipoli, how greatly they had regretted in Bulgaria the early ending of the offensive on Salonica, because the Bulgarian soldier, although excellent and unholdable in a steady offensive, is not suitable to support a long defensive and lead a necessitous and dangerous life in narrow trenches.

It is interesting to note that actually at this point, in the autumn of 1918, commenced the first collapse, which drew the whole structure of the Central Powers with it in its fall.

CHAPTER XVI
Conclusion

Thus the Dardanelles campaign of the Entente came to an unexpected end. What had commenced with a flourish of trumpets, ended as a charade.

If we glance once again at the varied incidents which pass like a cinematograph picture before our eyes, if we remember:

The first purely naval battles,
The fleet attempts to break through into the Dardanelles,
The approaching armada with an army on its decks,
The widely differing attempts to land, some successful, some beaten back,
The stubborn fighting on the dreary, of Gallipoli, ploughed-up ground
The brave *Asker*, sticking stubbornly to the soil of his homeland under the frightful combined fire of the Anglo-French fleet and the land forces,

if we review all these incidents in one single glance, I feel that the reader must agree with me that never in the course of the world's previous history has a campaign been fought so rich in dramatic pictures of such differing types of warfare which, in spite of its wealth of incidents, has been compressed into such narrow limits of time, and space, as in this particular case.

It is in itself a real treasure trove of experience in the numerous branches of military science, because every conceivable class of weapons were used here, including the floating, flying, and those below water, except cavalry, and it was just a born cavalryman who was our trusted leader.

The battle against land and sea mines and whole minefields, the battle of the ships against the land forts, their conduct in battle in confined spaces, their effect on the landing and in the land fighting later, the use of submarines, and the methods of protection used against these, long-range guns, or howitzers, the combination of land army and fleet, and the resulting distribution of responsibilities of command, the defence of long stretches of coastline, and the attack on these in the teeth of the enemy, and finally the months of bitter fighting between the field armies, the one magnificently equipped with most modern material, the other scantily equipped with anything that could be scraped together – these are all questions of great military importance. Here we find practical examples of them all.

Once we have escaped from the military writings of the immediate post-war period, which first concentrates on establishing in their proper relation the events of this vast world war, a period must naturally follow, during which the historically established incidents will be carefully studied to draw from them, for future use, the necessary strategic, tactical, and other lessons and conclusions.

Then this campaign will become more honoured. I have intentionally refrained from writing in any way from the point of view of military science. For one thing I lack the material, and perhaps the qualification. This must be the task of the Government archives, when possible, with the help of Turkish documents. I have here confined myself to
giving a general picture of the battles, as I promised in my introduction, drawn from my own notes, some comrades' diaries, and based on reports from authoritative sources.

The aim of this chapter is to awaken renewed interest for the Dardanelles operations from which so much can be learnt, and on the course of which German officers had such a definite influence.

The English take a far deeper interest in these battles. They already possess a great deal of literature on this subject. This is also understandable, because England regarded this campaign as one with which her own prestige was closely connected. Further, in England, at widely differing periods, there was still absolutely no doubt as to a successful issue of the campaign.

For instance, Churchill stated in Dundee on 5 June 1915:

The army of Sir Ian Hamilton, the fleet of Admiral de Robeck are separated only a few miles from a victory such as this war has not yet seen. When I speak of victory, I am not referring to those victories which crowd the daily placards of any newspaper. I am speaking of victory in the sense of a brilliant and formidable fact, shaping the destinies of nations and shortening the duration of the war. Beyond those few miles of ridge and scrub on which our soldiers, our French comrades, our gallant Australians, and our New Zealand fellow subjects are now battling, lie the downfall of a hostile empire, the destruction of an enemy's fleet and army, the fall of a world-famous Capital, and probably the accession of powerful allies.

To say that was at least hasty, to think it was in a sense justified, because, during these battles, all the advantages were in a quite exceptional manner on the side of the Entente. The more astonishing, therefore, was the victory of the Turks, and consequently the more interesting and instructive to follow the reasons which led to such a result now that we know the full course of events.

There were four factors on the Turkish side which were mainly responsible for the successful ending of the campaign. The energetic personality of the Marshal, the brave Anatolian *Asker*, the ample supplies of small arms ammunition and the beautiful, clear, flowing drinking water, available on the heights of Gallipoli even in the hottest summer.

The decisive influence of the Marshal, the Prussian Cavalry General Liman von Sanders Pasha, stands clearly revealed by the many varied critical turning points in the battles. He was tirelessly active, forceful, and full of capacity to take decisions. If a Turkish statesman in Constantinople is reported to have said: "It's a good thing that we have Liman Pasha on Gallipoli. The soldiers fear him more than they do the English," that is not quite true, but they had a wholesome respect for him, which was just as well.

This does not mean that I am in any way attempting to depreciate the merits of all the intermediary organisations, from the group commanders to the group leaders among the troops. They were absolutely necessary to success, generally achieved excellent results, and were often not merely executive organs, but, on their own initiative, without waiting for orders, organised resistance, heartened the troops, thought out improvements of positions and carried these out, in other words, worked creatively. But, when success stood trembling in the balance, it was always the Marshal on whose decision hung the whole, and he took the heaviest responsibilities on himself without the least hesitation. I need only point to the double withdrawal of all

troops from the Gulf of Saros. In comparison with these decisions the fighting on Gallipoli, like every other form of trench warfare, scarcely offered the leaders of lower rank any wide opportunities for individual activity or for the production of large decisions with far-reaching effect. Each was dependent on the telephone wire.

I often remember the quite excellent Anatolian soldier, the *Asker*. I don't want to repeat myself. I will only add one shining example of his simplicity and tenacity, that is the fact that the 19th Division, from 25 April to 20 December 1915, that is eight months long, and the 16th Division from 25 May until 20 December 1915, that is more than seven months, unceasingly, without a single calm day or without a single day of relief, from time to time engaged in very heavy fighting, remained constantly in the front line facing Ariburnu. Everyone who took part in the war knows what that meant.

Two factors considerably increased the resistance of the *Asker*. First, he always had ample ammunition for his rifle. That gave him a pleasant feeling of being able to defend himself. Even if he often fired without aim or purpose, he fired courage into himself. Finally, the Turk, who is accustomed to drink so much water, is quite impossible as a soldier without this most important element in life. If we also had been forced to bring our water in tank ships to Gallipoli, and then had to bring it up on donkeys' backs to the trenches, the bodily resistance of the Turk would have certainly completely broken down. The fact that these two necessary elements of war were and amply available, strengthened the physical power of the soldier to such an extent that he did not give way to other sapping influences.

As against this, the reason for the English failure, compressed into a short formula, was the many-headed War Council in London and the lack of peace time training of the English soldier – soldier here understood in its fullest sense, that is, inclusive of officers of all grades.

I discuss the English only here, because the French had occupied only a comparatively small section of the front, and took no part in the leadership. The English were magnificently equipped, and rationed, their bodies strengthened by sport, and they fought courageously. Their operations were based on correct principles, and were splendidly thought out, organised, and prepared, right down to the smallest detail, and were then carried out accurately and methodically. They all took place under the leadership of clear-thinking, energetic commanders. I name only Generals Hamilton and Birdwood. And yet, in spite of all these splendid preliminaries, although, as already stated, all advantages were on the side of the Entente, the final success did not come.

The English lacked the ability to extract the utmost from their success. Their Dardanelles campaign failed because of this. Their methods were responsible for it, because they were not based on any war experience. Experience of colonial wars was of no use here.

Their methods were mainly due to the constitution of the War Council. It reminds me of the time of the Vienna War Council of blessed memory, when I consider that a War Council in London, of repeatedly changing names, numbers, persons and competence, had the supreme command of the army and the fleet, and also that political considerations swayed the appointment of members, as, for instance, the admission of Bonar Law on 2 November 1915. In itself it was certainly an assembly of important men, but the greater part of them were civilians who were overwhelmed with other business, and understood more or less nothing of military matters.

Conversations, minutes and reports always preceded the decisive meetings, which again continually postponed the vital decision. So, valuable time was lost, and at the front that moment lost which contained the possibility of success. The leadership of a war cannot be entrusted to a limited liability company. So the June and August offensives of Hamilton were postponed for weeks, and months, because in London they were unable to agree, or because the political clearing of a governmental crisis must first be awaited.

From lists prepared by Churchill I take as an example, without being able to test the accuracy of the figures, that there could have been available at the moment on 7 July 1915, 150,000 English instead of 52,000 who were actually available against 70,000 Turks, whereas on 7 August, 1915, only 120,000 English faced 120,000 Turks. The Turks had thus been allowed sufficient time to prepare themselves for the Battle of Anafarta.

As here on a large scale, so on a smaller scale during the course of the tactical fighting, the right moment was often missed, and the lucky opportunity offered during battle not seized by the forelock. The methods were responsible for this. The English orders which we saw went exceptionally far into the smallest details. Everything was carefully thought out ahead, allowed for in advance, shortly, controlled right into the enemy's lines. In the conduct of the fighting the subordinate leaders clung resolutely to their given orders. This was just their method, and the English held stubbornly

Thus, however, they often missed the moment which an instinctive knowledge of the position offered, provided all methods, orders, and rules of war were consciously thrown
on one side, and the victory achieved by energetically driving forward.

'This feeling in one's finger-tips,' this instinctive recognition of a perhaps temporary weakening on the part of the enemy, can only be acquired in long years of peaceful training for a particular purpose, continuous from one generation to another. Experienced teachers are essential for this training, first who can draw on a fund of personal experience, second who tirelessly arrange situations during peace manoeuvres in which this lightning seizure of opportunities, this instinctive grasping, is steadily developed. Such faculties cannot be improvised or just ordered. They have to be reared, as plants with particular qualities are reared.

The Kitchener, the Territorial Divisions, and the colonial troops – these were all improvisations which – and this I gladly testify – moreover rendered excellent service.

But as a natural result, the men who composed the units lacked a systematic peace training, consequently they did not know how to grip the victory which was so often near them. That was our feeling during the course of the fighting on Gallipoli, and this we found confirmed in a later study of available writings.

Hence the reason why the Turkish Crescent fluttered triumphantly during the whole of those months on Achi Baba, the Kodjadschemendagh, and the Kiretschtepe, and later, in the cold January wind of 1916, again over the whole coast.

The military and political results of this achievement, which at the time astounded the whole world, were accordingly extraordinarily far-reaching.

At first, the open acceptance of their weakness resulted, for the Entente, in a loss of status and prestige, as compared with the generally described lowly Turk, particularly in the East. The Entente had therefore no longer any hopes of drawing in on their side those Balkan States which had still remained neutral.

Russia, however, received the heaviest blow, even if she had provided no men herself for the Dardanelles campaign. The dream of Byzantium was shattered. The year 1915 had already proved a disastrous year for Russia, and now came as a finish this shattering blow to their morale. They were finally cut off from their allies. Without Gallipoli they would probably have had no revolution.

England did not give up her aim on Constantinople, but was forced to take up the weary and difficult operations through Mesopotamia, and Palestine. This, in addition to work, cost money and blood for years, instead of months by the short route over Gallipoli.

On the other hand, the Central Powers had now a direct road to Constantinople, with connection to Asia Minor, from which they were able to obtain plentiful supplies for their struggling peoples, particularly copper, manganese ore and oil. Turkish armies, crowned with victors' laurels, stood ready for use in other directions.

Such was the importance of the fighting on Gallipoli. Firm will, stubborn devotion, unshakeable loyalty to their Sultan and Khalif, on the part of the Turks, gained them the victory against the superior might and crushing material of the Entente. Psychological powers triumphed over physical, the spirit over the material.

This is the lesson of the Gallipoli Campaign.

Battle Areas
of the
Dardanelles
and on
Gallipoli

Gulf of Saros

Aegean Sea

Dardanelles

ASIA MINOR

ERENKOI BAY

Suvla Bay

SALT SEA

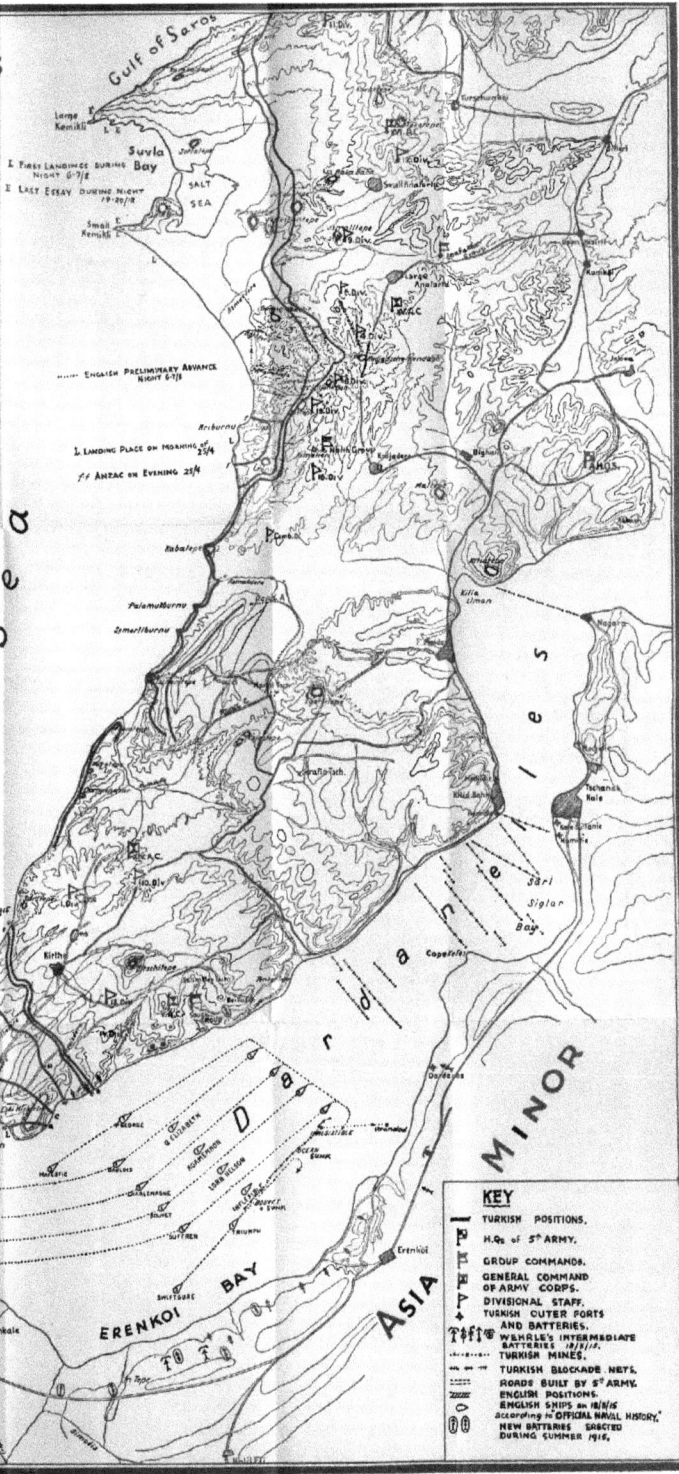

I First Landings during Night 6-7/8
II Last Essay during Night 19-20/8

Lampe Kemikli

Smail Kemikli

Anzac

Ari Burnu

Maidos

Kilia Liman

Krithia

Cape Helles

Sari Siglar Bay

Morto Liman

River Clyde

Kum Kale

Erenköi

L Landing Place on Morning of 25/4
ff Anzac on Evening 25/4

Engl. Preliminary Advance Night 6-7/8

cc Positions in Winter 1915
dd English Line June 1915
cc English on Evening of 27/4
b-b English on Evening of 26/4
a-a English on Evening of 25/4
L Landing Place on Morning 25/4
L Landing Place on 25/4 Morning
ff French from 25-26/4

KEY
TURKISH POSITIONS.
H.Q. of 5th ARMY,
GROUP COMMANDS.
GENERAL COMMAND OF ARMY CORPS.
DIVISIONAL STAFF.
TURKISH OUTER FORTS AND BATTERIES.
WEHRLE'S INTERMEDIATE BATTERIES 18/3/15.
TURKISH MINES.
TURKISH BLOCKADE NETS.
ROADS BUILT BY 5th ARMY.
ENGLISH POSITIONS.
ENGLISH SHIPS on 18/3/15 according to "OFFICIAL NAVAL HISTORY."
NEW BATTERIES ERECTED DURING SUMMER 1915.

Appendix 1

German Military Mission, Constantinople 2 August 1914

Chart of Military Duties of the Members of the German Military Mission in case of Mobilisation

No	Rank	Name	Post in Peace Time	Post in War Time	Remarks
1	Marshal	Liman V. Sanders	Head of Military Mission	Commander-in-Chief of 1st Army	Sick
2	Lieutenant General	Bronsart v. Schellendorf	Sub-chief of great General Staff	Chief of General Staff at G.H.Q.	
3	General	Posseldt	Inspector General Of Heavy Artillery		On Leave
4	General	Weber	Inspector General of Corps of Engineers & Pioneers	At disposal of Turkey	
5	Colonel	Back	Inspector General at Military School	At disposal of Military Mission	
6	Colonel	Trommer	Commander 10th Division	Commander 10th Division	
7	Colonel	Weidtmann	Commander and Staff Officer Depot Aleppo	At disposal of Turkey	
8	Colonel	Heuck	Commander 13th Division	Commander 13th Division	
9	Colonel	v. Sodenstern	Commanding Infantry Small Arms School	Commander 5th Division	
10	Colonel	Nicholai	Commander 3rd Division	Commander 3rd Division	
11	Colonel	v. Frankenberg und Proschlitz	Chief of General Staff, 1st Army Corps	Chief of General Staff, 2nd Army	
12	Colonel	Kannengiesser	Director Army Department in War Ministry	Director Army Department in War Ministry General H.Q.	
13	Colonel	Bischof	Inspector General Army Service Corps		
14	Lieutenant Colonel	v. Legat	Commanding Military Academy	Chief of General Staff, 5th Army Corps	
15	Lieutenant Colonel	Schlee	Inspector General Field Artillery	---	On Leave
16	Lieutenant Colonel	Wehrle	Commanding ranges for Heavy Artillery	At disposal of Military Mission	
17	Lieutenant Colonel	Rth. Kress v. Kressenstein	Chief of Army Department in War Ministry	Chief of operations section at G.HQ.	
18	Lieutenant Colonel	Potschernik	Inspector General of Transport	At disposal of Army Headquarters, 1st Army	
19	Lieutenant Colonel	Strange	Commanding 8 Infantry Regiment	Commanding 8th Infantry Regiment	
20	Lieutenant	Count v.	Inspector General of cavalry	At the disposal of Military Mission	

No.	Rank	Name			
21	Colonel	Hopffgarten Permet v. Thauvenay	Chief of Section II, Great General Staff	Chief of General Staff 2nd Army Corps	
22	Lieutenant Colonel	Albrecht	Chief of General Staff 6th Army Corps	Chief of General Staff 6th Army Corps	
23	Lieutenant Colonel	v. Feldmann	Chief of Section III, Great General Staff	Chief of General Staff 1st Army	
24	Lieutenant Colonel	Guse	Chief of General Staff 10th Army Corps	Chief of General Staff 3rd Army	
25	Lieutenant Colonel	Lauffer	Commanding Cavalry Officers Training School	Intelligence Officer, 2nd Army Corps	
26	Lieutenant Colonel	Kirsten	Commander 1st Cavalry Regiment	Commanding cavalry Brigade	
27	Lieutenant Colonel	Böttrich	Chief of Section IV, Great General Staff	Commanding A.S.C., G.H.Q.	
28	Major	v. Frese	Professor at war School	Commander at Headquarters 1st Army	
29	Major	Rabe	Commander 15 Infantry Regiment	Commander 15 Infantry Regiment	
30	Major	Binhold	Commanding 3rd Field Artillery Regiment	Commanding 3rd Field Artillery Regiment	
31	Major	Wilhelmi	Commander of modern Battalion of Heavy Artillery	Commanding Heavy Artillery 1st Army	
32	Major	Stange	Artillery Officer i/c Adrianople	At disposal of General Weber	
33	Major	Vonberg	Commanding 30th Field Artillery Regiment	Commanding 30th Field Artillery Regiment	
34	Major	Schierholz	Instruction Officer, Staff Officer, Depot	Commanding 9th Infantry Regiment	
35	Major	Welsch	Instructor at cavalry Officers Riding School	Staff of cavalry Brigade	
36	Major	Endres	Chief of 1st Section, Great General Staff	—	On leave
37	Major	Hunger	Commander 28th Infantry Regiment	Commander 28th Infantry Regiment	
38	Major	Eggert	Instructor at Military Academy	Chief of General Staff 1st Army Corps.	
39	Major	Effhient	Commander of 1st Pioneer Battalion	Commander of 1st Pioneer Battalion	
40	Major	v. Staczewski	Engineer Officer i/c Adrianople	At disposal of General Weber	
41	Major	Schroeder	Commanding 1st battalion A.S.C.	Commanding 1st battalion A.S.C.	
42	Major	Prigge	Commanding Cavalry Training School for NCOs	A.D.C. To Head of Military Mission	
43	Major	Lange	Instructor at Military Academy	Chief of General Staff, 10th Army	
44	Major	v. König	Staff of Military Mission	A.D.C. at Army H.Q. 1st Army	
45	Major	Mühlmann	A.D.C. to head of Military Mission	A.D.C. To Chief of General Staff at G.H.Q.	
46	Captain	Fischer	A.D.C. to Chief of General Staff at G.H.Q.		On Leave

No.	Rank	Name	Role	Assignment
47	Captain	v. d. Hagen	Commanding Physical Training School	Intelligence Officer, 1st Army Corps
48	Captain	v. Wrochem	Attached to Colonel Kannengiesser	Attached to Colonel Kannengiesser
49	Captain	Pohl	A.D.C. to Inspector General of engineer & Pioneer Corps	
50	Captain	Gerlach	Commanding 1st Pioneer battalion	Intelligence Officer 3rd Army Corps
51	Captain	Heibey	Battery Commander in Modern Battalion of heavy Artillery	Intelligence Officer 4th Army Corps
52	Lieutenant Colonel	Prof. Dr Mayer	2. Chief of Army Medical Section at the War Office	Surgeon General, 1st Army
53	Captain	Thieme	Attached veterinary Section	Army H.Q., 1st Army
54	Lieutenant Colonel	Burchardi	Attached Q.M.G.'s Department	Q.M.G., 1st Army
55	Major	Dr Huttner	Inspector of Army Medical Equipment	Attached to Q.M.G.'s Department 1st Army
56	Major	Schuch	War Office	War Office
57	Captain	Starke	Attached Q.M.G.'s Department	At disposal of Q.M.G., 1st Army
58	Lieutenant	Mainke	Attached to Engineer Officer Adrianople	At disposal of General Weber
59	Lieutenant	Weis	Attached to Engineer Officer Adrianople	At disposal of General Weber
60	Lieutenant	Jaenicke	Attached to Artillery Officer Adrianople	At disposal of General Weber
61	Lieutenant	Meier	Attached to Artillery Officer Adrianople	At disposal of General Weber
62	Paymaster	Brunberg	Paymaster with Q.M.G.	As in peace time
63	Ensign	Wagner	Secretary with 1st section, Great General Staff	Secretary at G.H.Q.
64	Ensign	Hardt	Secretary to Military Mission	Secretary to H.Q. 1st Army
65	Medical	Westermeier	Secretary to Medical Section	Attached to Surgeon General, 1st Army
66	Ensign	Heiden	Recruit Instructor, Field Artillery Regiment	At disposal of Officer Commanding Artillery Train
67	Ensign	Thiel	Recruit Instructor, to Modern Battalions of Heavy Artillery	At disposal of Officer Commanding Artillery Train
68	Ensign	Mühlbaur	Recruit Instructor to 8 Infantry Regiment	At disposal of Officer Commanding Artillery Train
69	Ensign	Mowitz	Recruit Instructor to 15 Infantry Regiment	At disposal of Officer Commanding Artillery Train
70	Ensign	Kutter	O/C Stables, Cavalry Officers Riding School	At disposal of Lieutenant Colonel Auffer
71	Medical Ensign	Bader	In Dispensary of Hospital at Gülhane	At disposal of Major Dr Huttner

APPENDIX II

Distribution of Troops and Commanders of 5th Army on Gallipoli during the winter of 1915

Supreme Command
Commander-in-Chief: Marshal Liman v. Sanders Pasha.
Chief of Staff: Lieutenant Colonel Kiasim Bey.
Commander of Artillery: General Gressmann Pasha.
Commander of Heavy Artillery: Lt Col Wehrle Bey.
Medical Officer: Surgeon Major Retzlaff Bey.
Q.M.G.: Major Musaffer Bey.

Anarfarta Group.
Commanding Officer: Colonel Mustapha Kemal Bey, later,
General Fehsi Pasha.
Chief of Staff: Major Izettin Bey.
Commander of Heavy Artillery: Major Lierau Bey.

XVIth Army Corps:
General in Command: Col Kannengiesser Bey.
Chief of Staff: Major Hunussi Bey.
Commander of Heavy Artillery: Major Senftleben Bey.
11th Division: Major Willmer Bey.
12th Division: Lieutenant Colonel Remsi Bey.
9th Division: Lieutenant Colonel Sabri Bey.

XVth Army Corps:
General in Command: General Ali Riza Pasha.
6th Division: Lieutenant Colonel Narif Bey.
4th Division: Lieutenant Colonel Djemil Bey.
8th Division: Major Nouri Bey.

Northern Group.
Commanding Officer: General Essad Pasha, later General Ali
Riza Pasha.
Chief of Staff: Major Fachreddin Bey, later Major Eggert Bey.
19th Division: Lieutenant Colonel Tschiflik Bey.

16th Division: Lieutenant Colonel Ruchti Bey.
Comb. Division: Colonel Abdurezan Bey.

Southern Group.
Commanding Officer: General Wehib Pasha, later Djewat Pasha.
Commander of Artillery: Lieutenant Colonel Assim Bey.

XIVth Army Corps:
General in Command: General Trommer Pasha.
Chief of Staff: Major Scheffket Bey.
1st Division: Lt Col Djaffer Tayar Bey.
10th Division: Lt Col Hüsni Salaheddin Bey.

Vth Army Corps:
General in Command: General Fehsi Pasha,
Chief of Staff: Lieutenant Colonel Albrecht Bey.
13th Division: Lieutenant Colonel Salaheddin Adil Bey.
14th Division: Lieutenant Colonel Kiasim Karabekir Bey, later
Colonel Von Sodenstern Bey.

Army Reserve.
3rd Division: Lieutenant Colonel Nourreddin Bey.
26th Division: Colonel Essad Bey.

APPENDIX III
Sources of Information

Helfferich Die Vorgeschichte des Weltkrieges. (History of the period preceding the World War.) Ulstein, Berlin

Hermann Stegemanns Geschichte des Krieges (Hermann Stegemann's History of the War) Deutsche Verlags Anstalt, Berlin-Stuttgart

Churchill, Winston, *Weltkrisis* (The World Crisis) volumes 1 and 2. K.F. Koehler, Berlin,

Daniels, Emil, *Der Kampf um die Dardancllen* (The Fight for the Dardanelles) Prussian Annuals, October 1920

Desmazes. 'Les Débarquements Alliés aux Dardanelles,' *Revue Mnilit. Francaise*, 1926

Kjellén, Rudolf, *Dreibund und Dreiverband* (Triple Alliance and Triple Association) Duncker & Hulmblot, Munich

Klinghardt, Karl, *Türkün Jordu.* Friedrichsen & Cie, Hamburg

Kugler, Ferdinand, *Erlebnisse eines Schweizers an den Dardanellen* (Experiences of a Swiss at the Dardanelles) Orell-Füssli, Zurich

v. Moltke. *Briefe und Zustände in der Türkei* (Letters and Conditions in Turkey) Berlin

Paléologue. *Am Zarenhofe Während des Weltkrieges* (At the Court of the Czar during the World War) Translation into German by Siebert

Pasha, Ahmed Djemal Pasha, *Erinnerungen eines Türkischen Stattsmanns* (Reminiscences of a Turkish Statesman) Drei Masken Verlag, Munich

Prigge. *Der Kampf um die Dardanellen* (The Fight for the Dardanelles) Kiepenheuer, Weimar

Sanders, Liman v., *Fünf Jahre Türkei* (Five Years in Turkey) August Scherl, Berlin

Schneider. *Die Deutsche Marine in den Dardanellen* (The German Navy in the Dardanelles) Mittler & Sohn, Berlin

Wehrle. 'Aus Meinem Türkischen Tagebuch' (Fron my Turkish Diary) *Die Schwere Artillerie* (The Heavy Artillery.) Year 1926, nos. 3 & 4, Munich

Weniger. *Der Flottenangriff gegen dic Dardanelles* (The Fleet Attack on the Dardanelles) *Naval Review*, 1925, nos 1–3

N.B.
The Fight for the Dardanelles, volume 16 of *The Battles of the World War*, Stalling-Oldenburg, could not be consulted as it only appeared after this book had gone to print.

9 781874 351313